THE
GRAND
TOUR

THE
GRAND
TOUR

Christopher
Hibbert

G. P. PUTNAM'S SONS
200 MADISON AVENUE
NEW YORK

For Billy and Jane

overleaf 'La Descente de M. de Saussure
de la Cime de Mont Blanc', 1785

First American edition 1969
© 1969 by Christopher Hibbert

Designed by Bruce Robertson
for George Weidenfeld and Nicolson Limited, London
Library of Congress Catalog Card No. 73-77547
Printed in West Germany

Contents

'Sir,' William Beckford was warned, 'your route is sure to be very perilous . . . the road's so deep and broken that if you go ten paces in as many minutes you may think yourself fortunate. There lurk the most savage banditti in Europe.'

Although the roads of Europe were much safer in the eighteenth-century heyday of the Grand Tour than they had been in the recent past, travellers were still liable to be attacked by gangs such as this.

INTRODUCTION
Precursors and Preparations

Sir Philip Sidney's three-year tour – the Grand Tour subsidised by the Queen as a training for a diplomatic career – the Tour a peculiarly English feature of aristocratic culture – sending an eldest son abroad to complete his education – the travelling tutor – 'if a young man is wild, and must run after women and bad company it is better he should do so abroad' – the traveller's rules of conduct – the importance of asking questions and avoiding one's own country-men – the expense, irritations, discomforts and hazards of Continental travel.

'Sir,' announced Dr Johnson with that uncommon animation he invariably brought to discussions of foreign travel, 'a man who has not been in Italy is always conscious of an inferiority, from his not having seen what it is expected a man should see. The grand object of travelling is to see the shores of the Mediterranean.'

To Johnson's contemporaries this seemed a sound enough judgment. The Grand Tour, whose climax was a visit to Rome and Naples, had long been accepted as an important, if not an essential, part of a gentleman's education. But although it was in the eighteenth century that it assumed its peculiar significance, the Tour was not an innovation of the Georgian era. In Elizabethan England – a century before Richard Lassels in his *Voyage of Italy* (1670) first used the phrase in a printed work – the Grand Tour had been recognised as a means of gathering information which would be turned to the nation's advantage, and of training young gentlemen to take their places in a world in which patriotic Englishness would not be enough.

Sir Philip Sidney, later to be appointed English ambassador to Rudolf II, Emperor of Germany, had been trained for this important post by a long tour of Europe. Following a preliminary education at Shrewsbury and Christ Church, Oxford, and a few months spent at Queen Elizabeth's court, Sidney left England in 1572 for Paris. Accompanied by a half-Italian tutor, three servants and four horses, he travelled through France, Germany, the Low Countries and Italy, learning the languages and the ways of foreign courts; and, after visits to Poland and Hungary, he returned home in 1575.

Journeys such as this were often subsidised by the Queen herself, who was concerned to establish a body of young courtiers fit to represent her at foreign courts, or by colleges which were anxious to profit from the knowledge imparted at foreign universities. Licences to travel had to be obtained from the Privy Council, and these stipulated the places the traveller was not to visit. Usually he was forbidden to go to St Omer, Rheims and Douai where he might fall under the influence of Roman Catholics at the Jesuit or Benedictine colleges; and often he was forbidden to go to Rome, nearly always so in the years before the defeat of the Spanish Armada when the English Cardinal Allen was plotting with the Catholic exiles there to overthrow the Queen's government.

After the defeat of the Armada, although less vigorous restrictions were imposed upon the movements of the English traveller, a journey abroad still entailed frustration, hardship and danger for all those who did not travel in a large retinue engaged upon some diplomatic or trade mission.

The *Itinerary* of Fynes Moryson, who left Peterhouse, Cambridge in 1591 with a grant of £20 a year to study the laws of the Continent, shows just how brave and enterprising the traveller needed to be.

Moryson sailed from Leigh-on-Thames on 1 May and, narrowly escaping capture by pirates from Dunkirk, he landed on the Netherlands coast after ten days at sea. Although at this time the coastal roads of Holland and East Friesland were infested with Spanish freebooters who robbed foreign travellers with impunity, Moryson's 'obstinate purpose to see the Cities upon this coast' induced him to disregard all warnings.

Since English travellers were the freebooters' favourite victims, Moryson thought it prudent to travel in disguise.

'So I bought an old Brunswicke thrummed hat,' he recorded, 'and made mee a poore Dutch suite, rubbing it in the dust to make it seeme old, so as my Taylor said, he took more paines to spoyle it, than to make it. I bought me linnen stockings, and discoloured my face and hands, and so without cloake, or sword, with my hands in my hose, tooke my place in a poore waggon. I practised as much as I could, Pythagoricall silence; but if any asked me who I was, I told him that I was a poore Bohemian, and had long served a Merchant at Leipzig, who left mee to dispatch some businesse at Stoke, and then commanded me to follow him to Emden. If you had seene my servile countenance, mine eyes cast on the ground, my hands in my hose, and my modest silence, you would have taken me for a harmelesse yong man.'

Wearing the clothes of a poor Bohemian, Moryson received scant respect at the inns where he stayed on the way; and he was as likely as not to be told that he must spend the night on a bench.

One night while he was washing his feet – which the gold concealed in his shoes had blistered – a maidservant caught sight of the good silk stockings he was wearing under his coarse linen and persuaded her mistress to find him a bed. But most nights Moryson dared not show that he had money to pay for one; and he would sit shivering in his wet clothes unable to change for fear lest, as he put it himself, 'my inward garments better than my upper, should betray my disguise to the Free-booters' spies; neither durst I call for wine and spend freely lest they should thinke I had store of money.'

Nor was Moryson any safer from thieves in France and Italy than he had been in Germany. In Italy, for instance, he found that it was highly dangerous to travel from Rome to Naples without a guard of sixty musketeers to offer protection against the *banditti* who, only the week before his arrival, had murdered many passengers on their journey south. Near Viterbo he came across the quartered bodies of numerous thieves which were stuck up beside the road as grisly but unsuccessful deterrents; while around Genoa he discovered that the countryside was ravaged by brigands and Turkish pirates. Advised to travel silently on foot in the darkness before dawn rather than on horseback in broad daylight, Moryson saw outside Genoa just before the breaking of day 'a Village all ruined by Turkish pirates [who] had spoiled the same and burnt it and had pulled downe the Churches and Altars, and, among other Prisoners, had taken away a most faire Virgine from her bridegroomes side, who had married her the day before.'

In France, between Metz and Châlons, Moryson was robbed himself by a gang of disbanded soldiers who took not only all his money which he had endeavoured to conceal in his inner doublet but also his sword, cloak, shirt and even his hat, giving him in exchange and to his disgust, a 'deep greasie French hat' in which he had to walk all the way to Paris.

Even when out of danger from freebooters, pirates, thieves, disbanded soldiers and starving wolves, there was still the ubiquitous Inquisition. Moryson travelled to Rome in the company of an English priest. But he thought it unwise to reveal his nationality to him; and when he came across a band of English pilgrims on their way to the shrine at Loreto he was 'much afraid lest some of them being Schollers of Cambridge' should recognise and denounce him. Although Moryson himself was able to enjoy the antiquities of Rome through the offices of Cardinal Allen – his visit took place some years after the failure of the Spanish Armada – other Protestant visitors thought it prudent to travel incognito, to change their lodgings every night, and to leave the city before Easter when the Inquisition kept a close watch on all inns to discover any guests who failed to take the sacrament.

Then there were the unexpected and unforeseen perils of the journey. A traveller could take care to keep out of the Inquisition's way, could walk rather than ride for fear lest a horse aroused a robber's cupidity, could disguise himself as a merchant's poor clerk (as Moryson did in Italy as well as in Germany); but there were some hazards he could not so easily anticipate. One day in Tuscany, Fynes Moryson broke off the bough of a mulberry tree and carried it over his shoulder, using its leaves to shade his head from the burning sun. Falling into the company of an Italian, he was told that he had broken a law and laid himself open to imprisonment and the payment of a heavy fine: 'since those trees planted in the high waies belonged to the Duke, who preserved them for silkewormes, and had imposed a great penalty upon any that should break a bough thereof'.

Despite the dangers and discomforts which attended a European tour, the numbers of Englishmen who travelled abroad increased year by year as the sixteenth century drew to its close, and as the establishment of permanent diplomats at foreign courts became an accepted practice. In 1592, and again in 1595, the Pope was induced to complain about the number of English heretics that were finding their way to Venice; and in 1612 James I's ambassador in Venice told the Doge that there were more than seventy Englishmen in the town whereas 'formerly' there had been only four or five. More and more Englishmen were finding it impossible to resist that 'certain tickling humour' to travel as described by Philip Sidney; more and more of them were beginning to agree with Thomas Coryat, a waggish frequenter of James I's court who believed that 'of all the pleasures in the world' travel was 'the sweetest and most delightful'. 'The mere superscription of a letter from Zürich' set Coryat up like a top, his friend Ben Jonson said, 'Basle or Heidelberg [made] him spin.'

There was still the danger of becoming involved with the Inquisi-

Portefeuilles, like this one made in Italy, were required for the great number of documents – passports, letters of credit, bills of health, and references – that the Tourist was required to carry with him.

John Evelyn, the diarist, left England on a continental tour in 1643, 'finding it impossible to evade doing very unhandsome things' in a country divided by civil war. He remained on the Continent for four years, travelling widely in France and Italy.

tion. John Mole, Lord Roos's Protestant tutor, died in the Inquisition's prison at Rome in 1638 at the age of eighty after spending thirty years of his life in confinement. But this was an exceptional case; and it was not difficult to avoid the attentions of the Catholic authorities provided the traveller did not extravagantly proclaim his distaste for popery or behave with the provocation of William Lithgow, a prejudiced Scotsman from Lanark, who indignantly tore the rich clothing off the images which offended him in a church. Even in Rome it was possible to stay quietly for a month or so, as Sir Edward Herbert did in 1614, having gone to the English College and introduced himself as a peaceable Protestant who only wanted to see the antiquities. After Charles I's marriage to the Catholic Henrietta Maria, sister of the King of France, in 1625, and the subsequent peace between England and France and Spain, the Inquisition became less and less of a hazard for the English traveller. John Milton, who toured Italy in 1638–9, did not trouble to conceal his determined Protestantism.

A greater hazard than the Inquisition in the later seventeenth century was the continuing danger of contracting some mortal disease. John Evelyn, for instance, caught small-pox in Geneva after having slept at an inn at Beveretta in a bed which had just been used by the landlady's daughter who had not yet fully recovered from the malady herself; and although Evelyn recovered after a long and painful illness there were many other seventeenth-century travellers who, having become seriously ill on their journey, never saw England again.

There was still the danger, too, in the seventeenth century, of being robbed by brigands or by marauding bands of soldiers returning from some campaign. During the Thirty Years War – and for several years after it ended in 1648 – travelling in Germany was an experience which few undertook for pleasure even during the intermittent periods of peace. Peasants as well as disbanded soldiers went about armed, cannibalism was common in Brandenburg county, and an intrepid traveller riding down the Danzig to Hamburg road in 1652 counted in a single day's journey thirty-four piles of faggots, each marking a spot where a previous wayfarer had been murdered. But the incidental dangers of Continental travel – the soldiers in Germany, the brigands in Italy, the wolves in France, the Algerian pirates in the Mediterranean – became less and less apparent as the century progressed; and many travellers returned from long journeys without having any experiences to relate remotely comparable with those of Fynes Moryson.

There were those, of course, who went abroad specifically in search of adventure, particularly military adventure. John Evelyn's first intention when he sailed from Gravesend to Flushing in 1641 was to gain some military knowledge and experience. He made for Genappe hoping to witness and perhaps to play an active part in the siege. Arriving five days after the town had fallen, he joined the army as a volunteer and for a few days trailed a pike round the horn-works

while the castle was re-fortified. But he had soon had enough of 'the confusion of armies', and having made a careful inspection of the trenches, approaches, mines, and wheel-bridge of the besiegers, he embarked on the Waal, 'in company with three grave divines', who, so he said, 'entertained us a great part of our passage with a long dispute concerning the lawfulness of church music.'

In 1643, when he was twenty-three, Evelyn returned to the Continent, this time, also, for a reason shared by many other English travellers of his generation: he did not want to become entangled with political disputes at home.

By the time of Evelyn's death in 1706, however, the Grand Tour had become firmly established not only as a convenient means of escape from unwanted involvements in England, not only as a training for diplomats, public servants and soldiers, not merely a way of satisfying youth's natural restlessness, curiosity and sense of adventure. It had become accepted as an ideal finishing school for a young gentleman of fortune after he had been whipped through a public school and acquired the doubtful benefits of its narrow curriculum. It had been recognised as an ideal means of imparting taste and knowledge and of arousing curiosity in the mind of a youth who might otherwise plunge unthinkingly into 'the brutalities of the Bottle and the Table' or even engage in such violent escapades as were practised by those aristocratic ruffians known as the Mohocks.

The Grand Tour had, in effect, already become an integral aspect of aristocratic culture.

Whether or not he was sent to a university after leaving school – and this was far from usual as the reputation of English universities at the beginning of the eighteenth century was very low – the Tourist was expected to return from his travels with a broadened mind as well as a good command of foreign languages, a new self-reliance and self-possession as well as a highly developed taste and grace of manner.

How frequently a parent's expectations were realised depended to

In the remoter parts of France and Germany and particularly in the south of Italy, the Tourist often had need of protection from bandits and gangs of disbanded soldiers. Here one rides through France guarded by a troop of musketeers.

Guide-books were an essential item in every Tourist's luggage. The most useful was *The Grand Tour containing an Exact Description of most of the Cities, Towns and Remarkable Places of Europe* by Mr [Thomas] *Nugent*. It was originally published in four volumes in 1743.

opposite The young Tourist was accompanied by his travelling tutor or 'bear leader'. Notable exceptions to Walpole's rule that travelling tutors were 'absurd animals', 'mischievous into the bargain', were Adam Smith, John Moore, Joseph Addison and Robert Wood. The second Duke of Northumberland's tutor, Lippyat, is depicted with his charge in this painting by Sir Nathaniel Dance.

a large extent upon the boy's travelling tutor, or 'bear-leader' as he was more generally called. An ideal tutor, in the words of a contemporary expert on education, Vicesimus Knox, was 'a grave, respectable man of mature age' who would, in addition to his duties as pedagogue and guide, 'watch over the morals and religion of his pupil', both of which, unless great care were taken, were sure to be 'shaken from the basis and levelled with the dust before the end of the peregrination'.

The good tutor would ensure, therefore, that his pupil's spiritual and moral fibre were sufficiently strengthened before exposing him to the corrupting influences of alien superstitions and licentiousness, to the Catholicism of Rome or the fashionable Satanism of Venice. Before setting out he would, also, ensure that the young man set himself to learn something about the countries through which their route would take them. He must begin to learn the languages – for Latin was no longer so widely understood on the Continent as it had been a century before – and he must consult the various guide-books that were published for his benefit. These contained lists of useful phrases, translated into a variety of languages, which he was enjoined to learn by heart.

One guide-book not recommended to their charges by conscientious tutors was *The Gentleman's Pocket Companion For Travelling into Foreign Parts*, the first edition of which was published in 1722. For although it contained maps no worse than those in other guides, and an accurate table of post routes, some of the useful phrases listed at the end were not considered such that a well-bred young man would employ. The section headed 'At the Inn' is in the form of a dialogue – given in French, German and Italian – between the Tourist, the innkeeper, and a chambermaid, named Joan:

'God keep you from misfortune, my host!'
'You are welcome, Gentlemen!'
'Shall we be well lodged with you for this night?'
'Yes, very well, Sir.'
'Have you good stable, good hay, good oats, good litter, good wine?'
'The best . . . .'
[The Tourist alights with his companions and enters the inn where he drinks too heavily with his meal.]
'By your leaves, Gentlemen, I find myself somewhat indispos'd.'
'Sir, if you are not well, go take your rest, your chamber is ready. Joan, make a good fire in his chamber, and let him want for nothing.'
'Sweetheart, is my bed made? Is it good, clean, warm?'
'Yes, Sir, it is a good featherbed. The sheets are very clean.'
'Pull off my stockings, and warm my bed, for I am much out of order. I shake like a leaf in a tree. Warm a Napkin for my head and bind it well. Gently, you bind it too hard. Bring my pillow, and cover me well; draw the curtains, and pin them together.

Where is the chamber-pot? Where is the privy?'

'Follow me and I will show you the way. Go strait up and you will find it on your right hand; if you see it not you will soon smell it. Sir, do you want anything else?'

'Yes, my dear, put out the candle and come nearer to me.'

'I will put it out when I am out of the room; what is your will? Are you not well enough yet?'

'My head lies too low, raise up the bolster a little. I cannot lie so low. My dear, give me a kiss, I should sleep the better.'

'You are not sick since you talk of kissing. I would rather die than kiss a man in his bed, or any other place. Take your rest in God's name. God give you a good night and good rest.'

'I thank you, fair maid.'

Apart from improving his grasp of French, Italian and German, the Tourist was expected to make sure that he had everything he needed for the journey. In the early seventeenth century the list of recommended items included – as well as such essential items as a book of Protestant prayers and hymns, note-books and crayons, swords and pistols – a linen overall to be worn over the clothes in bed at night, lice-proof, taffeta-lined doublets, plenty of handkerchiefs 'which come in useful when you perspire', a broad-brimmed hat, and either a pocket sun-dial or a watch (but not a striker, for that will give away the secret of your wealth). Later guide-books added to the list by recommending a prudent traveller to take at least a dozen strong shirts capable of withstanding the ferocious treatment of Continental washerwomen, a pair of waterproof buckskin breeches, an iron fastener for securing the door of his hotel room at night, a tinder-box to light a fire in case of an accident on the road at night, an inflatable bath with bellows, a pair of eye-preservers, a pocket inkstand, a tea caddy, a penknife, and a passport holder stamped with his name and rank and family crest. He must pack a box of medicines (for who would trust a foreign doctor?) and a box of spices and condiments (for who could trust a foreign cook?). Salt, mustard, pepper, ginger and nutmegs would all be needed, as well as tea, sugar, oatmeal and sago. Remedies against sea-sickness were essential, as there would be much rough travel by water even after the Channel was crossed; and the swaying, bumpy German post-wagons were also upsetting. A bag stuffed with powdered bay salt applied to the stomach was found efficacious in some cases; while other sufferers responded to pomegranates and mint, or the application to the belly of pulped quince and lemon peel. Reading the lists of items which were considered essential to the Tourists' comfort it is possible to believe that when the Earl of Burlington landed at Dover in the early part of the eighteenth century the pieces of baggage he had taken out with him and had since accumulated really did amount to the figure recorded in his accounts of 878 pieces.

The traveller, once abroad, was advised to follow these rules of

opposite Since foreign doctors were notoriously unreliable, 'quacks to a man', no prudent Tourist travelled without a well-stocked medicine chest. This one contained an entire apothecary's shop in miniature.

conduct: never travel by night and never travel alone; avoid the company of young women in the interests of virtue and of old women because they always want the best seats; if travelling by sea, keep clear of the sailors who are sure to be covered with vermin and take off your spurs otherwise they will be stolen while you are being sick; always have something to eat with you on a journey both as a means of assuaging your own hunger and of keeping off starving dogs; on reaching your inn at night look behind all the big pictures or looking-glasses in your room to make sure they do not hide secret doors.

When settling down to stay in any place the Tourist must remember that he has come abroad to gain knowledge and not to enjoy himself in idleness. He must make an effort not only to perfect his mastery of the language, but to learn all he can about the history, geography, trade, climate, crops, minerals, food, clothes, customs, fauna, flora, politics, laws, art and military fortifications of the district. On entering a strange town he should at once ascend the highest steeple to gain a good view of it and pick out the buildings worthy of further inspection.

Having inspected these buildings he must make drawings of them, take the necessary measurements, endeavour to learn how any curious details were executed, list their valuable contents and striking furnishings, constantly bearing in mind his future as inheritor and patron. 'Take particular note of the French way of furnishing rooms,' Lord Annandale advised his nephew who was making the Grand Tour in 1725 and who, some time after his return, could expect to become the owner of a fine country house, 'especially with double doors and windows and door curtains and finishing them with looking-glass, marble, painting, and gilded stucco.'

The Tourist must always be asking questions – one book makes 117 suggestions for those without natural curiosity – questions about the pay of the clergy, military training, funeral arrangements, grounds for divorce, water supplies, fire precautions, corporal punishment at the university or the care of paupers in the workhouse. And, having discovered the answers to his questions, he must write them down in his note-book. He must also form a collection of prints and drawings of the places and buildings and works of art he had seen, and of specimens of unusual plants, stones or whatever other natural phenomena struck his fancy.

He must avoid his own countrymen, so far as possible, choosing to pass his time with the polite society of the country he is visiting. He must obtain recommendations and letters of introduction to the best families, and must visit every eminent person prepared to receive him. He was reminded that the staffs of British embassies and consulates were always ready to help him in this respect. On his return he must keep up a correspondence with the distinguished people he had met; and let the polish that his foreign education has given him appear naturally in his conversation and manners rather than obtrusively in his clothes and gestures. He must, in the words of Francis Bacon, whose advice was quoted throughout the period of the Grand Tour, 'prick in some flowers of that he hath learned abroad into the customs of his own country.'

Although he must not travel alone for fear of bandits, the traveller was warned that 'familiarity with fellow travellers beyond a certain degree is very imprudent.' This advice in many cases was scarcely necessary. Tobias Smollett, the novelist, travelling through France in 1765, came across an English gentleman on the beach at Antibes who avoided him with great care although he knew that Smollett was also English. The gentleman's valet told Smollett's servant that his master had journeyed for three days in company with two other Englishmen and in all that time had not addressed a single word to either of them. Smollett also remembered an Englishman who was laid up at Auxerre with a broken arm. He asked him if there was anything he could do for him. No thank you, the man said, he did not choose to see any company and had no need of any help.

But despite their native reserve which made it quite unnecessary to advise some English Tourists not to spend too much time in the company of their fellow countrymen, few of them did travel alone. For although the roads in the eighteenth century were far less dangerous than they had been in the recent past there were still hazards enough. The *maréchaussée* in France kept the main roads reasonably safe from highwaymen; but in parts of Italy and Germany bandits still abounded.

Journeys began early in the morning so that the Tourist could be safely locked up in his room when darkness fell; and while on the road in daylight, so Thomas Nugent warned his readers in the most widely-read guide-book of the time, he must never take out any money in front of strangers. There were a 'great many villains on the roads', particularly in the Papal States, in the Kingdom of Naples and on the borders of small states where robbers committed their crimes in one of them before escaping into another.

Even in those parts of Italy where a man's life was secure, his baggage rarely was. It was essential, therefore, to strap it down well, and to keep a sharp eye on it. Many a traveller had arrived at his inn to find a nimble thief had cut his trunk from his post-chaise; and frequently, if a trunk arrived intact at its destination, it was only to fall victim to the pilfering fingers of a customs-officer in one of those anarchic *dogane* which held up the Tourist's entry into so many Italian towns.

It was often, indeed, impossible to get into many towns at all at night after the gates had been shut; and most of those towns which were not walled were protected by iron chains drawn across the roads leading into them. Once inside a town, it was as well to become immediately acquainted with its regulations. In some of them, for instance, it was an offence to walk about at night without a lantern; strangers who lost themselves in the badly lighted streets were likely to be arrested and imprisoned. One unfortunate Englishman who was imprisoned on suspicion in a small town in the Papal States and

Tobias Smollett, the novelist and model for Sterne's disgruntled traveller Smelfungus in *A Sentimental Journey*, spent two years on the Continent after over-work and the death of his only daughter had broken down his health. His acidulous *Travels* was published on his return in 1766.

Many French inns in the eighteenth century, even on the post route between Calais and Paris, were atrociously uncomfortable. Arthur Young, a writer on agriculture who toured France before the Revolution, described the floors as being permanently unswept, the kitchens as smoky and dirty, the straw mattresses as verminous.

who could provide neither the Roman passport nor the bill of health which the authorities demanded, was kept in prison for six weeks. On his release he was required to spend another forty days in the Lazaretto; and, when released from there, he returned to his inn to find most of the contents of his trunk had been confiscated and his post-chaise had been stolen.

Tourists fortunate enough to escape the notice of both police officers and thieves would almost certainly fall foul of a customs official, a money-changer, a toll-keeper or a postmaster. The regulations of the custom-houses which were to be encountered all over Europe seemed to the English traveller as wildly capricious, as the houses themselves were exasperatingly ubiquitous. The Tourist was constantly having articles confiscated or detained for inspection, and as constantly having to reach in his pocket for the customary bribe

Page 23 My Masters Expences at angers May the 15 1713

Brought over 3047 08

Sunday 15 Paid for 7 Bushels of oates at 23 pence pr bushel	08 01
Paid for Coffee and gave a poor women by order	01 12
Monday 16 Paid for 4 Bushels of oates	05 00
Thursday 18 Paid for one pound of Soap	00 12
Paid for one pound and halfe of Chocolat	06 00
Paid for a Letter	00 06
Paid for a suite of silke Cloaths for my master	160 02
Gave my master for his pocket	20 00
my master gave to a poor woman	05 00
Paid at the academy a month advance for	
Riding 4 Horss	55 00
for Riding at the Heads	20 00
Paid for Rods	01 10
Paid the Mathematick and french master for 2 month	40 00
Fryday 19 Paid la plant for a masquerade	05 00
Paid for Chocolat	01 00
Paid for a Chaise	300 00
Gave to Chevaliers Janeys servant	02 10
Saturday 20 Paid for 2 payor of thread stocking and Dying a pair black put	08 17
Paid for washing a flambeo payor mending Clocke	08 14
gave my master for his pocket	12 10
Monday 22 Paid for busquites and a Letter	00 15
Tuesday 23 Paid for 6 payor of Gloves	03 00
Paid for a Letter	00 08
gave to my master for his pocket	05 00
	3716 05

Page 24 My Masters Expences at angers may the 23 1713

Brought over 3716 : 05

Tuesday 23 Paid for oates 5½ Bushels	53 : 10
Paid to John Battis for small things that he bought at sometime	10 : 11 : 2
Paid the Dancing master one month	10 : 00 : 0
Paid for a Black silke bage for my masters periwig	03 : 00
Paid the whets Right	03 : 00
Paid the fencing master one month for mornings	
and after noones fencing and for a file book	22 : 10
Paid for a Canvis wast Coat for my master	20 : 10
Thursday 25 Paid for halfe a pound of Chocolat	02 : 00
gave the taylors man	01 : 05
Paid for a sett Horss at the academy one month	13 : 00
Saturday June Paid for 4 pound of sugar	03 : 14
3 Paid for a Letter	00 : 18
fryday 9 Paid for 7 payor of Gloves	04 : 07
Saturday 10 Paid for washing 5 weekes	21 : 14
Gave my master for his pocket	36 : 00
Tuesday 14 Paid for Inke	00 : 03
for a Payor of Shoe Buckles	10 : 00
for mending the servitore	01 : 10
Thursday 16 Paid for 2 Hates one for my master and one John	17 : 00
Saturday 18 Paid a Bill to Capeland for powder oyle and Jess at severall times	17 : 16
Paid to John Cockes a bill for small things that he bought for my master	11 : 11
for washing	10 : 00
for 2 payer of shoes	06 : 10
Paid to John Battis a bill of Extrordinarys for Horss this	26 : 00
Paid for Cards	01 : 12
	4004 : 06 2

---

which solved most arguments everywhere except Vienna and Dover. At Dover the officials were peculiarly strict. Horace Walpole angrily complained of having to pay seven and a half guineas on a 'common set of coffee things' that had cost him but five; and Thomas Townshend told George Selwyn that a friend of his had saved the coat and waist-coat of a new French suit from the clutches of the Dover customs men, 'but not having taken the same precaution for the breeches, they were seized and burnt.'

Nor were custom-houses the only cause of delay and expense on the road. Few travellers returned home without having paid more than they need have done to a grasping postmaster who insisted that, however many horses they had when they arrived at his post, one more would be required for the next stage of the journey. Then there were the keepers of locks and toll-houses. One exasperated Tourist

Amongst the items on this account sheet kept by Thomas Coke, the Earl of Leicester's valet, on their Tour in 1713 are the salaries of the drawing and fencing masters, of the 'mathematick and french masters', and sums for 'a masquerade', a 'Payor of Shoo Buckles', a 'Black Silk bag for my master's perriwig', and pocket money. The Earl of Leicester was then sixteen years old.

who travelled by canal and river in Lombardy and Venetia decided that there could not possibly be more delays on land. But afterwards he went to Germany where, in the sixty-three miles between Mainz and Andernach, there were no less than ten stops where tolls had to be paid in addition to all the other stops at post-houses and custom-stations.

Finally, there were the difficulties and complications of foreign currency and of arranging for transfers of credit from England. A Tour might last for as long as three or even four years without a return home, and few Tourists stinted themselves. John Evelyn managed on about £300 a year during his Grand Tour; and certainly there were those in the eighteenth century who managed on much less. As late as 1791 it was still possible to find a good apartment with eight rooms, a kitchen and cellar, near the Capitol in Rome for as little as £12 10s a year, when the same accommodation would have cost at least £200 a year in London; and Arthur Young, who travelled widely on the Continent before the Revolution, calculated that a man could live better on £100 a year in Italy than he could on £500 in England. Even in the early nineteenth century, when Crabb Robinson covered three hundred miles in Germany at a total cost of two and a half guineas, it was still considered possible to manage a Continental tour on seventeen shillings a day.

But the average eighteenth-century Tourist was not interested in economy. Indeed, he was advised to spend lavishly. The Tour was only done once, and, as one guide-book puts it, ''Tis the way to be respected.' With extravagant young men like Charles James Fox dissipating a far from modest fortune in such places as Naples and Spa, it is not surprising that prices went up wherever the English went.

Nor was extravagance the only cause of the Tourists' rapid consumption of money: there were almost fifty different sorts of coin circulating in Italy alone, some of them worth less in one part than they were worth in another or even having no value at all. Needless to say, all but the most wary traveller incurred a loss every time he had to change his money. Moreover, arranging for letters of credit and bills of exchange was a tiresome business. The mails were appallingly slow – a request addressed to a bank in London from, say, Pisa commonly taking six weeks to arrive, without any assurance that it would arrive at all.

Nevertheless, despite all the expense, the irritations, discomforts and hazards of Continental travel, despite the likelihood of the outbreak of a war preventing the return of a traveller when he intended to return, or the outbreak of a pestilence preventing his return altogether, the numbers of those who embarked on the Tour, married men as well as youths, continued to increase throughout the eighteenth century.

'Where one Englishman travelled in the reign of the first two Georges,' wrote one observer in 1772, 'ten now go on a grand tour. Indeed, to such a pitch is the spirit of travelling come in the kingdom, that there is scarce a citizen of large fortune but takes a flying view of France, Italy and Germany.'

Adam Smith, also writing in the 1770s, said in *The Wealth of Nations* that in England it had become 'every day more and more the custom to send young people to travel in foreign countries'. And some years later, Edward Gibbon, then in Lausanne, was told that in the summer of 1785, forty thousand English were on the Continent.

By then the Grand Tour had assumed a rather formal pattern. There was no set route, which wars in any case would have disrupted; there was not even a set order in which the countries visited should be seen, although most Tourists went down to Naples through France and Switzerland and returned through Germany and the Low Countries. But there were certain features common to nearly all itineraries, features which had gradually begun to be incorporated into the structure of the Tour in the middle of the seventeenth century after the end of the Thirty Years War had brought to Europe a period of relative peace and after the relations between Britain and the Catholic courts of the Continent had improved.

Spain and Greece and countries east of Prague or north of Hamburg were rarely visited, because the Tourist felt little drawn to territories where the comfort and society he was used to at home could not be enjoyed, or where, as he was led to believe, there were no sights or artistic treasures worth the exhausting effort of reaching them.

John Evelyn decided in 1645 that there was nothing to be gained in travelling farther south than Naples. 'This I made the *non ultra* of my travels,' he recorded in his diary; 'since from the reports of divers experienced and curious persons, I had been assured there was little more to be seen in the rest of the civil world, after France, Flanders, and the Low Countries, but plain and prodigious barbarism.' It was a sentiment which most Tourists – making a reservation in the case of parts of Germany and Switzerland – would have endorsed. When in 1776 Voltaire spoke about Spain to Martin Sherlock he expressed a common enough opinion. 'It is a country of which we know no more than of the most savage parts of Africa, and it is not worth the trouble of being known. If a man would travel there, he must carry his bed, etc. When he comes into a town, he must go into one street to buy a bottle of wine, into another for a piece of a mule; he finds a table in a third, and he sups.'

So the more inaccessible parts of Europe were ignored. Italy was the goal, and the highways and rivers of France the paths that led to it.

Although Dover was the most commonly used Channel port, there were as regular sailings from Southampton, Folkestone, Newhaven and Brighton as wind and tide allowed. Here Rowlandson depicts a party of apprehensive travellers about to be rowed to the Dieppe packet-boat from the Brighton shore.

FRANCE

Delays at channel ports – the road to Paris and the abundance of beggars – Normandy, Brittany and Amiens – the arrival in Paris and the purchase of French clothes – the beauty of the architecture contrasted with the poverty and squalor in the streets – the 'hideously painted faces' of French women – the delights of eighteenth-century Paris, the brothels, coffee-houses, taverns and theatres – the visit to Versailles and Blois – Lyons, Marseilles, Nice, Arles and Avignon.

Most Tourists made for Dover. They travelled in a coach that took a whole long day – and five changes of horses – to rattle its way from the Golden Cross in Charing Cross over the old London Bridge, down the old Kent Road, through New Cross and Blackheath to Shooter's Hill, where, at The Bull, the horses were changed for the first time. Then, with its fresh horses, the coach moved on to Gad's Hill, past the corpses of highwaymen rotting in their irons on the gibbets, past Rochester and the Medway flats to Canterbury, and then on through Barham to Dover.

The Dover to Calais, or Dover to Boulogne or Ostend routes, were, however, only three of many. You could sail from Southampton to Le Havre, Brighton to Dieppe, from Folkestone, Newhaven and Gravesend. Or you need not travel to the coast at all; for you could take a French trader from a London dock which landed you at Dunkirk. And although to sail from London cost twice as much as from Dover, a Tourist often found that he had saved money in the long run, since adverse winds might prevent a channel packet sailing for days on end. Dr Burney, the musical historian, once spent nine days in port in 1772 waiting for good weather; a week spent at Dover was not in the least uncommon. Nor was Dover a town in which a man would choose to stay if he could help it. Most Tourists found it a dismal place with scores of ramshackle inns kept by old sailors who found the life of a publican both more congenial and more profitable than a life at sea. There *were* good inns – both The King's Head and The Ship were comfortable – but they were usually full, and a delayed

traveller would often be obliged to seek a room in one of those lesser establishments that invited his custom by means of gaudily painted signs which swung above his head in almost every dingy street.

In the previous century delays at channel ports were even longer than in the eighteenth. In 1610 two ambassadors were held up for a fortnight before they could get away; and even then they were in danger, as frequently happened, of being blown back into a different harbour. Nor could a passenger be sure that the wind would allow him to be landed in France at the port he had chosen.

When the wind stood fair, Calais could be reached from Dover in three hours, and the passage rarely took longer than five or six. It often happened, though, that the packet could not get into the harbour because of the low tide. Then the passengers, nearly all of whom had been sick, would have to disembark, climb down into rowing boats to be taken closer in, and finally they would be lifted out and carried ashore by watermen. The cost of these rowing boats was a guinea, although the channel crossing itself was only half a guinea for a gentleman and five shillings for his servant.

But this was only the first of the Tourist's annoyances on arriving in France. He watched with consternation as his bags were tossed out of the packet by 'men and boys, half naked and in wooden shoes'; he was asked to pay what he considered exorbitant fees to the bare-legged porters, both male and female, who carried these bags to the custom-house; he was subjected to the importunate cries and ceaseless recommendations of the touts employed by the various inns; he might

Thomas Rowlandson, who went to live and study in Paris at the age of sixteen, thereafter made regular trips to the Continent. Here he displays the pleasures, discomforts and clumsy servants at a French table d'hôte.

well find that the gates of the town were shut, and would have to spend the night in one of the uncomfortable boarding-houses outside them. Yet as exasperating as any of these annoyances were the official formalities.

An Irish girl, Miss Catherine Wilmot, who accompanied Lord and Lady Mount Cashell on their European tour, described how tiresome these were:

'After a desperately rough passage of five hours, and a cruel delay before we were permitted to land, occasioned by our names being written down and reported to the municipality, we at length got on shore, reeling after our sufferings, and in that plight, we were taken to the Custom House, transferred from thence to the municipal officers, and then to the examination of the Commissaires. They were the most shocking sharks I ever saw altogether; even after trunks, Pocket Books, Writing Cases, Green baize bags, &c., were quietly delivered in, they put their hands into our pockets and then felt down our sides, even to our ankles, for contraband commodities.'

The personal examination was, fortunately, more rough and embarrassing than thorough. The examiner would think nothing of reaching down inside a woman's stays to search for some forbidden '*marchandise anglaise*'; but the entire inspection lasted only a minute or so, and little notice was taken of any additional clothes the traveller might be wearing, however obvious it was that these were intended as presents for some friend on the Continent. Also, a bribe would soon settle most arguments.

Calais   The inspection over, and a passport obtained for the onward journey through France – for his English passport would not be recognised on the Continent – the Tourist could seek out his inn. Although the inns at Calais were much better than those in most French towns, there were several very bad ones. One traveller was distressed to be shown to a comfortless room, 'but a step raised above the courtyard, a tiled floor without carpet and two very high windows, with very thin muslin curtains half-way up, opening into the public entrance, so that it was exactly like sleeping in the street. To add to which the upper half of the windows was overlooked by the huge kitchen on the opposite side of the court.'

The well-informed took care to avoid such places; and would choose either The Silver Lion, The Prince of Orange, or the Hôtel d'Angleterre which M. Dessin made famous during the second half of the eighteenth century. So famous did Dessin's, as it was usually called, become that the rich young man would not think of staying anywhere else, despite the fact that the drains of the military hospital ran beneath it and it was consequently often extremely smelly. By means of selling and hiring carriages, and changing money, as well as keeping an excellent and expensive table, its proprietor was said to have made a fortune of over fifty thousand pounds in the ten years between 1766 and 1776.

It was at Dessin's that Laurence Sterne stayed at Calais, being visited, as all new arrivals were, by a monk begging for something for his convent. It was at Dessin's that the Russian historian, Nikolai Karamzin, also stayed, asking for Laurence Sterne's room and being told that it was occupied by an old English widow and her daughter.

As Karamzin discovered, Dessin's was always full of Grand Tourists. When he arrived there in 1789 on his way to England, there were seven or eight Englishmen 'who had just crossed the Channel with the intention of travelling through Europe.' They were very noisy at supper, repeatedly calling out, 'Wine! Wine! The very best! *Du meilleur! Du meilleur!*,' teasing a talkative Italian who described the dangers he had encountered during his travels, and a long-nosed German who learnedly compared the pink champagne to the divine nectar which flowed from the horns of the sacred goat of Amalthaea.

Karamzin was woken up that night by the 'gay Englishmen who were shouting, stamping their feet, banging their fists on tables and so on' in a nearby room. Having endured the row for half an hour, he sent his servant to remind them that they were not the only guests in the hotel, and 'that perhaps their neighbours would like some peace and quiet.' Eventually, after 'several "God damns" were heard', there was silence.

Even those guests who found the noise of the rowdy young English Tourists intolerable had to agree that the food at Dessin's was the best in Calais. The fish was always excellent and the *spécialité de la maison*, the fresh sea crabs, were superb. Fortified by Dessin's fine food, and cheered by his cool and sparkling champagne, the Tourist left the hotel to explore Calais in an optimistic frame of mind. But he did not usually like what he saw.

It was a small town, consisting in the middle of the eighteenth century of but eight streets which all ran into the central market place, and having no more than four thousand inhabitants. The houses were low and looked 'bleak and poor', and in winter the air was damp and salty. 'I would not want to live here,' one disappointed traveller commented, 'for anything in the world.'

As a compensation, there was something 'very pleasing in the manners and appearance of the people' who were 'vastly obliging to strangers'. When Fanny Burney was staying there a band played 'God Save the King' outside her bedroom window, and the streets seemed full of 'innumerable pretty women and lovely children, almost all of them extremely fair', and all of them polite and affable.

Their pleasant manners and affability, as well as their fair skins and hair, were attributed to the fact that when Edward III had captured Calais he had turned out the old inhabitants and brought in English citizens in their place. For few English travellers could believe that the pleasant and friendly people they came across in the streets and shops could possibly be wholly French.

They were warned before they left home by Thomas Nugent's *Grand Tour* – first published in 1743 – that the French were 'fiery, impatient, inconstant, and of a restless disposition'; that they were so addicted to gambling that to play cards with them was 'the only means for a foreigner to ingratiate himself in their company'; that the young were 'debauched and irreligious'; and that they were all extremely talkative, 'especially those of the female Sex'. Moreover, according to another authority, 'swearing and cursing, with the addition of obscene words, are customary in both sexes'.

Many young English travellers scarcely needed these warnings. They had always been satisfied that the French were a grasping race and none too clean, that when they were not behaving like actors, they were acting like monkeys. It came as all the greater a surprise, therefore, when they gradually discovered for themselves that the French were far from being the blackguards they had always supposed them to be, that they were, in fact, a 'people of quick understanding and nice taste', courteous and charming, that the men were 'masters of good breeding', and the women 'of a graceful and winning deportment'. However atrocious his grammar and however ridiculous his accent, the Tourist was always listened to 'with the most serious attention, and never laughed at', even when he uttered the most absurd solecism.

'During the time we were in France,' William Wordsworth said after a visit in 1790, 'we had not once to complain of the smallest deficiency of courtesy in any person, much less of any positive rudeness. We had also perpetual occasion to observe that cheerfulness and sprightliness for which the French have always been remarkable.'

Everything was done with such grace, another Englishman confirmed. 'The lowest servant took your hat and gloves as if you did her a favour. Nothing struck us English more in the manners of the French than the sweetness of address in all classes.' Even the beggar boys were gracious. A London boy would flare up in anger on being pettishly repulsed. But not so in France. Here he would make a bow, saying '*Pardon, Monsieur, une autre occasion.*'

There were strange customs, of course, to which some Englishmen could never get used. As soon as he began his journey south from Calais, for instance, the Tourist would be forcibly reminded that travelling on the Continent was a very different matter from travelling at home, uncomfortable as *that* usually was. Ill-behaved and disagreeable children he was accustomed to; but in a French stage-coach 'it was impossible to suffer more from heat, from pressure' and from the overpowering smell of garlic-flavoured breath. And 'who but a Frenchman,' William Hazlitt complained, 'would think of carrying his dog! He might as well drag his horse into the coach after him.'

Then, for the more fastidious traveller there was the embarrassment of the conversations carried on in public carriages. To the Englishman's surprise there was little or no conversation at mealtimes in hotels. Expecting to find the French tirelessly voluble, he was

George Cruikshank's animated 'Life in Paris' displays the pleasures and excitements to which the Tourist could look forward in France – good food, good wine, *musique, la danse, le chant, l'amour, le jeu* in a society regulated by the rules of *l'honneur* and *la politesse.*

32

disconcerted to find them, when at table, 'more like an assembly of tongue-tied quakers, than the mixed company of a people famous for loquacity.' 'Of all *sombre* and *triste* meetings,' it was commonly agreed, 'a French *table d'hôte* is foremost.'

But on the road, the case was quite different. One prim young man found himself in a coach with a French lawyer, 'an elderly woman of genteel appearance, and a beautiful girl of sixteen . . . shall I record that in this company the most undisguised and shocking descriptions were given of the debaucheries of the capital, and particulars which would scarcely be whispered in English discussed with the utmost exactness.'

Few young men understood enough French at this stage of the journey to be shocked by conversation. But there were sights which were as shocking as sounds. A young lady, on stepping out of a carriage, 'discovered a lapse of stocking, and continuing her chat with the gentleman who had handed her out, she deliberately adjusted it and tied her garter!' It seemed that a French lady's knee was 'as modest as the elbow of an English lady'.

If the Tourist brought his own carriage from England with him or bought or hired one from M. Dessin, all such embarrassments and discomforts were avoided. This, he was advised, was the best way to travel. But it was an expensive way; and if he could not afford it, he had to choose between the *carrosse*, the *coche*, and the diligence.

The *carrosse* was a vehicle like the English stage-coach with room for six passengers; the *coche* was larger and heavier, carrying sixteen passengers, twelve in the body of the coach and two on each side of it by the door. Both carried a great deal more baggage than the English stage-coach, the *coche*, in fact, being equipped with two huge wicker baskets, one at the front and the other at the back, usually overflowing with trunks, bags, boxes, cases, cages, and, on occasions, additional passengers.

Since both these vehicles were so overloaded, and since both were pulled by very small horses – 'rats of horses', Nelson called them – they travelled extremely slowly.

Much quicker was the diligence, the big, public coach whose horses were changed every twelve miles and went at a gallop. Improved versions of the diligence could carry up to thirty passengers, all facing the front, and could cover as many as a hundred miles a day. But as they were not hung on springs until the last quarter of the eighteenth century, and as so many French roads were paved with large, uneven stones, diligences were exhaustingly bumpy.

'A more uncouth clumsy machine can scarcely be imagined,' wrote one dissatisfied passenger, 'all the carriages of this description have the appearance of being the result of the earliest efforts in the art of coach building.'

'They are detestable,' another passenger, Arthur Young, wrote. 'Overcrowded, badly sprung and fond of starting in the small hours of the morning.' The smaller ones, however, were not quite so

Changing horses outside a small and uninviting inn near Clermont, between Amiens and Chantilly on the post route from Calais to Paris. The French postilion, easily recognised by his gigantic boots, was, in Smollett's opinion, 'lazy, lounging, greedy and impertinent'.

disagreeable, and provided more comforts for the occupants:

'The inside, which is capacious and lofty, is lined with leather, padded, and surrounded, with little pockets, in which the travellers deposit their bread, snuff, night caps and pocket handkerchiefs … From the roof depends a large net work, which is generally crowded with hats, swords, and band-boxes; the whole is convenient, and when all parties are seated and arranged, the accommodations are by no means unpleasant.

'Upon the roof, on the outside, is the imperial, which is generally filled with six or seven persons more, and a heap of luggage, which latter also occupies the basket, and generally presents a pile, half as high again as the coach, which is secured by ropes and chains. The body of the carriage rests upon large thongs of leather, fastened to heavy blocks of wood, instead of springs, and the whole is drawn by seven horses.'

One advantage of the diligence was that the traveller was spared the irritation of having to deal personally with the postilion as he would have to do if he went by the post-route. For it was generally conceded that the French postilion was a rascal. He rode on a shaggy

pony beside the horse which drew the chaise; and in his dirty sheep-skin coat, his greasy night-cap and vast jack-boots – as big as oyster barrels and rimmed with iron to protect his legs in case of accidents – he looked as unsavoury as his mount.

Tobias Smollett, admittedly an implacable grumbler, decided that postilions in France, except in large cities, were 'lazy, lounging, greedy and impertinent. If you chide them for lingering, they will continue to delay you the longer; if you chastise them with sword, cane, cudgel, or horse-whip, they will either disappear entirely, and leave you without resources: or they will find means to take vengeance by overturning your carriage.'

The only way to deal with them, Smollett concluded, was to pay them an additional three sols (about threepence) each above the twenty sols they were customarily given for each post, a post being six miles. This forced the price of travelling by post-chaise up to 1s 11d a post – and there were thirty and a half posts between Calais and Paris – but it was considered the only way to travel without irritation. In any case, the slowness of the *carrosses* and the *coches* meant that the 183 miles to Paris could entail seven dinners and seven suppers on the road, so that the week-long journey might cost as

A model of the basket-work carriage that transported passengers, very slowly, between Paris and Versailles. It set out twice a day from the rue Saint Nicaise.

37

much as £2 10s. Moreover, some of the inns on the way made a quick journey all the more desirable.

The post-route went through Boulogne, Montreuil, Bernay, Abbeville, Amiens, Clermont, Chantilly and St Denis; the *carrosse*-route (after Abbeville), through Poix, Beauvais and Beaumont. And in only a few of the places where the coach stopped was there a first-class inn. Some inns, indeed, were atrocious.

At Marquise, two posts and a half (fifteen miles) from Calais, Nelson was taken to an inn – well, they called it an inn, he wrote, 'I should have called it a pigstye: we were shown into a room with two straw beds, and, with great difficulty, they mustered up clean sheets; and gave us two pigeons for supper, upon a dirty cloth, and wooden-handled knives – O what a transition from happy England!'

At St Omer (where Charles Burney was forced to spend the night in a 'miserable inn' outside the city walls, for he arrived there after the gates were shut), supper consisted of 'stale mackerel, a salad with rancid oil and an omelette made of raddled eggs'.

The niggardliness of the innkeepers in the smaller French inns was a frequent source of complaint: 'They have not heart to provide handsomely for their guests, and are so saving and penurious, the foible and habit of their nation, that they count every bit one puts into one's mouth. They are as well pleased to see their dishes not touched, as a hearty English landlord is displeased, when he thinks his guest does not like his victuals.' On Fridays – at the beginning of the eighteenth century at least – it was evidently even worse. ''Tis a great inconvenience to travel in France upon a fish-day,' a Tourist warned in 1701, 'for 'tis a hard matter to get anything to eat but stinking fish or rotten eggs.'

It was essential, therefore, Thomas Nugent warned in his guide, to know the price and quality of everything before you ordered it.

Arthur Young, who toured France shortly before the Revolution, agreed that the Tourist ought to make a bargain with the innkeeper, 'even for the straw, and stable; pepper, salt and table-cloth'.

This was but one of Young's complaints. He went on to condemn the furniture in French inns as 'such that an English innkeeper would light his fire with', the tawdry decorations – walls were either whitewashed, or covered in paper of different sorts in the same room, or hung with tapestries full of moths and spiders – the ill-fitting drawers and windows, the creaking doors, the lack of bells – 'the fille must always be bawled for; and when she appears is neither neat, well dressed nor handsome' – the smoky, dirty kitchen, the unswept floors.

The beds, however, he thought better in France than in England. But few other travellers agreed with him. Most complained that if they were of straw, the straw was damp or verminous, or both; if, in a more expensive inn, mattresses and feather beds were provided, they were piled up dangerously high: 'Two of them are always placed in the same room: they consist of a bed of straw at the bottom, then a large mattress, then a feather-bed, then another large mattress, upon which are the blankets, etc., with all which, the bed is so high, that a man with great difficulty climbs into it; and, if he were to tumble out of it by mischance, he would be in danger of breaking his bones upon a brick floor.'

As for the coffee, in some inns Lord Macaulay thought it was worse than any cook 'could make for a wager'. While the soap, when he found soap provided, made him think that he ought to take a piece of it away 'that men of science might analyse it'.

Most intolerable of all to some Tourists was the way French inn-keepers carved and served at their own tables d'hôte. William Hazlitt found this peculiarly distasteful:

'The master is such a Goth too, a true Frenchman! When carving he flourishes his knife about in such a manner as to endanger those who sit near him, and stops in the middle with the wing of a duck suspended on the point of his fork, to spout a speech out of some play. Dinner is no sooner over than he watches his opportunity, collects all the bottles and glasses on the table, beer, wine, porter, empties them into his own, heaps his plate with the remnants of fricassees, gravy, vegetables, mustard, melted butter, and sops them all up with a large piece of bread, wipes his plate clean as if a dog had licked it, dips his bread in some other dish that in his hurry had escaped him, and finishes off by picking his teeth with a sharp-pointed knife.'

Few travellers were unfortunate enough to come across such a distressing landlord as this. Indeed, it was often the English guests whose manners were the more exceptionable. Beaujolois, the rather prim but highly observant fourteen-year-old daughter of Lady Charlotte Campbell, while on her way to live in Italy with her family, came across some 'most vulgar' Englishmen at the table d'hôte at Meurice's Hotel at Calais – 'impossible to guess what rank but their manners could only be those of a very under class. They were perfectly civil but eating off their knife leaning back upon their chair with elbows upon the table was too vulgar.'

The innkeepers she came across were, on the other hand, courteous and well mannered. At Amiens where the guests sat down to the table d'hôte dinner at four o'clock, the landlady was 'a middle-aged woman not handsome, nicely dressed, and with a sufficient degree of self approbation to appear perfectly at her ease'.

In fact, as all but the most prejudiced travellers agreed, the owners of the better French inns were quite as polite and competent as their English counterparts. And, although they roasted 'everything to a chip if not cautioned', French cooks were considered perfectly adequate. As Thomas Nugent advised his readers:

'The French diet is not near so gross as ours. Their bread is exceedingly good, and so is their beef and mutton ... They boil and roast their meat much longer than we do, which exempts them from the gross humours to which the crudity of our meat subjects us. They are fond of soups, ragoos, and made dishes, which they dress the best of any people in Europe. Their vegetable food consists of kidney-beans, white lentils, turnips, red-onions, leeks, lettuce, white-beets, and asparagus. They have scarce any potatoes, but great quantities of sorrel and mushroom, especially the latter, of which they are very fond.'

A typical dinner might consist of soup served by the landlord or his wife and passed round the table to the various guests, then a fish course served in the same way, then a *bouillie*. Afterwards the corner dishes on the table would be uncovered and might reveal duck stewed with cucumber, tongue with tomato sauce, and fricandeau of veal. When these dishes were removed, others containing stewed fruit, sweetmeats and puddings would take their place; and, at the same time, fresh fruit and cakes would be placed directly upon the cloth.

Even in the more modest inns there was usually a good variety of dishes to choose from; and if many Tourists missed the good English beer, 'French liqueurs were not to be despised'. Bad wine was occasionally encountered, but in general it was 'far better than English inns give'.

To some disgruntled travellers all French inns were an abomination because they were not English. Thomas Gray, for instance, thought that they were 'terrible places indeed', and longed to get his journey finished; and to other travellers, even if the inns themselves caused no offence, the crowds of beggars who swarmed around them did.

At the beginning of the eighteenth century, all the country villages of France, according to Lady Mary Wortley Montagu, were full of beggars. 'While the horses are changed,' she wrote, 'the whole town comes out to beg with such miserable starved faces, and thin tattered clothes, they need no other eloquence to persuade one of the wretchedness of their condition.' Nor had conditions changed seventy years later. 'The whole kingdom swarms with beggars,' a traveller recorded shortly before the Revolution. 'This observation was confirmed at every inn I came to, by crowds of wretches. I have often passed from the inn door to my chaise through a file of twenty or thirty of them.'

'There is always a little matter to compound at the door, before you can get into your chaise,' Laurence Sterne confirmed in *A Sentimental Journey*, 'and that is with the sons and daughters of poverty who surround you ... I always think it better to take a few sous out in my hand; and I would *consel* every gentle traveller to do likewise; he need not be so exact in setting down his motives for giving them – They will be register'd elsewhere.'

These sons and daughters of poverty were, however, as Catherine Wilmot said, 'the merryest beggars' in the world, humpbacks shouting good-natured insults at each other, cripples congratulating blind men on the excellence of their legs, blind men praising the fine sight of mutes, and mutes dancing about in pretended fury at their inability to answer, till two or three coins flung from the window of the carriage would make them all wave their arms or join in the common cry of '*Bon voyage! Vive les voyageurs!*'.

In view of the number of beggars, the fertility of the fields of Normandy and the Ile de France came as all the greater surprise. The vast cornfields and rich pastures amazed most Tourists who expected to find the same sort of contrast between their own country and France as Hogarth, with his firm determination to be displeased at everything he saw out of Old England, depicted in his 'Roast Beef at the Gate of Calais'. 'In my life,' exclaimed a seventeenth-century traveller, 'I never saw Cornfields more large and lovely.' It was a sentiment continually repeated.

There was surprise, too, though less universal, at the military aspect of the towns. Boulogne, Montreuil, Abbeville and Amiens had all been fortresses, like Calais, and they still retained much of the character of garrisons, with strong walls, and gates that denied entry during the hours of darkness. Then there was the pervasive atmosphere of Roman Catholicism, the numbers of monks and priests, the people praying at shrines, the processions following the Host through the streets, the clothed and painted images, the tinkling of bells, and the occasional 'Pilgrim dressed in dark brown with cockleshells upon his hat and cloak, a bag for his provisions, a staff in his hand and a wooden bottle by his side for his drink'.

A few Tourists took the opportunity while in northern France to explore Normandy and Brittany; to cross the Seine at Rouen and to travel up to Cherbourg through Lisieux, Caen and Bayeux; to see the medieval towns around the Golfe de St Malo or to traverse the foothills of the Côtes du Nord to Brest and Quimper, calling on the way at the Trappist abbey at Mortagne where 'the severity is very surprising, for the monks are obliged to perpetual silence, to live upon vegetables, bread and cyder, with several other amazing practices of austerity. Strangers are received here with great civility and entertained at the expense of the convent.'

Some Tourists remained at Amiens where monks taught French for half a guinea a month; others stayed a few days in Rouen, a big, sad, grey town, where they looked down at the bridge of boats across the Seine, up at the Gothic vaults and arches of the great cathedral, admired the famous bell of Cardinal d'Amboise, and made notes in their diaries about the palace of *parlement* and the burning of Joan of Arc. Others went down to Nanteuil to get on the post-route to Rheims and so visit 'one of the most elegant cities of France'. A few preferred to tour western France before entering Paris and, passing through Rambouillet to see the Count of Toulouse's castle, 'one of the finest buildings in the neighbourhood of Paris', and through Orléans where many English students attended the university, they joined the Bordeaux and Bayonne post-route at Cléry. The rare Tourist who got as far as Bordeaux was usually displeased with what he saw –

Thomas Gray, the poet, toured the Continent in 1739–41 with Horace Walpole, who had been one of his closest friends at Eton and Cambridge; but they quarrelled at Reggio and returned home separately.

Immediately upon his arrival in Paris the Tourist was besieged by all manner of touts offering their wares and services, in particular by men hoping to be employed as valets.

a large and sprawling port, 'none of the most beautiful, the streets being narrow, and the buildings old'.

Anxious to reach the capital as soon as possible, most Tourists followed the direct post-route to Paris, stopping perhaps at Chantilly to visit the castle of the Prince of Condé, and to see his famous gardens, 'laid out in a most elegant taste', with their canals and fountains and waterfalls, the ornamental birds flying about the walks, and the aviaries almost hidden in the groves. They might stop again at St Denis to see the white marble sepulchres of the French kings in the Benedictine abbey, the tomb of Marshal Turenne, and Paolo Poncio's bas reliefs of the victories of Louis XII. If they went to the abbey they would be shown the French crown jewels, Charlemagne's golden crown, his diamond-encrusted sword and spurs and his ivory chess men, Roland's hunting horn, the sword of the Maid of Orléans, and a variety of holy relics which John Evelyn conscientiously listed as 'a nail from our Saviour's Cross … a crucifix of the true wood of the Cross, carved by Pope Clement III … a box in which is some of the Virgin's hair … some of the linen in which our blessed Saviour was wrapped at his nativity … some of our Saviour's blood, hair, clothes, linen … one of the thorns of our blessed Saviour's crown … with many other equally authentic toys, which the friar who conducted us would have us believe were authentic relics.'

Having quickly marked these items down in his note-book, the Tourist turned impatiently towards Paris.

The entrance into Paris was beset with formalities and hindrances. There were barriers with iron gates stretching across every approach road, and, once these were passed, there were the tiresome and meticulous custom officials in the Bureau du Roi who examined every part of the post-chaise as well as the visitors' baggage for forbidden articles. Also while the search was being conducted, and throughout the drive from the Bureau to his hotel, the Tourist would be besieged by elegantly dressed young men, wearing earrings and bag-wigs, who pleaded in broken English to be employed as valets, who thrust through the windows of the chaise references written in English by their previous employers, and who, after demanding fifty or sixty sols a day would eventually agree to accept thirty, or 2s 6d in English money.

The Tourist was strongly advised not to enter into any contract with a valet until his references had been verified; and he was as strongly advised not to accept either his advice or that of the postilion as to a suitable hotel. The best hotels were in the Faubourg St Germain outside the old city walls – the Imperial and the Anjou were both in the rue Dauphin. Other recommended hotels were the

John Crome's painting shows the Boulevard des Italiens, which took its name from the Théâtre Italien, as it appeared at the beginning of the nineteenth century. It contained one of the most interesting of Paris's street markets.

43

Hambourg, the Orléans, and the Picardie in the rue Mazarin, the Hôtel d'Espagne in the rue de Seine, the Doge of Venice in the rue de Boucherie, the Grand Hôtel de Luine on the Quay des Augustines, three hotels in the rue St Denis (the Croix Blanche, the Croix Dorée, the Croix de Fer), and the Hôtel du Dauphin in the rue de Teranne where James Boswell stayed in 1766.

Paris If a long stay in Paris were intended, however, the Tourist was recommended to take furnished rooms and dine out at one or other of the numerous public *ordinaires*. The most favoured quarter was where the best hotels were, in the Faubourg St Germain. Here the Rev. William Cole paid four guineas a month for two rooms, one for himself and another for his servant; and here also Edward Gibbon took an apartment in 1763, paying six guineas a month for the four rooms it comprised.

Some Tourists preferred to board with a private family with whom they could expect a neat room, a hot dinner and supper with a pint of wine at each meal for £2 12s 6d a month.

Having settled in at a hotel or in rooms, the Tourist's first thought was to buy new clothes. Even Dr Johnson, when he visited Paris in 1775 at the age of sixty-six, abandoned the black stockings, brown coat and plain shirt he customarily wore in London, and appeared in white stockings, a new hat and a 'French-made wig of handsome construction'.

Robert Adam, the young Scottish architect who arrived in Paris with the Hon. Charles Hope in 1754, described to his mother the transformation of her 'once plain friend' into the most elegant of Tourists:

'A most Frenchified head of hair, loaded with powder, ornaments his top: a complete suit of cut velvet of two colours, his body – which is set off by a white satin lining: white silk stockings and embroidered silk *gussets*, his legs: Mariguin pumps with red heels, his feet: stone buckles like diamonds shine on his knees and shoes. A gold-handled sword, with white and gold handle knot, ornaments his side: Brussels lace, his breast and hands: a solitaire ribbon his neck ... I often burst out a-laughing upon this single thought – of what you would all say were I for a moment to show myself in the drawing-room thus metamorphosed.'

'When an Englishman, comes to Paris,' Smollett said, 'he cannot appear until he has undergone a total metamorphosis! At his first arrival it is necessary to send for the taylor, perruquier, hatter, shoemaker, and every other tradesman concerned in the equipment of the human body. He must even change his buckles, and the form of his ruffles.'

Moreover, so *The Gentleman's Guide* of 1770 warned, 'you will meet nowhere with greater cheats than the French taylors, it is therefore my advice to you to buy everything yourself: and, even at the merchant's, be very careful not to give so much as they ask you.' Fair

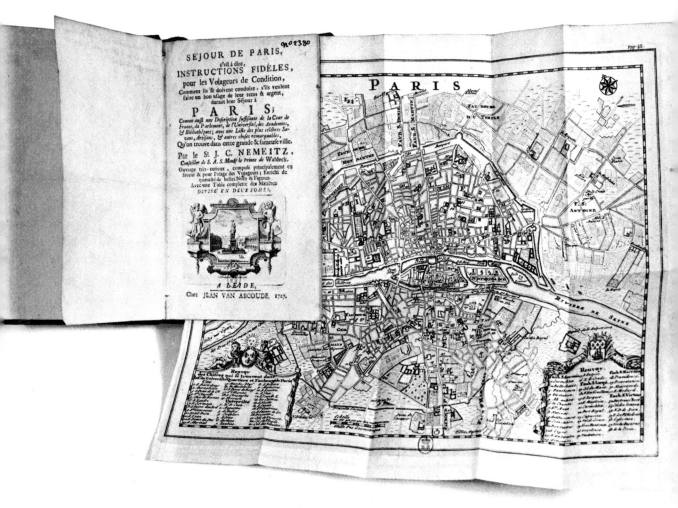

prices ranged from eighteen shillings for 'a plain suit of clothes' to sixteen guineas for 'a black velvet suit with very rich gold waistcoat and two pairs of breeches'.

In his fine new clothes the conscientious Tourist now set out with his tutor to begin exploring the wonders of the city. He had already and immediately been struck by the noise and the bustle, the astonishing speed with which the carriages and people moved through the streets. Before the Revolution there were 'an infinity of one-horse cabriolets, driven by young men of fashion and their imitators, alike fools, with such rapidity as to be real nuisances and to render the streets exceedingly dangerous.' It was not an uncommon sight to see a child run over and probably killed; and since it was impossible to walk about without being splashed by the mud thrown out of the gutters, practical-minded Parisians wore black stockings out of doors in winter and usually black suits as well.

After the Revolution the streets were just the same.

Nemeitz's *Séjour de Paris*, which contained 'reliable instructions for tourists of quality', was published in 1727 and was the most popular and useful guide of the period. The map shows the well-defined limits of the early eighteenth-century city which was, nevertheless, the most populous on the Continent.

45

The Gardens of the
Tuileries, the palace begun
by Catherine de' Medici
and finished by Louis XIV.
'Here it is that the quality
and citizens of Paris walk in
fine evenings as they do in
the Mall at London.'

'The numerous coaches, chaises and cabriolets drive with amazing rapidity over an irregular pavement with a deafening noise, splashing through the gutters which run in the middle of the streets,' wrote Dr Peter Mark Roget, travelling tutor to the two sons of a Manchester cotton merchant in 1802. 'The total want of foot pavement renders it really dangerous to walk in the streets, till you are trained to feats of agility. You are required every instant to hop from stone to stone and to dart from one side of the street to the other. The poor foot-passengers are driven about by the cabriolets like a parcel of frightened sheep. The only security is large stones close to the houses, which scarcely allow you, by sticking close to the wall, to escape being hit. Accidents are frequent. The pavement consists of large round stones, very far from being level and very irregular. They are either covered with mud or, which is generally the case, greasy and very slippery.'

The speed with which the four thousand hackney-carriages and the innumerable two-wheeled carts were driven through the streets was matched by the quick movements of the people. 'Descartes's vortex theory could have been conceived only by a Frenchman, a Parisian,' the Russian traveller Karamzin decided in the year of the Revolution. 'Here everyone is hurrying; seemingly they are all trying to outstrip each other; they hunt out and snatch at ideas. They guess at what you want, so as to be rid of you as quickly as possible … Before you have finished your question, the Parisian has answered you, bowed, and taken his leave.'

'Picture yourself twenty-five thousand houses, four or five stories high, filled with people from top to bottom!', Karamzin continued excitedly. 'In spite of all the geographical almanacs, Paris has a greater population than Constantinople or London, containing, according to the latest calculation, 1,130,450 inhabitants, including 150,000 foreigners and 200,000 servants. Go from one end of the city to the other. Everywhere there are crowds of people on foot or in carriages; everywhere noise and hubbub, in large and small streets, and there are about a thousand streets in Paris! At ten, at eleven o'clock at night there is still life, movement, noise everywhere. At one and two o'clock many people are still about. At three and four you hear the occasional rattle of a carriage. Yet these two hours can be called the quietest of all. At five the workmen, Savoyards and artisans begin to appear in the streets, and little by little the whole city comes alive again.'

Paris had quite as many street performers as London. The itinerant *violoneux* was a characteristic type.

It was a city of contrasts, as well as of speed and noise and constant activity. There were the magnificent churches and palaces, the impressive stone houses of the nobility of the *ancien régime* – glimpsed for a moment through the ironwork gates of their *portes cochères* – the fine wide bridges over the Seine and the gardens by its banks, the expanse of grass that led to the trees of the Champs-Elysées, the beautiful gardens of the Tuileries, the Luxembourg and the Palais Royal, the domes and cupolas, spires and turrets of the Louvre, the Sorbonne, Notre-Dame, Ste Marce and Les Invalides, the vanes of the countless windmills rotating in the wind above Montmartre.

But there were also the frightfully dirty streets, the poverty and squalor. Often visitors were compelled to hold their noses and close their eyes. Near to a glittering jewelry shop or one of the many houses where scent, pomade and hair-powder were sold, there would be a pile of rotten apples and herrings, 'monstrous black sausages in great guts or bladders and boiled sheep's heads'. Everywhere there was 'filth and even blood streaming from the butchers' stalls. You must call Paris', the young Karamzin decided, 'the most magnificent, the most vile, the most fragrant and most fetid city.'

To many Englishmen it seemed fetid and vile, without being either magnificent or fragrant. In his *Instructions for Forreine Travell* (1642), the earliest of continental hand-books, James Howell described it as 'that hudge (though durty) Theater of all Nations'. And later commentators were more explicit. 'It is the ugliest beastliest town in the universe,' Horace Walpole thought. 'A dirty town with a dirtier ditch calling itself the Seine ... a filthy stream, in which everything is washed without being cleaned, and dirty houses, ugly streets, worse shops and churches loaded with bad pictures ... Trees cut into fire shovels and stuck into pedestals of chalk compose their country.' Hazlitt agreed with him: 'Paris is a beast of a city. Rousseau said well, that all the time he was in it, he was only trying how he should leave it.'

47

Even those who were happy there agreed that the shops were mostly very disappointing, and that the poor people who walked by them – the women in wooden clogs, the men unshaved and all of them dirty – were a distressing sight. Ten years after the Revolution, the shops which sold wine or bread, indicated by a garland or a loaf painted outside them, still had 'an iron grating before the windows to defend them from the mob'. At night the narrow streets, badly lit – until argands came into use towards the end of the century – by dimly flickering lamps hanging from ropes suspended overhead, chilled the blood of many a nervous stranger walking back to his room after supper.

To add to his distress, the newly arrived Tourist probably had not enjoyed his supper. To the eighteenth-century Englishman's palate, Parisian food was far too highly seasoned. He had been warned about this before he came. The eatables in Paris, so Nugent's *Grand Tour* cautioned, 'are not so good as in London ... for wholesomeness they are inferior to ours, most of their dishes being too high seasoned, and some of them a perfect hodge-podge, or according to the vulgar proverb, *a medicine for a sick dog*'. Henry Thrale 'justly observed' to Dr Johnson that 'the cookery of the French was forced upon them by necessity; for they could not eat their meat unless they added some taste to it'.

The wine, Nugent had to admit, was 'the best in Europe and very reasonable'. But, then, it had need to be as 'the water they bring in buckets from the river Seine, is neither well tasted nor very wholesome, as appears from the effect it has sometimes in giving violent gripes and purging.' The *Eau de Roy* from Ville d'Avray was excellent but very expensive.

Having found fault with their food, their shops, their traffic and their streets, the Tourist now turned his attention upon the Parisians themselves. He soon found grounds for complaint with them, too.

'I see nothing here that we have not finer and better in England,' Lord Chesterfield wrote from Paris to the Duchess of Marlborough. 'I shall not give you my opinion of the French, because I am very often taken for one; and many a Frenchman has paid me the highest compliment they think they can pay to anyone, which is – "Sir, you are just like one of us". I shall only tell you that I am insolent; I talk a great deal: I am very loud and peremptory; I sing and dance as I go along; and lastly I spend a monstrous deal of money in powder ...'

The Parisians were even more derisive of a man's strange appearance than Londoners were.

'Accident has given me what may be esteemed a comparative test of politeness,' Thomas Holcroft observed. 'Being short-sighted I began to wear spectacles nearly thirty years ago when the custom of walking the streets in them was scarcely introduced. The English populace, when I passed, would often call me Mr Four Eyes, but I never met a greater instance of rudeness from them than this;

Rowlandson's 'La Belle
Liminaudière au Caffee de
Mille Collone, Palais
Royale, Paris' was a well-
known refreshment-room
keeper of the period whose
voluptuous proportions
were much admired by her
customers.

whereas in Paris, the first time I went there *Voilà les quatre yeux* was much more frequently repeated, and with an air of great rudeness and contempt. One day a youth, who was nearly a man, tolerably dressed therefore not of the lowest order, suddenly darted his two fingers almost to my face, uttering the same exclamation.'

In addition to being considered rude, the Parisians were thought arrogant. 'If something foreign arrives at Paris,' said Walpole, 'they either think they invented it, or that it has always been there ... Their boasted knowledge of society,' he complained in another letter, 'is reduced to talking of their suppers, and every malady they have about them, or know of.' Admittedly Gibbon, who was considered sufficiently entertaining and distinguished to be admitted to Mme Geoffrin's salon, and who 'heard more conversation worth remembering' in a fortnight in Paris than 'in two or three winters in London', did not agree with Walpole. But the majority of those few Tourists who could take part in any sort of French conversation claimed to have derived no more benefit from it than Walpole did.

Then, worse than the frivolity and the arrogance of the Parisians' talk, was their 'odious custom of spitting about the Room, which they certainly do to such an excess, that they look like a parcel of Tritons with eternal water spouts plying from their lips; sometimes even when the pocket handkerchief is produced, it is such a flag of abomination that one feels little redress from the exchange.'

'The French are an indelicate people,' Dr Johnson confirmed; 'they will spit upon any place. At Madame ————'s, a literary lady of rank, the footman took the sugar into his fingers, and threw it into my coffee ... The spout of the tea-pot did not pour freely, she bade the footman blow into it. France is worse than Scotland in every thing but climate.'

Almost as distasteful to English visitors as seeing French ladies spitting on the floor was having to look at their 'hideously painted faces'.

'When the Indian chiefs were in England everybody ridiculed their preposterous method of painting their cheeks and eyelids. But this ridicule,' Tobias Smollett thought, 'was wrongly placed. Those critics ought to have considered that the Indians do not use paint to make themselves agreeable, but in order to be more terrible to their enemies ...

But to lay it on as the fashion in France prescribes to all the ladies of condition, who indeed cannot appear without this badge of distinction, is to disguise themselves in such a manner, as to render them odious and detestable to every spectator, who has the least relish left for nature and propriety. As for the *fard*, or white, with which their necks and shoulders are plaistered, it may be in some measure excusable, as their skins are naturally brown, or sallow; but the rouge, which is daubed on their faces, from the chin up to the eyes, without the least art or dexterity, not only destroys all distinction of features, but renders the aspect really frightful, or at best conveys nothing but ideas of disgust and aversion. You know, that without this horrible masque no married lady is admitted at court, or in any polite assembly; and that it is a mark of distinction which no bourgeoise dare assume. Ladies of fashion only have the privilege of exposing themselves in these ungracious colours. As their faces are concealed under a false complexion, so their heads are covered with a vast load of false hair, which is frizzled on the forehead, so as exactly to resemble the wooly heads of the Guinea negroes.'

It would not have been so bad, the Rev. William Jones considered, if the paint had been applied with some care and dexterity, instead of being slapped on in 'great blotches as well defined as the circumference of a circle, and as red as the Saracen's Head upon a sign-post'.

Many Parisian ladies, it had to be admitted, were wonderfully vivacious. Yet even this was far from being a universal trait; and Smollett was exasperated by three languid girls who lived opposite his room and did nothing at all from morning till night. 'They eat grapes and bread from seven till nine,' he reported. 'From nine till twelve they dress their hair, and are all the afternoon gaping at the window to view passengers. I don't perceive that they give themselves the trouble either to make their beds, or clean their apartment. The same spirit of idleness and dissipation I have observed in every

After the Revolution the Louvre became a well-known meeting place for English tourists who were often 'more concerned with their conversation than the pictures', as Cruikshank suggests.

part of France, and among every class of people.'

Twenty years later, in 1781, Samuel Romilly also found the Parisians not nearly so gay as he had always believed them to be. He was in Paris the day the dauphin was born, and, in honour of the birth, the citizens were ordered to illuminate their houses and the police were commanded to ensure that the order was obeyed:

'At night I walked about Paris to see the illuminations; the streets were crowded with people, and the public edifices were well lighted up; but in many of the private houses there appeared only one glimmering lamp at each window, hung up, not in a token of joy, but of reluctant obedience to the Sovereign's will; and some of the citizens were daring enough not to illuminate their houses at all. In many of the squares were little orchestras with bands of music playing to the populace, some of whom danced about in wild, irregular figures ... But they were noisy rather than merry, and none seemed happy.'

After the Revolution the poor people did not appear to be any happier. On Sunday evenings sometimes a Tourist would come across a group of workmen drinking wine and singing vaudevilles on the grass in the Champs-Elysées, or see a party of gay shopkeepers' wives dancing round the trees. But for most of the poor, life was still hard and cheerless, while church congregations were still mostly composed of 'starved Hairdressers, disconsolate Tailors, moaning musicians, and old rheumatic men and women smelling brimstone'.

Of course, not many Tourists allowed the condition of the lower classes to interfere with what pleasures the city afforded. In the jaundiced view of Lord Chesterfield these pleasures were all selfish ones.

Chesterfield's typical *milord Anglais* rose very late, breakfasted with other *milords Anglais* ('to the loss of two good morning hours'), went by coach to the Palais, then on to the English coffee-house where a party was made up for dinner. 'From dinner, where they drink quick, they adjourn in clusters to the play, where they crowd up the stage, drest up in very fine clothes ... From the play to the tavern again, where they get very drunk, and where they either quarrel among themselves, or sally forth, commit some riot in the streets, and are taken up by the watch.' In between times they make love to an Irish laundry-woman or to some itinerant Englishwoman who has escaped either from her husband or her creditors.

Although most Tourists did not behave in the irresponsible way Lord Chesterfield suggested, few derived such intellectual benefit as the young Sir Thomas Pickering did in the seventeenth century, if his tutor is to be believed. This tutor, the Rev. Thomas Lorkin, reported that his charge spent two hours in the morning 'on horseback', one hour reading French, one hour translating a Latin author into French, and a fifth hour practising his swordmanship. At twelve o'clock he dined; and afterwards he spent an hour or so 'in discourse or some

'From nine till twelve they dress their hair,' reported Smollett of the languid girls who lived opposite him in Paris. Fanciful as were the adornments provided for Parisian ladies by the feather-workers, the *perruquier* offered almost as exotic creations for men.

honest recreation perteyning to armes'. From two to three he was at his dancing lessons, then retired to his room with his tutor for two hours of Latin. At five he translated more Latin into French. After supper he and the tutor took 'a brief survey of all'.

In the eighteenth century tutors rarely found it possible to impose so strict a curriculum upon their young charges, who were more likely to spend the early part of the day with a barber than with a riding-master. The barber would sprinkle the *milord*'s head with fine white powder, and with pomade and scent from Provence. Then the young man would wander out in his new coat and breeches, stroll about the Tuileries, sip coffee, throw a handful of coins to the singing-women and musicians who went from table to table, watch the washerwomen scrubbing linen by the banks of the Seine, take a ride in a man-drawn two-wheeled chair, look into a jewelry shop in the arcades beneath the Palais Royal, or into one of the curio shops near Notre-Dame, or browse amongst the books at Didot's, read the English newspapers at the Cabinet Littéraire in the rue Neuve des Petits Champs, eat a heavy meal at noon, perform a little undemanding sightseeing in the afternoon but not too much – for, as Thomas Gray remarked, 'it is not the fashion here to have curiosity' – and look forward to the evening, when he could escape the observation of his tutor and make his way to one or other of the fashionable brothels.

James Boswell, unencumbered by a tutor, asked at the custom-house where the good brothels were, and was directed to one of Mme Charlotte Genevieve Hecquet's two establishments where he was introduced to a Mlle Constance, a 'tall, quite French lady'. The next day he visited Mlle Dupuis's brothel at the Hôtel Montigny, but found his experiences there 'sad work'. So two days later he returned to Mme Hecquet's 'as in fever. Constance elegant'.

Unlike so many of his contemporaries, Boswell did not find pleasure in Paris only in the brothel, coffee-house and tavern. He conscientiously toured the sights of Paris, as Dr Johnson did ten years later.

Dr Johnson's intinerary might well, indeed, have served as a model for his juniors. He went to the Tuileries to walk in the famous gardens redesigned by Le Nôtre in 1665, and noted in his diary that the walks were not open to 'mean persons', for here it was that the upper classes paraded in their finery 'dripping powder and paint' onto their embroidered clothes. He went to the Palais Royal, 'very grand, large and lofty – A very great collection of pictures – Three of Raphael – One small piece of M. Angelo – One Room of Rubens.' He went to the *Ecole Militaire*, and the Observatory, to several *hôtels* and to many churches, to the courts of justice, and to the King's cabinet, a natural history museum which displayed a wonderful variety of shells, fossils, dried animals and 'candles of the candletree'. He went to the King's library, too, and to the libraries at the Sorbonne and St Germain. Never speaking anything but Latin – for 'it was a maxim with him that a man should not let himself down by speaking a language which he speaks imperfectly' – he bought himself two pairs of stockings, a hat, a wig, a snuff box, a table-book and three pairs of scissors. He watched the rope-and-egg-dancing on the boulevards; he inspected the statue of Louis XIV in the Place de Vendôme; he looked into the dried-up moat of the Bastille; he dined with the Marquis Blanchetti, with Count Manucci and with the Benedictine monks who gave him 'soup meagre, herrings, eels, both with sauce; fryed fish; lentils, tasteless in themselves'. He went to see the Gobelins tapestry factory, the porcelain works at Sèvres, and M. Sans-terre's brewery. He went to Gagnier's house where he saw rooms 'furnished with a profusion of wealth and elegance' such as he had never seen before – 'Vases – pictures – dragon china – lustre said to be of crystal and to have cost 3,500l – the whole furniture said to have cost 125,000l – Damask hangings covered with pictures – Porphyry' – and he went to court to see the King and Queen at dinner, and noticed that the King 'fed himself with his left hand as we'.

Although few young Tourists covered Paris as thoroughly as Dr Johnson, they were all as interested as he was in seeing the royal family at the dining-table. After the outbreak of the Revolution, however, Louis XVI and his family did not dine in public any more; and the curious had to be content to look at them in the royal chapel, wondering how long they would be allowed to survive.

Karamzin, who saw them there a few months after the fall of the Bastille, thought that the King's 'countenance bespoke composure, gentleness, and kindness', that Marie Antoinette was 'born to be a queen'.

'Her air, her glance, her smile – all denote an uncommon soul,' he wrote. 'Her heart must be suffering, but she knows how to hide her sorrow, and not a single cloud is to be seen in her bright eyes. Smiling like the Graces, she leafed through her prayer book, glanced first at the King, then at the princess, her daughter, and again turned to the book. Elizabeth, the King's sister, prayed with great fervour and devotion. She seemed to be weeping.'

When the second Lord Palmerston saw Mme Elizabeth two years later, however, she 'looked as if she was going to spit in the people's face', which he understood she was 'almost ready to do upon every occasion'. The Queen, though much changed, was 'an agreeable looking woman. She seemed to possess herself well and showed no emotion … The King himself came rolling along and looked as if he did not care a farthing about it if they would but let him alone.'

A spectacle almost as popular as the royal family was the Paris theatre. Karamzin went every night for almost a month. And although Dr Johnson was disappointed – not only because he could neither see nor hear, but also because of the 'drunken women' he encountered there – few Tourists shared his distaste.

To be sure the Théâtre Français was considered 'a gloomy place,

top Although the palace itself came as a disappointment to most Tourists, the gardens of Versailles, planned by André Le Nôtre, were a delight. Particularly popular was the labyrinth, a number of walks leading into each other and surrounded with pallisades.
bottom A fancy-dress ball in the Galerie des Glaces at Versailles. The gallery, 253 feet long and over 40 feet high, was built by Mansart in 1678. Its numerous chandeliers and looking-glasses made it one of the most glittering rooms in Europe.

56

A *divertissement pantomime* given at the Théâtre Italien. The scene is a *guinguette* near Montmartre.

dirty and black', and the performances there 'outré, fantastic, and full of nonsensical grimace'. Admittedly when Charles Burney went to the Théâtre Italien to see a comic opera, the performance – quite rightly in his opinion, for French music was at a very low ebb in 1770 – was 'thoroughly damned' by an audience who hissed and booed and laughed at it, 'in short condemned it in all the English forms, except breaking the benches and the actors' heads; and the incessant sound of *hish* instead of *hiss*'. But there were over twenty other theatres, and the Opéra was a delight. The performances there, Catherine Wilmot thought, exhibited 'more grace, dexterity of pointed toes, variety and elegance of attitude, and sparkling show of dress, &c., than any spectacle I ever saw in my life … The ballets are enchanting … I had heard of the public decorum in France and indeed the Opera was a striking instance of it, for during the length of the entire performance not a whisper was to be heard! Every eye was turned upon the stage, with most devotional attention.'

After the theatre the well-behaved Tourist would go to the Café de Valois or the Café de Caveau for a cup of *bavaroise*, and then return to his diary and his bed. But others, if they did not find their way to Mme Hecquet's, or Mlle Dupois's, would seek out a house where they could gamble. Such houses were easy enough to find, for the Parisians were devoted to gaming and welcomed into their drawing-rooms young English gentlemen with money to play with and to lose. Indeed, Dr John Moore, who was introduced into 'some of the most fashionable circles' in Paris by a French marquis, thought that nothing could give greater proof of the marquis's influence and standing in society than that he should presume to present to his acquaintances an Englishman who did not have a title and who did not gamble.

But, in fact, most Englishmen, whether titled gamblers or not, were rarely made to feel unwelcome. Both before and after the Revolution the houses of the rich usually contained in a corner of the saloon 'an English tea equipage', which was brought into use when visitors arrived; and even after the end of the Napoleonic wars young Beaujolois Campbell noticed how 'Englishified' France seemed to be.

The Napoleonic wars halted the inflow of English Tourists into Paris. But in the early days of Napoleon's power, Englishmen were as welcome in Paris as they had always been. Many of them were invited to dine with him at the Tuileries and were delighted by the polite conversation and charming smile of the man whose features were so familiar a part of the Parisian scene, adorning ladies' reticules, stamped on barley sugar, and reigning supreme (in plaster of Paris) over every gingerbread stall.

A more intimidating host than Napoleon, so ruthless yet so gracious when he chose to be, was the Turkish ambassador whose dinners were famous and in whose dining-room the English ambassador, eating little, and Talleyrand, gobbling like a duck, were frequent guests.

Lord and Lady Mount Cashell and Catherine Wilmot were there once when a bottle of champagne burst with so much violence that some heretical drops were sprinkled on the ambassador's Mohammedan sleeve.

'Really,' Miss Wilmot reported, 'I never saw anything so dreadful as a Turk in a passion! His eyes flashed forth fire, and I thought he would have been tempted to draw his diamond dagger upon the unlucky offender. After deprecating the Prophet's wrath, by mumbled expiations, he strode into the drawing-room, with his robes flying wide behind him, like a tragic King and seated himself cross-legged upon the sofa, after having flung his yellow slippers on the floor. There he held himself in deepest meditation for an hour, and on seeing us amusing ourselves by quaffing liqueurs and coffee, to my amazement he started up and drank down without stopping six glasses of the strongest Liqueurs upon the board. He then walked with measured pace about the room, called all his merry musselmen about him, and departed to offer to Mahomed the contaminated robe as a sacrifice to appease his vengeance.'

After paying a visit to this formidable but entertaining Turk, a Tourist's visit to Napoleonic Paris was not complete without calling upon Tom Paine, the famous author whose *Rights of Man* had provoked the British government to have him sentenced as an outlaw.

Paine had been living in exile in Paris since 1792, and in 1802 he was occupying a set of mean rooms up half a dozen flights of stairs in a remote part of the town. 'A friend of his lives in the house with him, whose two little boys, children of four and five years old, he has adopted,' reported one of his visitors.

'During the entire morning that we spent with him, they were playing about the room, overturning all his machinery and putting everybody out of patience except himself, who exhibited the most incorrigible good temper. His appearance is plain beyond conception; drinking Spirits has made his entire face as red as fire and his habits of life have rendered him so neglectful in his person that he is generally the most abominably dirty being upon the face of the earth … In spite of his surprising ugliness, the expression of his countenance is luminous, his manners easy and benevolent, and his conversation remarkably entertaining. Vanity is his ruling passion, and praise in any way infatuates him.'

Versailles

Sooner or later during his stay in Paris, the Tourist would go out of town to visit Versailles, either by the *coche*, which left twice a day from the rue Saint Nicaise, by *carrosse* or post-chaise, or by water as far as Sèvres and then along the great causeway beneath the heights of Viroflé.

Although described by Nugent as 'one of the finest palaces of the world', few Tourists found that Versailles lived up to their expectations. Hoping to encounter there all the magnificence of Louis xiv's dream, they professed themselves disappointed to discover what Horace Walpole termed 'a lumber of littleness, composed of black brick, stuck full of bad old busts, and fringed with gold rails'. Walpole found particularly distasteful the 'mixture of parade and poverty … In the colonnades, upon the staircase, nay in the antechambers of the royal family, there are people selling all sorts of wares. While we were waiting in the Dauphin's sumptuous bedchamber, till his dressing-room door should be opened, two fellows were sweeping it, and dancing about in sabots to rub the floor.'

'The apartments are dirty,' a later visitor observed in 1773, 'which cannot be wondered at when you are told that all the world rove about the palace at pleasure. I went from room to room as my choice directed me, into the King's bed-chamber, dressing-room, etc., in all of which were numbers of people, and many of them indifferently clad.'

Two years before the outbreak of the Revolution Arthur Young discovered men in tattered shirts and wooden shoes wandering about the private apartments; and even in the chapel ragged crowds pressed to watch the King at Mass.

'The King laughed and spied at the ladies; every eye was fixed on the personages of the Court ... while the priest, who in the mean-time went on in the exercise of his office, was unheeded by all present. Even when the Host was lifted up, none observed it; and if the people knelt, it was because they were admonished by the ringing of the bell; and, even in that attitude, all were endeavouring to get a glimpse of the King.'

The surroundings of the palace seemed all of a piece with the vulgarity of life inside it.

'Ramble through the gardens, and by the grand canal, with absolute astonishment at the exaggerations of writers and travellers. There is magnificence in the quarter of the orangerie, but no beauty anywhere ... The extent and breadth of the canal are nothing to the eye; and it is not in such good repair as a farmer's horse-pond. The menagerie is well enough, but nothing great.'

'The palace is a huge heap of littleness', Lord Macaulay decided in the following century, echoing Walpole's disappointment.

'On the side towards Paris the contrast between the patches of red brick in the old part and the attempt at classical magnificence in the later part is simply revolting. Enormous as is the size of the Place des Armes, it looks paltry beyond description ... In the middle of the Court is an equestrian statue of Louis XIV. He showed his sense, at least, in putting himself where he could not see his own architectural performances .... I doubt whether there be anywhere any single architectural composition of equal extent ... yet there are a dozen country houses of private individuals in England alone which have a greater air of majesty and splendour than this huge quarry.'

Less disappointing than a visit to Versailles was the trip down the Seine in a *coche d'eau* to Saint-Cloud and the Duke of Orléans's palace which, 'for situation, waters, woods, architecture, sculpture, and paintings, [was] reckoned one of the finest in the Kingdom'. Other trips by *coche d'eau* might be taken to Sèvres; to Marli where the grand cascade 'resembles a river tumbling from a precipice', and where the machine which pumped the water sixty-two fathoms high for all the spouts and basins at Versailles was 'look'd upon as the most stupen-dous thing of its kind in the whole world'; or to Fontainebleau.

Indeed, a trip up the Seine as far as Fontainebleau was a common prelude to a journey down the Loire from Orléans to Nantes where the Hôtel de Henry IV was described by Arthur Young as the 'finest inn in Europe'. The towns of the Loire valley were famous for the purity of their French; and many Tourists spent several months in

Passengers climb aboard the *coche d'osier* in the 1770s for the journey to Versailles. The *coche* was designed to carry sixteen passengers, but frequently took almost twice that number, many of them on the roof.

one or other of them, attempting to acquire a satisfactory accent. Blois, then considered 'one of the pleasantest cities in France', and Tours, which John Evelyn thought was exceeded in beauty and in delight by no other town in France, were the most favoured of all. But it was at Saumur that Robert Montagu, later third earl of Manchester, spent over a year during his Grand Tour in the middle of the seventeenth century. He learned fencing and singing there, how to dance and to play the guitar, as well as to speak French and Latin. Saumur was full of Huguenots, and no Protestant traveller who passed through the town in the earlier half of the century was content to leave it without paying his respects to that greatest of Huguenots, Philippe de Mornay, Seigneur du Plessis-Marly, founder of the Protestant university at Saumur which was suppressed by Louis XIV in 1683. Towards the end of his life, however, Mornay was shattered by the loss of a dearly loved wife; and when Thomas Wentworth, Earl of Strafford, visited him at his castle he found 'a little, old, man, great ills, purblinds, melancholly, and hath had a red beard'.

From Saumur as his base, Robert Montagu visited Angers, La Flèche, Richelieu, Poitiers, and Loudun, where there still lived the famous old nun whose devils the Jesuits had driven out. He also visited La Rochelle to see the sugar refinery, and Chinon to see the birthplace of Rabelais. He hunted in the woods of the duc de la Trémouille and on the estate of Cardinal Grimaldi.

Going back to Paris in November 1650 by way of Orléans, where

A 1767 list of the posting
inns of France published by
order of the Duc de
Choiseul d'Amboise, the
Grand Master and
Superintendent of the
'Couriers Postes et relais de
France'.

he met Louis XIV's armies returning from the siege of Bordeaux,
Montagu then set off for Lyons through Briare, Pouilly (famous for
its mineral waters), Nevers, Moulins and Roanne.

Although this remained the post-route throughout the eighteenth
century, many Tourists preferred to take the longer road through
Dijon, and then down the Saône past Châlon, Mâcon and Ville-
franche. Alternatively, a diligence ran every other day from the
Hôtel de Sens in Paris to Lyons, going through Melun, Joigny,
Vermenton and Arnay le Duc. As on the journey from the coast to
Paris, so on the road further south, the inns were sadly disappointing.
Dr Roget – plagued on the way by women begging him to buy gloves,
trinkets, knives and corkscrews and by smiths who appeared very
cross that his chaise needed no repairs – said that he and his pupils
'never met with comfortable inns at the time' they wanted them; and
since they found their chaise more comfortable than the stuffy inn
rooms they were shown into, preferred not to stop for a midday meal.
Many other Tourists did the same. Even so the journey often took
as long as six tiring days.

Lyons, unfortunately, was not at that time considered a pleasant
place to rest. Particularly obnoxious were the 'extreme narrowness
of the streets, which [were] badly paved and ever dirty; and the
villainous ragged paper windows, with which every house (except
those of the richest merchants) [was] defaced'. There were, admittedly,
several good inns, of which the three best known were the Three
Kings, the Dauphin and the Auberge au Parc, while the *ordinaires*
were considered as good as those in Paris and were less expensive.
There were also in Lyons several good shops; and Robert Adam, for
one, wrote admiringly of their varied stock which included 'the
prettiest things for ladies'.

'The inhabitants of this city are industrious, and civil to strangers,'
Nugent told his readers. 'The women would be very handsome, were
it not for their losing their hair and teeth so soon, which some
attribute to the frequent fogs that cover the town.'

Although there were 'a great many remains of antiquity' in Lyons,
for most Tourists it was but a stopping-place and a terminus. They
were anxious to move on south to Marseilles and Toulon, or to cross
the frontier into Switzerland or Italy. Some of those who planned to
go home from Italy through Germany and the Low Countries took
the opportunity to see the south of France now.

The coastal towns and villages along the Côte d'Azur were largely
ignored. The only places in Nugent's guide which were considered
worthy of mention on the journey between Aix en Provence and Nice
were Brignole ('a very ancient place, noted for its fine fruit, particularly
prunes'), Fréjus (which 'has some old fortifications, indifferently
built ... the old harbour is now a flat shore') and Antibes ('the last
town in France toward the frontier of Italy ... pretty well built').
The road from Antibes to Nice was 'very bad, bordered with precipices
on the left, and by the sea to the right.' There was nothing worth

remark at Cannes which could only be approached 'on the sides of great stony mountains thick covered with pines and firs'. Monaco in 1785 constituted, so Dupaty noted, 'two or three streets upon precipitous rocks; eight hundred wretches dying of hunger; a tumble down castle; and a battalion of French troops.' While the countryside around Menton, in Swinburne's opinion, was

'a calcined, scalped, tasped, scraped, flayed, broiled, powdered, leprous, blotched, mangy, grimy, parboiled, country *without* trees, water, grass, fields – *with* blank, beastly senseless olives and orange-

A map of French post routes. There were six miles to a post, and the cost of travelling in the middle of the eighteenth century was not much less than two shillings a post if the postilions were to be kept content with the large tips they expected.

65

trees like a mad cabbage gone indigestible; it is infinitely liker hell than earth, and one looks for tails among the people. And such females with hunched bodies and crooked necks carrying tons on their heads, and looking like Death taken seasick.'

Nice, however, by the 1780s, at that time part of the kingdom of Piedmont, was quite fashionable. 'The place is flourishing,' Arthur Young thought, 'owing very much to the resort of foreigners, principally English who pass the winter here, for the benefit and pleasure of the climate.' Indeed it had altogether 'too much the air of an English watering-place' for the taste of James Edward Smith who confessed himself 'disgusted with the gross flattery paid here to strangers, and to the English in particular'.

Marseilles

The only other places along the coast frequented by foreigners were Marseilles and Toulon. Marseilles, a busy and populous port with one hundred thousand inhabitants, could be reached in three and a half days by mule-drawn diligence, or more quickly, and more dangerously, by the boats which went down the Rhône at great speed, sometimes striking the piers of the Pont Saint-Esprit. Upstream they were drawn by oxen which trudged along the bank and swam between the arches of the bridges with their drivers sitting between their horns.

The harbour at Marseilles was the town's main attraction for here the king's galleys were stationed.

John Evelyn, on his visit to the galleys, was given most courteous entertainment by the captain of the Galley Royal:

'The spectacle was to me new and strange, to see so many hundreds of miserably naked persons, their heads being shaven close, and having only high red bonnets, a pair of coarse canvas drawers, their whole backs and legs naked, doubly chained about their middle and legs, in couples, and made fast to their seats, and all commanded in a trice by an imperious and cruel seaman … The rising-forward and falling-back at their oar is a miserable spectacle, and the noise of their chains, with the roaring of the beaten waters, has something strange and fearful in it … They are ruled and chastised on their backs and soles of their feet, on the least disorder, and without the least humanity.'

Yet, as Evelyn was pleased to notice, they were 'cheerful and full of knavery', and there was hardly one but had 'some occupation, by which, as leisure and calms permitted, they got some little money, insomuch as some of them have, after many years of cruel servitude, been able to purchase their liberty.'

In the eighteenth century many of them dealt in toys and cutlery, and even had their own little shops along the quay.

Sometimes a Tourist recorded in his diary a conversation with a slave, and many listed in their note-books the wonderful variety of Marseilles's export trade – almonds, cloth, salted eels, figs, anchovies, cotton waistcoats and stockings to Italy; taffetas, box-combs, dimities,

V. J. Nicolle's 'La Seine vue du Louvre' represents ideally the kind of picture the Tourist sought to take home with him, a view of a town in which he had stayed combined with details of architectural motifs.

paper, gum arabic, hardware and drugs to Spain.

Toulon also kept the conscientious Tourist busy copying out its statistical marvels, the vast size of its rope-yard, the number of naval cannon cast each year in the foundry, the huge proportions of the hall of arms and the artillery park.

But it was not so much the towns of the French Mediterranean coast as the Provençal hinterland that caught the Tourists' fancy. Aix was much admired and much visited, its squares and fountains being considered more beautiful than any others in France save those in Paris. *The Gentleman's Guide* of 1770 went so far as to suggest that 'this town will perhaps please you better than any you have yet seen in France ... in winter it is extremely pleasant.'

Arles was also very popular, since 'no city in France is so remarkable for its antiquities, insomuch that it is generally called a second Rome'. Further north was Avignon, 'the residence of a vast number of handsome English gentlemen', some, so the dowager Countess of Carlisle assured George Selwyn, of 'very good sort'. Many of them came down to Avignon from Lyons by the Rhône *coches d'eau*, and were startled on stepping ashore by the crowds of bronze-coloured sailors on the banks. Catherine Wilmot described the fringed sashes tied about the waists of these sailors and 'the talismans suspended on their bare necks to guard them from shipwreck ... This was almost all the dress they wore except their Trousers. The women, in the midst of rags and tatters, were glittering in dropt gold ear-rings, and Holy Ghosts in the shape of a dove, which they all dangled from their necklaces; the crowd through which we elbowed our way from the Boat to the Inn, really looked like a Pawnbroker's shop, suddenly kindled into animation.'

Montpellier Both Avignon and Arles were recommended as summer resorts for those whose health could not withstand the rigours of the English winter. But the university town of Montpellier was more renowned as a health resort than either. 'Vast numbers of consumptive people flock hither from all parts of Europe, especially from England, to breathe this air.' The number of apothecaries who set up business to attend to them was 'incredible; some say near two hundred, who all live very well on the many compositions they make'. In the opinion of the *Gentleman's Guide*, though, the reputation of Montpellier was wholly undeserved: 'This town has long been famous for (what it does not in the least degree possess) a salubrious air and skilful physicians.' Also, according to Smollett, it was atrociously expensive.

'Put up at the Cheval Blanc, counted the best auberge in the place, tho' in fact it is a most wretched hovel, the habitation of darkness, dirt, and imposition,' Smollett wrote in his *Travels*. 'Here I was obliged to pay four livres a meal for every person in my family, and two livres at night for every bed, though all in the same room ... This imposition is owing to the concourse of English who come hither, and, like simple birds of passage, allow themselves to be

plucked by the people of the country, who know their weak side, and so make their attacks accordingly. They affect to believe that all the travellers of our country are grand seigneurs, immensely rich and incredibly generous; and we are silly enough to encourage this opinion, by submitting quietly to the most ridiculous extortion, as well as by committing acts of the most absurd extravagance. This folly of the English, together with a concourse of people from different quarters, who come hither for the re-establishment of their health, has rendered Montpellier one of the dearest places in the south of France.'

Montpellier was as far west as most Tourists ventured. A few found their way to Carcassone, though the medieval town and fortifications aroused little interest; and the dismissive opinion of one disgruntled visitor was not an uncommon one: 'Carcassone is in two parts, but

The *coche d'eau* was a pleasant way of travelling for those in no great hurry. Halts to take on extra passengers and baggage might last for anything up to three hours.

neither of them worth notice, nor yet the Castle: the country here is
stony and barren.' A few others reached Toulouse and were tempted
by the cheap food and lodgings to extend their stay. Lady Knight,
who could not afford to live so well anywhere else, was one of those
who were delighted with the cheapness of Toulouse. In 1776 she
wrote home to say, 'I gave a dinner ... two days since to an Irish lady
and a French gentleman; we had a soup and a dish of stewed beef,
a very fine large eel, mutton chops, a brace of red partridges, an
omelet with peaches in it, grapes, peaches, pears, and savoy biscuits;
a bottle of Bordeaux – sixteen pence – a bottle of our own wine, value
three half-pennys. The whole expense amounted to ten shillings, wine
included and a very fine cauliflower.'

But little time was spent in any of the towns in southern France, and
by the time he had reached Lyons the average Tourist was already

planning his journey into Italy or Switzerland.

Those who did not want to battle with the Alps could go down the Rhône valley to Marseilles or Toulon and there take a boat to Genoa or Leghorn. But even though all vessels kept close to the shore, a sea voyage in the Mediterranean was always open to interruption by Barbary pirates. An alternative means of avoiding the Alps was to take the post-route to Nice, and then the winding road which ran along the coast at the foot of the Ligurian Alps. But this road was appallingly rough and so beset by bandits that James Boswell – who went that way in 1765 when his felucca was obliged to put ashore by an adverse wind – felt so nervous when he got to Ventimiglia that he slept at the post-house fully clothed, with his ill-treated dog Jachone clasped in his arms.

Most Tourists, therefore, chose to cross the Alps, either through Grenoble, Briançon and Cesana, or through Geneva and Switzerland. The Grenoble route provided an opportunity both to see this town, 'generally ranked among the chief cities of the Kingdom', and to visit the Grande Chartreuse, the stark and isolated mother house of the

The sea voyage into Italy by felucca from Marseilles to Genoa was always open to interruption by Barbary pirates; but even this was considered a safer route than the winding coast road at the foot of the Ligurian Alps, beset as it so often was by bandits.

top A diligence, packed with travellers, creeks out of the Coq en Pâte. Rowlandson's beggars were inevitable attendants on such occasions.
bottom Catacombs at St Denis, where Cruikshank's farceur is frightening four English Tourists.

The naïve young English Tourist, accompanied by tutor and valet and clutching a copy of Chesterfield's *Letters*, arrives at a French country inn where '*la grenouille traiteur*' stands ready to fleece him. The caricaturist Henry William Bunbury, son of the Rev. Sir William Bunbury, had himself made the Grand Tour in the 1760s and had studied drawing in Rome.

Boots similar to the vast pair worn by the postilion in Bunbury's picture – almost as big and rounded as oyster barrels to protect the legs in case of accident – were brought back from the Continent by the Tourist as mementoes of his travels.

A common sight in the villages of south-eastern France was a roving family of musicians. A little girl accompanying her mother on the triangles may also be seen in Rowlandson's picture of a table d'hôte on page 29.

The Grande Chartreuse

severely ascetic Carthusian monks.

The approach to their monastery was as forbidding as their rules. 'Scituate in the most solitary place that can be found in the world,' Clenche wrote of it, 'amongst horrid mountains, worse than the Alps and the way from Chambéry, hewn out of the side of rocks in steps, with continual precipices, a roaring torrent in the bottom, and through the melancholy shade of pine and fir-trees.' 'But the road, West, the road!' exclaimed Walpole in a letter to his friend of Eton days, 'winding round a prodigious mountain, and surrounded with others, all shagged with ranging woods, obscured with pines, or lost in clouds! Below, a torrent breaking through cliffs, and tumbling through fragments of rocks! ... Now and then an old foot-bridge, with a broken rail, a leaning cross, a cottage, or the ruin of a hermitage!'

The millionaire William Beckford – despatched on the Grand Tour in 1780 by a family concerned by his emotional entanglements both with a young boy and a married cousin – was entertained by the monks at the Grande Chartreuse in the noblest manner, served with 'the best fish, the most exquisite fruits ... a variety of dishes, excellent, without the assistance of meat, and Burgundy of the happiest growth and vintage.' In the dining-room a marble fountain played, casting its clear water into a porphyry shell; and in his bedroom, there was a delicious smell of pine 'with which the little apartment was roofed, floored and wainscotted'.

Wild as the country around the Grande Chartreuse was, the scenery across the border of Savoy to the east was wilder and more rugged still. Here the vast black perpendicular sides of mountains, streaked with the foam of torrents roaring from ledge to ledge, rose high above the rough road, and awed every Tourist who passed by them. Thomas Gray spoke for all Tourists when – remembering his perilous and frightening journey on mule-back in the shadow of the Grande Chartreuse – he wrote of the Savoyard scene, 'Rocks and Torrent beneath; Pine trees, and snows above; horrours and terrours on all sides ... scenes which would awe an atheist into belief, without the help of other argument.'

The Savoyard peasants, picturesque as they looked at a distance in their laced jackets and bordered petticoats, were a fitting accompaniment to this awesome landscape. 'Meagre, ragged, barefooted, with their children in extreme misery and nastiness', these peasants horrified Gray. While Catherine Wilmot found them 'frightful', with 'terrific' goitres on their throats. They seemed quite unselfconscious about these goitres which they decorated with gold trinkets making themselves look 'so stupid'. Miss Wilmot was sometimes 'at a loss to discover which was the Guatar, the Face or the throat'.

The men who carried her across the mountains were nevertheless full of gaiety and high spirits. 'They went full speed, running races with one another, bounding down the Rocks from cliff to cliff ... In coming into the little towns, or rather villages, scattered on the Mountain, they set up a wild song which brought out all the guatar'd villagers, and after setting us down, like old disabled Beggarwomen, they went in to regale themselves with Vin-du-Pays.'

With such companions as these the journey through the mountains lost much of its terror. And those Tourists who chose to enter Switzerland by way of the steep but good post-road through Montluel, Nantua and Collonges had little idea as yet of the discomforts and shocks that lay ahead in the Alpine passes.

An engraving by Brockendon showing the hazardous journey over the Simplon pass.

The St Gotthard pass. The
wild, chaotic and terrible
beauty of Alpine scenery
held little appeal for the
eighteenth-century
traveller.

SWITZERLAND

Geneva – high prices due to gullibility of English – the visit to Voltaire at Ferney – the pleasures of Lausanne society – Basel – William Windham's expedition to Chamonix to see the glaciers – the dangers and excitement of crossing the Alps – dismantling and storage of carriages – Walpole's spaniel devoured by a wolf.

Informed by Nugent that the Swiss were a handsome, well-made, industrious and honest race whose reputation for heaviness was undeserved, the Tourist entered the independent city state of Geneva in hopeful anticipation. He was rarely disappointed.

The common people, who spoke a 'very bad dialect of the French tongue', were, it was admitted, of a 'clownish disposition'. But the people of condition were polite, friendly and hospitable. Most evenings – since playhouses were not permitted in Geneva – assemblies were held in the larger houses, and although games of chance were prohibited by law in other parts of Switzerland, in Geneva cards were played even on Sundays. James Boswell, after attending a service one Sunday in 1764 at the Eglise de St Germain, walked for a while 'on the Bastion Bourgeois, an excellent airy place, where the Genevois and Genevoises assemble'. He then called first on a banker, and afterwards on a 'society of young folks', where he was 'amused to see card-playing, and a minister rampaging amongst them. O John Calvin, where art thou now?'

The main complaint of most Tourists was that prices were so high. This was commonly attributed to the numbers of Englishmen who were always to be found there. Everywhere on the Continent, but particularly in Geneva, it was assumed that every Englishman must be rich and should be charged accordingly. Often this was the Tourists' own fault.

'The English,' said Lady Knight, 'pay double for everything in every country.' 'If they do not find things dear,' Dr Moore confirmed,

Berne was 'a beautiful city', Samuel Romilly's sister thought, 'the streets wide, regularly built with arches, that you may walk round the town in bad weather without being wet.'

'they soon make them so.' The *Gentleman's Guide* agreed with them. 'How frequently,' its author wrote, 'did I with concern see our young nobility and gentry ... collecting mobs in the street by throwing money from the windows ... People in trade find the English custom so vastly beneficial, that they have their lookers-out on purpose to bring them to their shops and taverns.'

In Samuel Foote's *The Capuchin*, a revised version of *The Trip to Calais* which the Lord Chamberlain banned at the instigation of the Duchess of Kingston, there is a scene which derides this exhibitionistic extravagance. Sir Harry Hamper is making the Tour with a tutor:

'Hamper: Come, come! Come along, Doctor! Give the postilions 30 sous apiece.
Tutor: 'Tis put down they are to have but five in the book.
Hamper: No matter; it will let them know we are somebody.
Tutor: What significations that? Ten to one we shall never see them again.
Hamper: Do as you are bid.
Tutor: Then! See how they grin. I dare be sworn you hadn't seen such a sum this many a day.
1st Postilion: Serviteur! Bonne voyage! Monsieur, my Lor!
Hamper: There, there! '*My Lord*'! I have purchased a title for tenpence. That is dog cheap, or the Devil's in it!'

Ferney

It was such Englishmen as Sir Harry Hamper, who, by driving out of Geneva to Ferney merely to stare at him, antagonised Voltaire.

The young James Boswell, depicted opposite in a portrait by George Willison, visited Voltaire at Ferney in 1764. Above the bust of Voltaire is an engraving of the church with the inscription noted by Boswell.

'Well, gentlemen, you now see me,' the great man cried out in exasperation to one group of gaping Tourists. 'Did you take me for a wild beast or monster that was fit only to be stared at as a show?'

Provided a request were made, however, Voltaire was always glad to allow English Tourists to see round his house and gardens; and they, for their part, could scarcely contemplate a visit to Geneva without paying a call upon the grand old philosopher, who bought the estate of Ferney four miles outside the town in 1758.

A few years later Boswell, that disarmingly inveterate tusk-hunter, made his famous call:

'I was in true spirits; the earth was covered with snow; I surveyed wild nature with a noble eye … The first object that struck me was his church with this inscription: "Deo erexit Voltaire MDCCLXI". His chateau was handsome. I was received by two or three footmen, who showed me into a very elegant room. I sent by one of them a letter to Monsieur de Voltaire which I had from Colonel Constant at The Hague. He returned and told me, "Monsieur de Voltaire is very much annoyed at being disturbed. He is abed."'

The inauspicious beginning dampened Boswell's spirits; and the subsequent conversation between the two men, when they did meet, was not an easy one. They spoke of Scotland; and Boswell, conscious of his awkwardness, remarked that an Academy of Painting had been established in Glasgow, but that it was not a success. 'No,' said Voltaire. 'To paint well it is necessary to have warm feet.'

After some discussion of Lord Kames's *Elements of Criticism*, Boswell

then brought up his intended tour of the Hebrides with Dr Johnson.

'Very well,' Voltaire commented. 'But I shall remain here. You will allow me to stay here?'

'Certainly.'

'Well then, go. I have no objections at all.'

Boswell asked him if he still spoke English. He replied, 'No. To speak English one must place the tongue between the teeth, and I have lost my teeth.'

Although Boswell remained at Ferney for dinner, Voltaire was not one of the company. 'Madame Denis, his niece does the honours of his house very well. She understands English. She was remarkably good to me. I sat by her and we talked much. I became lively and most agreeable. We had a company of about twelve ... The gates of Geneva shut at five, so I was obliged to hasten away after dinner without seeing any more of Monsieur de Voltaire.'

Despite his cool reception, Boswell determined to see Voltaire again; and he wrote to Mme Denis a 'very lively letter' asking to be allowed to spend a night under the master's distinguished roof. His request was granted, and although Voltaire rebuked him for speaking too fast – 'How fast you foreigners speak!' 'We think that the French do the same.' 'Well, at any rate *I* don't. I speak slowly, that's what I do.' – on this occasion Boswell enjoyed a long and stimulating *tête-à-tête*.

'When the company returned, Monsieur de Voltaire retired. They looked at me with complacency, and without envy. Madame Denis insisted that I should sup; I agreed to this, and a genteel table was served for me in the drawing-room, where I ate and drank cheerfully with the gay company around me. I was very lively and said, "I am magnificence itself. I eat alone, like the King of England." In short this was a rich evening.'

'There is at Ferney,' Boswell concluded, 'the true hospitality.' It was a verdict which many another Tourist echoed. Edward Gibbon – despite his unflattering portrait of the grotesquely thin, seventy-year-old Voltaire acting the part of a tartar conqueror in one of his own

plays 'with a hollow broken voice, and making love to a very ugly niece of about fifty' – echoed it for one:

> 'The play began at eight in the evening,' Gibbon wrote, 'and ended (entertainment and all) about half an hour after eleven. The whole Company was asked to stay and sat Down about twelve to a very elegant supper of a hundred Covers. The supper ended about two, the company danced till four, when we broke up, got into our Coaches and came back to Geneva just as the Gates were opened. Shew me in history or fable, a famous poet of Seventy who has acted in his own plays, and has closed the scene with a supper and ball for a hundred people. I think the last is the more extraordinary of the two.'

From Geneva the Tourist usually made his way round the shores of the lake to Lausanne which was also crowded with young Englishmen, who went there, in Karamzin's opinion, not merely to study French but also to play 'various stupid and capricious pranks' and to 'make progress in mischief'. With its narrow, dirty and exhaustingly steep streets it was not considered an attractive place. And Edward Gibbon, although he was to return there to write the last three volumes of his *Decline and Fall of the Roman Empire*, was at first miserably unhappy in the 'unhandsome town'. On his second visit in the 1760s, however, he rather enjoyed himself.

His friend, John Baker Holroyd, afterwards Lord Sheffield, described the pleasures of Lausanne society:

> 'All the world is come to town and we are eminently brilliant, not an evening scarce without one or two Assemblies. We are not troubled with Playhouse, Ridottos or such like. There is a sort of Club Coffee House the members of which are chosen by ballot. The number is confined to Eighty and is at present full. It is a very good collection ... There is another society which pleases me very much. It is called the Spring because it consists of Young Women. It is held every Sunday at the house of one of the young ladies.

Although many Tourists complained of its poorly paved streets overgrown with weeds, Thomas Nugent described Basel as 'the largest, fairest and richest city of Switzerland ... the squares are spacious, adorned with no less than 300 fountains. The public and private buildings are quite magnificent.'

Lausanne

Swiss country women seen
at work outside a farm-
house in the canton of
Berne.

I attend most devoutly. After cards we generally amuse ourselves
with some innocent recreations which are nearly the same as what
you call in your country Blind Man's Buff, Questions and Commands, etc., etc. At the same time I must observe that notwith-
standing the Gayety of the Misses there never happen any impro-
prieties. Occasionally they have balls. They are much addicted to
English country dances.'

From Lausanne the Tourist would usually make his way up to Basel
through Neuchâtel. While in Neuchâtel he would hope to catch a
glimpse, at least, of Rousseau who was living at Motiers in the 1760s.
But Rousseau was tired and ill, and did not encourage visitors. Only
those as flatteringly enthusiastic and persistent as Boswell actually
managed to see him.

After Neuchâtel came Basel. But although Basel was then the
largest and richest city in Switzerland, and although its university
was described by Nugent as being in a very flourishing condition,
few Tourists remained there long. When Karamzin passed through it
in 1789, its only two fine buildings were the two enormous houses of
Sarrasin, the banker. The streets were poorly paved, and overgrown
with weeds; and the women, in the Russian's estimation, were
uniformly ugly: 'I have not seen a single attractive one, nor even
one who is passable.'

Berne was much more to Karamzin's taste. It made a strong
appeal, also, to Samuel Romilly's sister, Catherine.

'Berne is a beautiful city,' she wrote during a visit in 1783, 'the
streets wide, regularly built and with arches, that you may walk
all round the town in bad weather without being wet; under these
arches are the shops; in the middle of the street runs a small stream
of water, which with the well-built fountains and the cleanliness of
the whole is very agreeable. The streets are kept clean by the
criminals, who drag carts through the streets every morning,
sweeping up all the rubbish they find and even (with small brooms)
dusting all the public gates and iron rails. The one we saw was
drawn by women.'

But in Berne, as in so many other towns in Switzerland, there was
little exciting to do after dark. 'I do not know whether cards are on
sale in Zürich,' Karamzin wrote, 'but I do know that the people here
never play cards and seem unaware of this wonderful way of killing
time (forgive me this Gallicism), which has become almost indis-
pensable in other countries.'

Social gatherings began at four or five o'clock in the afternoon,
and were over at eight. As Boswell had discovered at Geneva, it was
quite usual to close a town's gates at five o'clock when drummers
would march along the ramparts calling the wanderer home. Also
to many travellers' astonishment, sumptuary laws were still in
operation as late as the 1780s. Certain classes of people were pro-

hibited to keep carriages in Zürich; and at Basel, though every citizen might keep a carriage, no servant was allowed to run behind it.

Yet for the less sybaritic Tourist, Switzerland had its compensations. Wandering from town to town, as Gibbon did, visiting the 'Churches, arsenals, libraries, and all the most eminent persons' in each; riding through the lovely villages of the lowlands; eating and drinking in the clean neat little inns, was a delightful way of passing a summer. Although more expensive than France, you could 'live much better than in England for the same money', Archdeacon Coxe decided; and in many places cheerful, simple-hearted peasants asked the traveller to share their meals. Karamzin once dined with a family of shepherds 'seated on a log, for their huts contain neither tables nor chairs. Two gay young shepherdesses kept staring and giggling at me. I told them that their simple, carefree life pleased me very much, and that I should like to remain with them to milk the cows. They replied only with laughter.'

Karamzin enjoyed his day on the slopes of the Wengernalp. But it was only recently that the mountains of Switzerland had begun to be appreciated by foreign visitors. Writing of the tour he had made thirty years before, Gibbon said that at the time 'the fashion of

Much of the work in the streets of Berne, as in other cities in Switzerland, was done by gangs of female convicts.

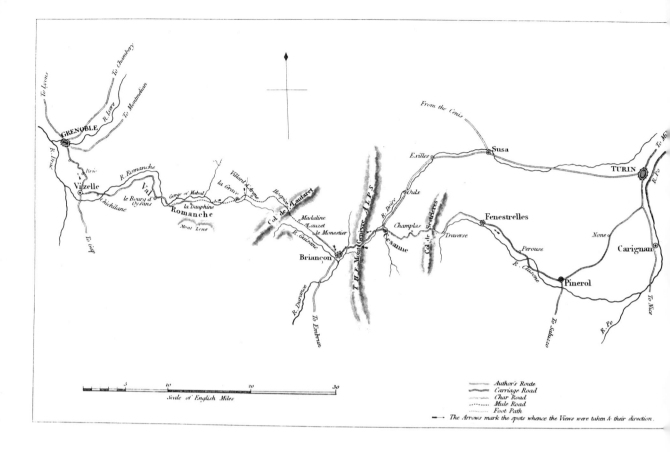

Crossing the Alps was a hazardous and uncomfortable enterprise, a 'horrid necessity'. The route shown here from Grenoble to Turin crossed the Col de Lautaret and the Mount Genèvre.

climbing the mountains and viewing the *Glaciers* had not yet been introduced'. Addison, on his tour at the beginning of the century, had left the Alps severely alone.

The wild chaotic and terrible beauty of Alpine scenery made little appeal to the early eighteenth-century eye, trained as it was to appreciate the nice regularities of controlled forms, more responsive as it was to the pastoral scene than the reckless grandeur of the wilderness.

Misson, in the seventeenth century, found it 'matter enough of astonishment, that any one should venture himself among the cliffs and precipices of such dismal mountains'; Misson's contemporary, Dr Northleigh, wrote with horror of the 'frightful Alps'; and a hundred years later a traveller 'started with affright' as he obtained his first glimpse of their 'awful and tremendous amphitheatre'; Addison, though he admitted to 'a sort of agreeable shuddering' at the sight of it, described it as 'this most misshapen scenery'.

The Alps   It was not until the middle of the eighteenth century that the Tourist first began to be persuaded that the Alps might perhaps offer something more than a *frisson* of horror. In 1744 there appeared in London a short work entitled *An Account of the Glaciers or Ice Alps in*

The Mount Cenis pass on the route from Lyons to Turin, the most usual way into Italy. At Lanslebourg the Tourist's coach was sometimes dismantled and packed in pieces on the backs of mules.

Savoy, which described how eight gentlemen, together with five servants, horses, baggage, provisions, arms, and tents – the whole presenting 'very much the Air of a Caravan' – had actually made a six-day expedition to Chamonix.

Organiser of the expedition was a determined young Tourist who had come to Geneva with his tutor, and was not to be put off by the warnings of the mountain people that such an excursion could never be accomplished in safety. Windham's *Account* advised those who cared to follow his example to equip themselves with pocket compasses, quadrants, thermometers, barometers, plenty of horse-shoes with nails and hammer, and 'victuals ready dressed'. And then they 'might do many things which we have not done,' he wrote. 'All the merit we can pretend to is having opened the way to others who may have Curiosity of the same Kind.'

As it happened others eventually did have curiosity of the same kind; and by the 1760s muleteers were running excursions up the Alpine paths, and revealing to their customers, at a price of three shillings for a day's trip, magnificent views of waterfalls and ice-capped summits.

In 1765 a widow felt it worth her while to open an inn at Chamonix.

Fifteen years later there were inns also at Grindelwald and Lauter-brunnen, and there were as many as thirty visitors a day to the Montanvert, most of them English. By the turn of the century the Tourist was making excursions, as a matter of course, to the Mer de Glace, the Glacier des Bossons, and the source of the Arveyron, taking with him his kettle to boil water to determine heights, his botanist's handbook to help him study Alpine plants, and even his personal painter to provide him with a permanent record of the sights he had seen. In 1790 Wordsworth was walking for pleasure in the Swiss mountains.

But although the Tourist gradually lost his horror of the Alps, the crossing of the passes into Italy remained a 'horrid necessity'. The most usual route was by way of Lanslebourg and Susa over Mont Cenis; and Mont Cenis, in Thomas Gray's opinion, carried 'the permission mountains have of being frightful rather too far'. It was here at two o'clock on a cold clear afternoon that Horace Walpole's King Charles's spaniel, while 'waddling along close to the head of the horses', was snatched away and devoured by a wolf.

At Lanslebourg the Tourist's coach was either dismantled and packed in its separate pieces on the backs of mules, or stored in one of the large sheds in the town until the day of his return. He himself, wrapped up in bear skins, muffs, hoods, boots lined with hare skins, beaver masks, and taffety eye-shades, was placed in a kind of straw sedan chair with long poles which the porters grasped or rested on their shoulders as they leaped from rock to rock. The chair had no floor which, as Mariana Starke discovered, was very uncomfortable when the porters put it down for a rest and she was left sitting in the snow, clutching for warmth a little lap dog and a heated bag of semolina.

Those who crossed by the Col di Tenda were often obliged, as Smollett was, to alight near the top and clamber up as best they could supported by two guides, known as *coulants*. Even the mules, sure-footed as they were and shod with specially nailed shoes, constantly slipped and fell, so that the inexperienced traveller could scarcely be surprised when he too found it quite impossible to keep his balance on the packed and frozen snow. The St Gotthard Pass was even worse:

'The mountain is two miles high, and very dangerous in winter, because of the great heaps of snow and stones, which the violence of the wind rolls down the precipices. But the most hazardous part is the bridge on the Russ, called the bridge of hell from the horrid noise the water makes as it tumbles from the rocks, and from the slipperiness of the bridge which renders it difficult even to foot passengers who are obliged to creep on all fours, lest the fury of the wind should drive them down to the rocks.

When Beaujolois Campbell crossed by the Simplon route in 1817, the age of Alpine road building had begun. But even then the crossing

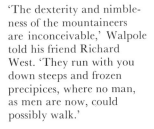

'The dexterity and nimbleness of the mountaineers are inconceivable,' Walpole told his friend Richard West. 'They run with you down steeps and frozen precipices, where no man, as men are now, could possibly walk.'

Although sometimes held to be of a 'clownish disposition', the Swiss struck most Tourists as being far from the 'heavy generation' of traditional legend. Friendly and hospitable, they were 'always ready to share a meal or a glass of wine'.

It was usual to be carried through the snow in 'low arm-chairs on poles', but sometimes the descent was made by sledge, 'quite the most frightful way of travelling in the world'.

was uncomfortable enough. She was called at three o'clock in the morning to ensure an early start from Brig, and it took over eight hours to reach the top. On either side of the road tall fir trees had been knocked down by avalanches; and melting snow formed torrents which ran 'furiously down the mountain in various directions'. At several places workmen were mending the road.

Where the Alpine tracks permitted it, a *char-à-banc* was sometimes used, 'a species of jolting wheel barrow, the most infernal vehicle ever invented', or, on occasions, the descent was made on a sledge; and while some Tourists found the sledge a frightening means of transportation, at least one of them was so exhilarated by it that he remained on the mountain eight days so as to enjoy the experience repeatedly.

But it was unusual to stay in the Alps for long. For the inns were appalling. There were only two inns at Lanslebourg; and both of them were 'scarcely habitable'. The inn on the Col di Tenda was still in 1792 'a crazy hovel, containing scarcely one whole window, and no sitting-room, except that which serves in common for postilions, porters, gentlemen, poultry, and hogs.' At Simplon, even half a century later, the post-house was 'dear and dirty; damp sheets, hard bread, hard water, hard old hens, and of course hard eggs'.

But by the time the Tourist had slid down the Simplon towards Domodossola, the worst of his journey was over; the Italian lakes, and the Plain of Lombardy lay beneath him; and the beauties and treasures of the south were his to enjoy at last.

The gentle beauty of the
Plain of Lombardy, seen
here in a landscape by
Fragonard, was a delightful
contrast to the desolation of
the Alpine passes. The
Tourist could enjoy an
alfresco meal in the shade
of the trees.

ITALY

The goal of the Grand Tour – Genoa – boiled snails, fried frogs and garlic – the delights of Florence: horse racing, theatres, the Uffizi, the Pitti Palace, the Boboli Gardens – Milan – Venice, 'the brothel of Europe' – Padua, Bologna – crossing the Apennines to get to Rome – Gibbon inspired by Coliseum to write Decline and Fall *– Evelyn's visit to the Catacombs – Naples, the most captivating city in Europe – the gaiety and exuberance of the Neapolitans – watching the excavations at Pompeii – the ascent of Vesuvius.*

opposite Giuseppe Maria Crespi (1664–1747), the brilliantly versatile painter of the late Bolognese school, was known as 'Lo Spagnuolo' because of his passion for exotic clothes. Here he depicts the salon of a Venetian courtesan.

Whether he came down into Italy by Domodossola and the shores of Lake Maggiore, or further east by way of Bolzano, the delighted Tourist was immediately struck by the contrasting gentleness and fertility of the Plain of Lombardy and the Adige valley after the desolation of the Alpine passes.

The air was 'sweet and temperate' in the valley of Bolzano, the vineyards 'all green', 'a true spring in the air in the midst of winter'. William Beckford noticed how the rocks were 'mantled with vines and gardens. Here and there a cottage, shaded with mulberries, made its appearance; and we often discovered on the banks of the river, ranges of white buildings, with courts and awnings' giving shade to peasants making silk. At Bolzano there were terraces of melons and Indian corn, 'gardens of fig trees and pomegranates hanging over walls'.

Beaujolois Campbell thought how beautiful the scenery was as she drove into Sesto Calende, how comfortable the houses looked with their large projecting roofs, how much more attractive than the Swiss was the Italian way of cultivating vines by planting them against fruit trees and posts and allowing them to 'twine almost naturally from the one to the other'.

Catherine Wilmot was enchanted by the hair of the Piedmontese countrywomen which, combed back from their foreheads and wound in a large knot at the back, was pierced by big pins almost a foot long with gold or white beads at the ends. They wore huge ear-rings and necklaces, and jackets 'worked in gold threads, and as much ornamented as the wearer can afford, white shift sleeves are tied over all,

Turin, the capital of Piedmont, was one of the most formal and cere-monious places in Italy, but it was also, Nugent said, one of the finest 'for the magnificence of its buildings, the beauty of its streets and squares and for all the conveniences of life'. A pleasant excursion was to Stupinigi where the Villa Reale was built by Filippo Juvarra in 1729–31.

with bunches of the gayest coloured Ribbands. The only thing they have as a Hat, is a vast number of folds of white linen laid flat and square upon their heads about the size of a stiff pocket handkerchief with a tassle at one corner.'

After this pleasant introduction to the beautiful countryside and attractive people of Piedmont, the capital was a disappointment. Like so many Italian towns in the eighteenth century (only four of which – Naples, Rome, Venice and Milan – contained more than one hundred thousand inhabitants), Turin seemed curiously under-populated. It was also dull.

'I hardly think you will like Turin,' Gibbon warned a friend. 'The court is old and dull; and ... everyone follows the example of the court. The principal amusement seems to be driving about in Your Coach in the evening and bowing to the people you meet. If you go when the royal family is there, you have the additional pleasure of stopping to salute them every time they pass. I had that advantage fifteen times one afternoon. We were presented to a Lady who keeps a public assembly, and a very mournfull one it is. The few women who go to it are each taken up by their Cicisbeo; and a poor Englishman, who can neither talk Piedmontese nor play at Faro, stands by himself, without one of their haughty nobility doing him the honour of speaking to him.'

Turin One evening out was like any other: 'If there is any pleasure in watching a play which one does not understand,' Gibbon sardonically continued after an evening at Mme de St Gilles's, 'in listening to a

ITALIAN AFFECTATION
Real Characters

'Italian Affectation', by Rowlandson. It was the fear of many parents that their sons would return home having picked up the 'antick manners' of an Italian. It was proposed in a London magazine that an 'Act Against Rambling' should be passed making it an offence 'to make any unmeaning grimace, shrug or gesticulation'.

Piedmontese jargon of which one does not take in a word, and in finding oneself in the midst of a proud nobility who will not speak a word to you, we had a most amusing time in this assembly.'

James Edward Smith agreed with Gibbon that a carriage seemed to be essential; for 'persons of any sort of figure' used their legs very little. When Smith wanted to make a friendly visit without ceremony, he was warned that it would ruin his reputation for ever to go on foot. 'Nor are the Turin people less ceremonious in dress,' Smith went on. 'A visit to a superior cannot possibly be made without a sword and a *chapeau de bras*.'

The town itself, particularly the Piazza San Carlo, was perfectly agreeable, having been rebuilt with broad streets and pleasant squares after the devastating siege by the French in 1706; but it was distasteful to find, as in so many Italian towns, that to lessen the heat of the sun, the windows of even the larger houses were made not of glass but of oiled paper. And after visits to the king's palace, the various handsome churches, the Jesuits' college, and the chapel of the Holy

Handkerchief – named after the handkerchief which Saint Veronica gave to Christ to wipe His face with as He was carrying the cross – most Tourists were content to remain in their inns, of which there were two particularly good ones, The Duke of Florence and The Spit.

It was fortunate that these inns *were* good, for the Tourist was rarely asked out to dine in a private house. This was the case in other towns in Italy. At Florence, for instance, Arthur Young complained, 'no one ever received guests for dinner'. Marquis Riccardi had forty servants in his palace many of whom had their own servants to wait on them; but an invitation to dinner there was very rare. 'The Ranuzzi,' Young continued, 'are even richer and more people live at their expense; but there are no dinners, no parties, no equipages and no comfort.'

At Genoa, a French traveller wrote indignantly, 'to give one a meal is unheard of. You would not believe how far the parsimony of these princes goes.'

In Turin, the position was even worse than in Florence and Genoa. Montesquieu said that a dinner given for a foreigner there was 'a great novelty in the Town . . . no one eats anything in Turin . . . M. de Cambris was never invited anywhere in three years . . . the Marquis de Prie, who had kept five or six Piedmontese with him for years in Flanders and Vienna, was at Turin when I was. Not one of them offered him so much as a glass of water.'

Most Tourists accordingly stayed in their inns in the evening, planning the rest of their *Giro d'Italia*.

It was possible to go all the way to Venice by boat, and a few travellers did so. But it was considered advisable to make arrangements at Turin for a carriage. The best type of carriage, it was commonly agreed, was a *calesce*, which had room for two people inside and two trunks behind, and was drawn by two horses, one of them running between the shafts to bear the stress. The ideal *calesce* was 'strong, low-hung, double-perched with well-seasoned corded springs, and iron axle-trees, two drag chains with iron shoes'. It allowed the Tourist to be his own master, to go where he liked when he liked, and relieved him of the necessity of changing carriages at the various posts and therefore of having to untie all his bags, portmanteaus, bedding and trunk. Those who travelled this way often employed a *vetturino* who drove the *calesce* and looked after the horses, agreeing with his employer a fixed sum to include meals and accommodation on the way, and so saving him 'the annoyance of quarrelling with cheating landlords'.

James Edward Smith was quite satisfied with this method. 'We engaged [a *vetturino*] to conduct us both from Pisa to Florence, forty-nine miles, for fifty pauls (not twenty-five shillings) to be fed by the way into the bargain. To our astonishment we were excellently accommodated; and we made use of this same honest fellow to carry us over most parts of Italy … We never had a word of dispute all the way.'

There were others, though, who felt that the *vetturini* were worse cheats than the landlords.

William Hazlitt was one of these.

'Vetturini,' Hazlitt wrote, 'bargain to provide you for a certain sum, and then billet you for as little as they can upon the inn-keepers ... who consider you as common property or prey, receive you with incivility, keep out of the way, will not deign you an answer, stint you in the quantity of your provisions, poison you by the quality, order you into their worst apartments, force other people into the same room or even bed with you, keep you in a state of continual irritation and annoyance all the time you are in the house.'

Even when the *vetturino* was as honest as James Edward Smith's, this method of travel was tediously slow. Smith did not cover more than about four miles in the hour, and sometimes, as Shelley discovered, it was impossible to cover even three.

Those who were in a hurry, therefore, chose to ride post-horses, or to travel by *cambiatura* where the system operated, and this, Nugent warned, was 'only in the ecclesiastical state, in Tuscany and in the duchies of Parma and Modena. The price of the *cambiatura* is generally at the rate of two julios (about one shilling) a horse each post. The greatest conveniency of this way of travelling is, that you may stop where you please, and change your horses or calash at every *cambiatura* without being obliged to pay for their return.'

Stage-coaches ran regularly between a few of the principal towns, and the passengers, transported cheaply but uncomfortably, paid for tickets which included all expenses *en route*.

Whichever way he travelled the Tourist expected, and almost invariably had to endure, a tiresome journey. There were very few good roads, except in Tuscany and parts of Piedmont; secondary roads were rarely more than tracks; in many hilly districts the passenger had to alight and continue his journey on horse or mule-back; in the south the draught animals were sometimes buffaloes, 'ugly, stubborn, and sometimes mischievous Animals', while the average Italian post-chaise, Goethe complained, was no better than an ancient litter. 'They have put two wheels on them without adding a single improvement. You are tossed about as you would have been centuries ago.'

Travelling by water was often as uncomfortable. When Arthur Young had to take a boat from Venice to Bologna because the roads were too bad even for the *vetturini*, he found the conditions on board appalling: 'The skipper takes snuff, wipes his nose with his fingers, cleans his knife with his handkerchief at the same time as he is preparing the food he offers you.'

Contemporary accounts retail the discomforts and perils of travelling in Italy with resignation. 'The coach,' recorded Smollett, for example, 'had been several times in the most imminent hazard of being lost

'A scene of enchantment', wrote Hazlitt of Florence, 'a city planted in a garden... Everything on the noblest scale, yet finished in the minutest part.' Most Tourists contrived to find rooms overlooking the Arno, seen here from near the Porta S. Niccolò.

with all our baggage; and at two different places it was necessary to hire a dozen of oxen and as many men, to disengage it from the holes into which it had run.' The Rev. J. C. Eustace, trying to pay a visit to Petrarch's last home, said, 'a little way beyond the village of Cataio, we turned off from the high road, and alighting from the carriage on account of the swampiness of the country, we walked and rowed occasionally through lines of willows, or over tracts of marshy land, for two or three miles, till we began to ascend the mountain ... We passed through the village and descended the hill. [Then we were] overturned by a blunder of the drivers, and for some time suspended over the canal with imminent danger of being precipitated into it.' The comte de Caylus was overturned three times between Parma and Modena by drunken postilions.

Also, in many districts it was necessary to start the journey at dawn to avoid the heat of the sun by day and the roaming *banditti* at night; while the numerous states into which Italy was then divided – kingdoms, grand duchies, republics, and the states of the pope – forced upon the Tourist the need for repeated custom inspections and therefore the repeated payment of bribes.

In some towns the actual inspection was dispensed with altogether, and the Tourist was merely invited to pay for '*la buona mancia per il signor ufficiale della dogana*'. Any indignation displayed by the Tourist, or any pretence that the invitation was not understood would be greeted with threats of confiscation or even of imprisonment.

Nor was it only the customs officials who were constantly demanding tips:

'You cannot find a man who does not ask you for money,' Montesquieu grumbled in Verona; 'a shoemaker asks me for alms after selling me a pair of shoes; a man who has sold you a book asks for the buonamano; the man who tells you the way or a piece of news asks for a reward. This is quite different from Holland where they ask for money for drink; here it is to live. Cheating, the companion of poverty, is rampant: if you have agreed on a price with someone, he will make you pay more.'

Charles de Brosses confirmed this: 'For the smallest things you are surrounded with men asking for tips; even a man with whom you have made a bargain for a *louis* would find it very odd if he was not given an *écu* for a tip when he carried it out.'

Edward Gibbon had the same trouble. Having tipped some porters a guinea with which they seemed perfectly well satisfied, one of them soon afterwards asked him for more money as he had lent him a pair of gloves.

As well as being constantly bothered with the importunities of customs officials, the Tourist had to put up with repeated checks on his various passports, his certificates of health, his letters of credit, his *lascie passare*, and, in several towns, documents signed by the authorities and giving the Tourist's name, nationality and 'station of life', without which he would not be allowed to sleep at any inn.

'We left Ravenna,' runs a typical complaint, 'with a double fede (or testimonial), one to certify that we were well, the other that we were sick; the former on account of their fear of the plague, to get us entrance into their cities; and the other (it being Lent) to get us some grasso (flesh-meat) in the inns.'

Then, there was the need to change money, and to understand the difference between the astonishing variety of coins in use in the different parts of Italy, an exact knowledge of which must have been denied even to the most experienced bankers and expert numismatists.

In Venice alone, for instance, the Tourist was faced with mastering the worth of lire, soldi, pichioli, grosses, louis d'ors, sequins, ducatoons, silver crowns, genoins, philips, testoons, julios, three sorts of pistole, and four sorts of ducat, after having only just learned in Tuscany, perhaps, the difference between the sequin, the scudo, the livre, and the paul.

Muddled as he invariably was by all this different specie, the Tourist was likely soon to fall prey to the dishonest *vetturino* or innkeeper; and, in the almost paranoic opinion of some Tourists, nearly every Italian innkeeper was a grasping rogue.

As elsewhere on the Continent, it was advisable to make a bargain beforehand. James Edward Smith, staying at the same 'execrable' inn at Lerici that Smollett had already condemned, was charged on his bill an amount for coffee 'about as much as all the rest put together. On complaining, [he was] told with the utmost effrontery, that coffee was not in the original bargain'. Breval, who protested at the exorbitance of his bill at an inn near Naples was threatened by the landlord with a shotgun. 'The common people', commented Jérôme de Lalande after a long visit to Italy in 1765–6, 'look on foreigners as their dupes and frequently cheat them outrageously, not caring twopence what one says to them.'

What most Tourists failed to realise was that the Italian innkeeper, and particularly the innkeeper in the south, just like any other Italian tradesman, loved bargaining. In his autobiography Leigh Hunt emphasised the importance of understanding this, as William Hazlitt had done before him, and as Norman Douglas was to do after him.

'If you paid anybody what he asked you,' Leigh Hunt observed, 'it never entered his imagination that you did it from anything but folly. You were pronounced a *minchione* (a ninny), one of their greatest terms of reproach. On the other hand, if you battled well through the bargain, a perversion of the natural feeling of self-defence led to a feeling of respect for you. Dispute might increase; the man might grin, stare, threaten; might pour out torrents of argument and of "injured innocence", as they always do; but be firm, and he went away equally angry and admiring. Did anybody condescend to take them in, the admiration as well as the anger was still in proportion.'

It was essential, Norman Douglas confirmed in *Old Calabria*, to show that you were not *scemo* (a worthless nincompoop). 'You may be a forger or cut-throat – why not? It is a vocation like any other, a vocation for *men*. But whoever cannot take care of himself – i.e., his money – is not to be trusted in any walk of life; he is of no account, he is no man.'

A friendly and honest landlord, however, did not always denote a comfortable inn. It is, indeed, rare that an English traveller in his diary or letters refers to an inn with approbation. Even in the large towns and in such expensive hotels as the Scudo d'Oro in Rome, the Louvre at Venice, or the White Cross at Genoa, the Tourist usually stayed no longer than it took him to find lodgings or a furnished house. In the smaller country inns the beds were damp or dirty or broken, the mattresses full of wet leaves, potatoes or peach stones, the ceilings covered with spiders, the meals 'cooked in such a manner that a Hottentot could not have beheld them without loathing'.

At San Remo the inn was 'so dirty and miserable that it would disgrace the worst hedge ale-house in England'; there was one near Parma which Beaujolois Campbell thought so uncommonly bad 'that all one could do was laugh at it' – in the main room there was an altar and the picture of a man being flayed alive. The Hotel di San Marco, supposedly the best in Piacenza, provided dinners which were 'scarcely eatable [having] a great profusion of oil but a general taste of dirt'; at Carrara the few inns were still 'only fit for labourers' a century after Fynes Moryson had pronounced them so; near Turin a traveller was still likely to pay an enormous price as Peter Mundy

'The captain of the Hampshire grenadiers . . . has not been useless to the historian of the Roman Empire.' It was on 15 October 1764, as Edward Gibbon sat musing amidst the ruins of the Capitol, that the idea of writing *The Decline and Fall of the Roman Empire* first started to his mind.

105

had done for 'an egg, a frog, and bad wine'; at Tenda 'the only inn [was] frightful, black, filthy and stinking' without a single window pane; at Bologna the Tre Mauretti was nothing but 'an appalling hovel'; at an inn between Florence and Pavia, so Catharine Wilmot gloomily reported:

'For our supper they brought us up a patriarchal cock, with stiff black legs, which seemed to have died of the gout a month before, and Macarno in a bowl writhing into a hundred serpents. The door was then locked and we were to await our doom till morning. You may imagine the kind of night we spent. The wind was roaring a hurricane, and the rain pattering frightfully against the windows; there were no shutters to prevent our seeing bright blue flashes of lightning fork across the room, or hearing the crashes of thunder breaking in hollow echoes amongst the Apennines, which eternally reminded us of these Mountains being the resort of legions of Banditti.'

Between Terni and Rome, according to Smollett, the inns were 'abominally nasty', generally destitute of provisions; and when provisions *were* found the guests were 'almost poisoned by the cookery'. Sharp confirmed this verdict:

'Give what scope you please to your fancy, you will never imagine half the disagreeableness that Italian beds, Italian cooks, Italian post-houses, Italian postilions, and Italian nastiness offer to an Englishman in an Italian journey; much more to an English woman. At Turin, Milan, Venice, Rome, and, perhaps, two or three other towns, you meet with good accommodation; but no words can express the wretchedness of the other inns. No other bed but one of straw, and next to that a dirty sheet, sprinkled with water, and, consequently, damp; for a covering you have another sheet, as coarse as the first, and as coarse as one of your kitchen jack-towels, with a dirty coverlet. The bedsted consists of four wooden forms, or benches; and English Peer and Peeress must lye in this manner, unless they carry an upholsterer's shop with them, which is very troublesome. There are, by the bye, no such things as curtains, and hardly, from Venice to Rome, that cleanly and most useful invention, a privy; so that what should be collected and buried in oblivion, is forever under your nose and eyes.'

These opinions were not peculiar to Englishmen. The comte de Caylus, when at Modena in 1714, stayed 'in an unspeakable tavern, although it is the best in the town'. The inn at Narni he thought 'infamous'. Charles de Brosses considered the inns at Florence 'detestable beyond measure', full of small midges 'a hundred times more damnable' than the ones at home. While Father Labat, who chose to sleep on a table in Siena rather than venture into the bug-ridden bed, overheard a servant impertinently reply to his fellow-guests, who complained that they had spent the night scratching

The Cathedral of Boschetto and Rinaldo and the leaning tower of Pisa, whose gradually increasing deviation from the perpendicular was $15\frac{1}{2}$ feet in 1829. William Beckford thought the tower as 'perfectly awry' as anyone had a right to expect.

themselves, that 'the only bugs in the beds were the ones they had brought with them'.

South of Rome the inns were even worse. Charles de Brosses complained of the impossibility of 'finding even a semblance of a bearable lodging' between Rome and Naples. And George Gissing discovered that the Two Little Lions at Cosenza was still the same at the end of the nineteenth century as it had been over a hundred years before:

'Over sloppy stones, in an atmosphere heavy with indescribable stenches, I felt rather than saw my way to the foot of a stone stair-case; this I ascended, and on the floor above found a dusky room, where tablecloths and an odour of frying oil afforded some sugges-tion of refreshment. My arrival interested nobody; with a good deal of trouble I persuaded an untidy fellow, who seemed to be a waiter, to come down with me and secure my luggage. More trouble before I could find a bedroom; hunting for keys, wandering up and down stone stairs and along pitch-black corridors, sounds of voices in quarrel. The room itself was utterly depressing – so bare, so grimy, so dark.'

Despite his extravagant complaints it was not always so much that the food in the better sort of Italian inn was as bad as the Tourist implied it was, as that it was unfamiliar – which for an Englishman was often something worse.

The *antipasto* might comprise a dish of giblets boiled with salt and pepper and mixed with white of eggs. This was likely to be followed by two or three different sorts of ragout, then *minestra di grasso* or *di magro*, then fruit. 'They are fond of boiled snails served up with pepper and oil, and fried frogs dressed in the same manner,' *The Traveller's Guide Through Italy* distastefully informed its readers. 'They frequently eat kites, hawks, magpies, jackdaws, and other lesser birds, not used with us; and drink their wine in winter as well as summer out of snow. Between Rome and Naples travellers are sometimes regaled with buffaloes and crows; the buffalo's flesh is black, stinking, and hard.'

And 'what do you think?' Shelley exclaimed in horror. 'Young women of rank actually eat – you will never guess what – garlick!'

Those who ate in the private houses of the rich laid themselves open to a further hazard, in addition to the strange food. The payment of vails was fairly common in London; but in Italy the servants in many households had so extended the practice that the guest at a dinner party was solicited for a *buonamano* not only after the meal but upon each subsequent visit. Sometimes, even – as was the case at the house of the governor of Milan in the 1730s – guests were besieged by 'a multitude of domestics' although they had only called to pay their respects to him and had not been offered so much as a drink. And as Montesquieu complained in Rome, 'You go to see a man: immedi-ately his servants come to ask you for money, often even before you

Drawings made in Italy and at Diocletian's Palace at Spalato in the 1750s gave Robert Adam the inspiration for such designs as these on tureens made for Sir Watkin Wynn.

have seen him. Men better dressed than I have often asked me for alms. In short, all this rabble is constantly after you.'

But in spite of such irritating customs, and all the annoyances to which the Tourist was subject during his journey, the better he knew Italy and the Italians the more, in general, he liked them. At first he was ready to find fault everywhere. The country girls, so dirty, brown, and overworked, except in parts of Piedmont, could not be compared with their English counterparts, 'unquestionably the handsomest in the world'; the people of Milan were 'a miserable race' – the opinion is Shelley's – they looked 'like a tribe of stupid and shrivelled slaves'; the Italians generally – this is Joseph Addison talking – 'notwith-standing their natural fieriness of temper, affect always to appear sober and sedate, insomuch that one sometimes sees young men walking the streets with spectacles on their noses, that they may be thought to have impaired their sight by much study.'

'The whole lump want backbone, serious energy, and power of honest work,' a later commentator observed. 'I am tempted to take the professors I see in the schools by the collar, and hold them down to their work for five or six hours a day – so angry do I get at their shirking and inefficiency.'

But soon, when all their indolence, affectation, dissimulation and cunning *sleatta* was admitted and condemned, the Tourist, as often as not, fell victim to the Italians' insidious charm and fundamental friendliness; and even those who found them less constantly cheerful than they had expected, agreed that they were scarcely ever drunk – although when John Wilkes arrived in Rome he found only two of the twelve officials in the customs-house sober enough to do their work.

In northern countries drunkenness, being widespread, was commonly cited as a principal cause of violent crime. In Italy, even though drink could not nearly so often be held to blame, there was as much violent crime as anywhere.

The body of a murdered man lying in a ditch aroused so little interest even at the beginning of the nineteenth century that 'the people passed along, looked at it and appeared very little affected by the sight'. Arthur Young counted fifty crosses indicating the places where murders had taken place on the road from Brescia to Verona. A group of murderers being escorted along the road in chains, or a glimpse of condemned convicts gambling behind a prison grille, caused the traveller no more than a sudden and soon-forgotten shock of fear or pity, or the guilty thrill of *Schadenfreude*.

'What astonishes all foreigners and is the talk of the town again to-day,' Goethe wrote in his diary in Rome in 1786, 'are the murders which are an everyday occurrence. Four people have been murdered in our quarter within three weeks. Today a worthy Swiss artist named Schwerdimann, a medallist, was murdered just like Winckelmann [the distinguished German archeologist who had been murdered at Trieste some years before]. The murderer with whom Schwerdimann grappled, struck him as many as twenty blows with a dagger and as the guard ran up the villain stabbed himself. Incidentally, that is not the fashion here; the murderer escapes to a church, and that is the end of the matter.'

When executions did take place they provided the Tourist with a dramatic and, for him, often unusual spectacle; for it was rarely that an Englishman at any rate witnessed anything more esoteric than a public hanging in his own country. In Italy death was inflicted in various other more exciting ways.

In the sixteenth century – when several aggravated forms of the death penalty were tolerated in England, too – Fynes Moryson saw two young men, the sons of senators, punished for spending a too wildly uninhibited night in Venice. First they had their hands cut off, then their tongues were ripped out at the place where they had sung blasphemous songs, then they were beheaded. In the next century, William Lithgow was in Venice when a friar was burned alive for getting fifteen nuns pregnant within a single year.

'Mine associate and I were no sooner landed,' Lithgow wrote, 'and perceiving a great throng of people, and in this midst of them a great smok; but we began to demand a Venetian what the matter was? who replied there was a grey Friar burning quick at St Mark's pillar for begetting fifteen young Noble Nuns with child, and all within one year; he being also their Father confessor. Whereat, I sprang forward through the throng, and my friend followed me, and came just to the pillar as the half of his body and right arm fell flatlings in the fire.'

Such punishments were not so frequently to be seen in the eighteenth century, although in 1794 at Caserta, in the kingdom of the Two Sicilies, a man, whose crime had been to shout, 'Long live Paris! Long live Liberty!' three times during a church service, was condemned not only to be hanged, but also to have his hand, tongue and head cut off. In Rome the authorities still punished miscreants by having them tied face downwards on the *cavalletto* while blows were struck at their spines with a bull's penis. For serious crimes they still used the *martello*,

'which is to knock the malefactor on his temples with a hammer while he is on his knees, and almost at the same time to cut his throat and rip open his belly. Lesser crimes are frequently punished by the gallies or the *strappado*: the latter is hanging the criminals by the arms tied backwards, and thus bound they are drawn up on high, and let down again with a violent swing, which, if used with vigour, unjoints their backs and arms.'

Few Tourists did not witness at least one public execution during their travels, and in the seventeenth century there were few who did not go to watch a prisoner being tortured. John Evelyn visited the Châtelet prison in Paris to witness the torture of a suspected robber.

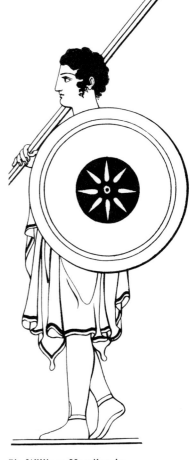

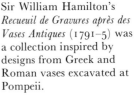

Sir William Hamilton's *Recueil de Gravures après des Vases Antiques* (1791–5) was a collection inspired by designs from Greek and Roman vases excavated at Pompeii.

'First they bound his wrist to an iron ring made fast to the wall, about four feet from the floor, and then his feet with another cable, fastened about five feet farther than his utmost length to another ring on the floor of the room. Thus suspended, they slid a horse of wood under the rope which bound his feet, which so exceedingly stiffened it, as severed the fellow's joints in miserable sort, drawing him out at length in an extraordinary manner, he having only a pair of linen drawers on his naked body …

In this agony, confessing nothing, the executioner with a horn (just such as they drench horses with) stuck the end of it into his mouth, and poured the quantity of two buckets of water down his throat and over him, which so prodigiously swelled him, as would have pitied and affrighted any one to see it; for all this, he denied all that was charged to him. They then let him down, and carried him before a warm fire to bring him to himself, being now to all appearance dead with pain. What became of him, I know not … It seems they could not hang him, but did use in such cases, where the evidence is very presumptive to send them to the galleys, which is as bad as death.'

Evelyn also watched the *martello* used in Rome, saw a gentleman hanged for murder in his cloak and hat, and, in St Mark's Square in Venice, witnessed the execution of a 'wretch who had murdered his master, for which he had his head chopped off by an axe that slid down a frame of timber.'

Byron thought that an Italian execution was far more dramatic than a Tyburn hanging.

'The ceremony,' he wrote, 'including the *masqued* priests; the half-naked executioner; the bandaged criminals; the black Christ and his banner; the Scaffold; the soldiery; the slow procession, and the quick rattle and heavy fall of the axe; the splash of blood, and the ghastliness of the exposed heads – is altogether more impressive than the … dog-like agony of affliction upon the sufferers of the English sentence.'

There was no need to make any particular plans to witness such a drama, the Tourist was advised, whatever route he chose he was sure to see an execution at some time during his travels.

In planning his *Giro d'Italia* the Tourist was advised to arrange his journey so as to be in Venice for the Carnival, in Bologna for the Octave of the Sacrament, and in Rome for Holy Week. But the route he could follow between these towns was open to infinite variations.

It was common practice to make straight for Venice across the Plain of Lombardy, going through Milan, and then – as Dr Burney did – through Bergamo, Brescia, Verona and Vicenza. Some, however, chose to cross the Ligurian Apennines to Genoa and then to go down

An illustration from Sir William Hamilton's *Recueuil de Gravures après des Vases Antiques.*

the coast road through Pisa, Lucca and Pistoia to Florence, and to see Venice on their way back from Rome and Naples.

Everyone wanted to see Florence, of course; but there were few towns by the coastal route from Genoa that appealed to the average Tourist. Genoa itself, with its magnificent harbour and fine palaces luxuriating in the shade of orange trees, was admittedly beautiful, though the Tourist was advised not to stay very long. For, as James Howell warned in his *Instruction for Forreine Travell*, 'the very worst Italian dialect [was] spoken there'. Also, being like Venice, a city in decline, it was full of beggars; indeed the multitude of mendicants sometimes made walking in the narrow streets an ordeal. Mrs Piozzi said that it was necessary to be carried in a chair even for a dozen steps, otherwise 'you are likely to feel shocked at having your knees suddenly clasped by a figure hardly human, who, perhaps, holding you forcibly for a minute, conjures you loudly by the sacred wounds of our Lord Jesus Christ to have compassion on his wounds'. Moreover, the enjoyment of the harbour was overcast by the evil-looking hulks in which Turkish prisoners were kept locked up in tiny cages in which there seemed scarcely room to breathe. The air, in any event, was not considered too healthy. 'The climate is by no means a fine one,' warned Mariana Starke, 'especially for consumptive persons.' Nor did Miss Starke approve of the Genoese people, especially the 'ill-educated nobles'. These nobles, as de Brosses noticed, were all uniformly dressed in black and all of them wore 'a small wig tied to the ears'. Their wives also wore black, except in their first year of marriage, as, indeed, did most of the ordinary citizens, numbers of whom, more than one Tourist noted with displeasure, used a special wash to dye their hair an unnatural shade of ochre.

The Genoese were not highly regarded even by the Italians themselves who had a proverb that at Genoa you found 'sea without fish, men without conscience, and women without shame.' The Italians also said that the reason why there were so few Jews at Genoa was that the Genoese were 'so cunning that it would be impossible for a Jew to earn his bread amongst them'.

Pisa   The air at Pisa, like that at Genoa, was also considered 'unwholesome and obnoxious to strangers'. And although the fountain-water that flowed through the aqueduct, and was transported about the town on the backs of camels, was the finest in Italy; although the Tower, in William Beckford's opinion, was as 'perfectly awry' as anyone could expect, Pisa was considered to have little else to recommend it. It had once been a powerful and prosperous place with 150,000 inhabitants; but there was about it in these later years an air of decay. Hundreds of houses stood empty, grass grew in the streets; the Earl of Cork and Orrery, who had thought of settling there in 1754, decided against it. 'In its present state, chameleons only can inhabit this city. Horses indeed may graze and fatten in the streets. Human creatures, unless they are Italians, cannot find lodgings or subsistence.'

Leghorn, though inhabited by several English and Scottish merchants, was similarly dismissed. So was Lucca. 'Happy for me,' wrote William Beckford, 'that the environs of Lucca were so beautiful; since I defy almost any city to contain more ugliness within its walls. Narrow streets and dismal alleys; wide gutters and cracked pavements; everybody in black, according with the gloom of their habitations which having all grated windows, they convey none but dark and dungeon-like ideas.'

Even the charms and treasures of Pistoia went unappreciated. On his way to Florence from Lucca, Evelyn stopped to dine there and commented laconically in his journal, 'besides one church, there was little observable'. 'There is nothing in Pistoia that deserves either the trouble or charge of going out of the way to see it,' wrote Misson; while de Brosses considered that the only thing worth looking at in the town was the baptistery – the cathedral had 'the air of a village church'. A later traveller, Northall, remarked in 1752 that 'ruin, desolation and indolence' were to be seen in every street.

But after Pistoia came Florence; and Florence, despite 'the medieval gloom' of so many of its buildings, was admired by all – as indeed it always had been.

'I live in Florence,' wrote Toby Mathew in August 1608, 'in an excellent coole terrene, eate good melons, drink wholesome wines, looke upon excellent devout pictures, heer choyse musique.'

Fynes Moryson had been equally delighted during his stay a few years before, particularly by the Florentine inns which, unlike those in so many other parts of Italy, were 'most neate':

> 'From morning to night the Tables are spread with white cloathes, strewed with flowers and figge leaves, with Ingestrars or glasses of divers coloured wines set upon them, and delicate fruits, which would invite a Man to eat and drink, who otherwise hath no appetite, being all open to the sight of passengers as they ride by the high way, through their great unglased windowes. At the Table, they touch no meate with the hand, but with a forke of silver or other mettall, each man being served with his forke and spoone, and glasse to drinke. And as they serve small peeces of flesh (not whole joints as with us), so these peeces are cut into small bits, to be taken up with the forke, and they seeth the flesh till it be very tender. In Summer time they set a broad earthen vessel full of water upon the Table, wherein little glasses filled with wine doe swimme for coolenesse.'

Even Horace Walpole, who had found so much that was distasteful in his journey south, thought that Florence was enchanting, infinitely the most agreeable of all the places he had seen since London. He remained there over a year. Many other Englishmen did the same. William Hazlitt never forgot his time there, nor that first sight of the town in its circle of surrounding heights on which the white villas, olive groves and vineyards, sparkled in the sunlight. It was 'a scene

A punch party at Charles Hadfield's *pensione* in Florence in 1760. Sir Charles Bunbury stands making a toast on the right; Sir Henry Mainwaring sits at the opposite end of the table; Lord Grey, for whom Thomas Patch painted the picture, is shown on the near side of the table in front of Hadfield himself holding aloft the punch bowl. Patch lived in Florence from 1755 until his death in 1782.

Florence

Charles Hadfield's *pensione* was near the S. Spirito with views across the Arno. Beyond the Ponte S. Trinità, one of the four bridges across the river at this time, is the palazzo of the Marchese Roberto Capponi.

of enchantment, a city planted in a garden ... Everything was on the noblest scale, yet finished in the minutest part.' The most popular inn in Florence in the 1750s and 1760s was the one on the left bank of the Arno opposite Palazzo Corsini which was kept by a convivial Englishman, Charles Hadfield. This was a recognised meeting-place for his countrymen, a party of whom could always be found there, eating, drinking or playing cards, providing subjects for a conversation piece by the English artist, Thomas Patch.

If he could not be traced at Hadfield's a visiting Englishman could almost certainly be found by making enquiries at Sir Horace Mann's house on the Lungarno, near the Ponte di Santa Trinità.

Mann, an agreeable fellow, 'quiet and polished', in Edward Gibbon's opinion, had been appointed minister in Florence in 1740 and remained there for thirty years. The best and most obliging person in the world, according to Thomas Gray, Mann knew everybody of importance in Florence, went out of his way to introduce the English Tourist into the best society, and gave frequent dinner parties himself.

There were disadvantages to life in Florence, though, as elsewhere. For instance, women, never much in evidence in other Italian towns, were 'almost invisible'; and the nobility, while polite enough to foreigners, rarely – despite Mann's relentless activities – asked a Tourist to anything more exciting than a card party or a *conversazione* at which lemonade, coffee or tea would be served with ice-cream.

Yet there was so much to occupy his time at Florence that the Tourist was rarely bored. After a day spent driving in the beautiful country outside the town, up to Fiesole, or along the Arno valley beside the rows of mulberry bushes, he returned, perhaps, to a reception at the Grand Duke's court in the Pitti Palace, the theatre, or for a walk with friends across the bridges, listening to the street musicians, delighted by the brilliance of the fire-flies. Another evening he might drive on the Cascine and buy a basket of carnations, mignonettes, yellow roses and orange blossom; or go to buy wine from one of the palaces of the nobles who advertised themselves as vintners by hanging bottles from their windows and gates; or he might stroll in the Boboli gardens where cypress and ilex cast shadows in the moonlight across the crumbling statues.

Judged worthy of special attention were the fine mosaic works in the chapels and palaces, 'the sparks of gems and minute pieces of the finest-marble'; and, although the baroque churches were rarely to the Tourists' taste, it was usual to visit the mausoleum of the Medici family in the chapel of St Lawrence, to gaze at the walls of jasper, agate, touchstone, lapis lazuli and alabaster, at the tombs of the great dukes made of marble and oriental granite topped with jasper pillows enriched with jewels and ducal crowns – though Byron dismissed it all as 'fine frippery in great slabs of various expensive stones, to commemorate fifty rotten and forgotten carcases'.

For those who preferred more lively entertainments there were the

Zoffany's painting of the Tribuna in the Uffizi Gallery in Florence was done under the patronage of Queen Charlotte between 1772 and 1778. Beneath the array of works on the walls, paintings by Raphael, Rubens, Holbein, Rembrandt and

Michelangelo – some of them transported by Zoffany from the Pitti to the Tribuna – are portraits of numerous English Tourists, diplomats and collectors. Sir Horace Mann, Envoy Extraordinary to the Grand Duke of Tuscany, is seen, wearing a star, beside Titian's 'Venus of Urbino'. Sitting down beside him is the Hon. Felton Hervey; holding the picture is Thomas Patch; George, third Earl Cowper, stands at the far left beside 'Cupid and Psyche'. Next to him, wearing a star, is Sir John Dick, British Consul at Leghorn; to his left is the sixth Earl of Plymouth; and, looking round Raphael's Madonna, Zoffany himself. Sitting on the stool is Charles Loraine-Smith, and bending down behind him, Richard Edgcumbe. On the far right, standing with his arms behind his back beneath the 'Venus de Medici', is James Bruce, the African traveller. Standing immediately beneath the right arm of the 'Satyr with the Cymbals' is George Legge, Lord Lewisham.

Visitors entering and leaving the court of the Pitti Palace in Florence, the palace of the Grand Duke of Tuscany, begun in the fifteenth century by one Luca Pitti, a member of a wealthy family which opposed Lorenzo the Magnificent.

horse races in the Corso; the Grand Duke's 'combat of wild beasts'; the games of Calcio, a kind of football, 'performed by persons of quality'; the Palio de' Cocchi, the chariot races in the Piazza di Santa Maria Novella on the eve of the Festa of San Giovanni; and the sight of agitated ladies of the court, in imitation of the Pope's washing the pilgrim's feet, scouring the feet of old women brought in from the streets 'with a fervour and devotion according to the extent of their own crimes'. Then, of course, there were the long walks round the 89 convents, the 84 fraternities, the 152 churches, the 18 halls belonging to merchants, the 72 courts of justice, the 17 palaces (unhappily disgraced by paper windows), the 7 public fountains, the 6 columns, the 2 pyramids, the 160 public statues, the unnumbered pictures in the Grand Duke's gallery at the Pitti palace, and the treasures of the Uffizi.

Some of those who made no pretence of being *conoscitori* had grown rather tired of looking at pictures now, particularly those who had come to Tuscany after a tour of Lombardy and Venice and had gone to Milan after Turin instead of to Genoa.

Milan   In Milan, alone, there were, so Nugent advised in his admonitory way, 'a great many excellent paintings to be seen', and went on to list two pages full of Baroccis, Titians, Raphaels, Leonardos, Caraccis,

Gallitias, Bassanos, Ceranis and Renos. Most of the best of these were in 'the famous cabinet of Signor Manfredo Settala'. Later the Brera collection was assembled; and it was at the Palazzo Brera that the *laquais de place* infuriated Beaujolois Campbell by telling her mother there were certain works of art it would not be proper for a young girl to see. 'He was a blockhead for his pains. I was very provoked at him. Mamma laughed heartily but not to scandalise him we did not ask to see them.'

It was not so much Milan's pictures, however, that impressed the Tourist as the splendid theatre, the largest in the world; the vast Ambrosian Library with its fourteen thousand manuscripts, seventy-two thousand printed volumes, medals, antique sculpture and Leonardo's mechanical drawings; and the cathedral, begun in 1386 and not yet finished four hundred years later.

'I think in all my life I never saw anything to come up to the beauty of the Cathedral,' Catherine Wilmot thought. 'It is entirely built of white polished Marble, both inside and outside. One chapel is in pure silver, all the panels carved, and beautifully representing different stages of the Saint's life to whom it is dedicated. Mysteriously veiled before the Altar, is an original relique of a tooth set in

The Gothic cathedral at Milan – after the cathedral of Seville and St Peter's the largest church in Europe – was begun in 1386 and not finally completed until the beginning of the nineteenth century. The baroque façade, started in 1615 and finished on the orders of Napoleon, was removed in 1900.

diamonds, and framed in gold and mother of pearl. The Friar who walked about the aisles with us, was a delightful sketch of a whole-sale camel swallower. He believed in the most extravagant miracles performed at the Shrine of the Tooth, and recapitulated them to us, with the most devout gravity.'

As in many other cathedrals and churches in Italy, the supplications of the beggars considerably alloyed 'the pleasure one might otherwise enjoy'. Ignoring the well-dressed Milanese women with their fine black hair and veils arranged 'with skilful abandon', and hurrying past the Milanese young men who dramatically threw their 'dark assassination cloaks' over their shoulder and most of their face so as to reveal but one black and brilliant eye, the mendicants swarmed round the *Inglesi* with relentless importunity. So did pimps. 'You cannot take a step into the squares without meeting the most obliging pimps in the world,' de Brosses commented. 'They always offer you women of whatever colour and country you want; but there is no doubt that the girl who appears is not always as magnificent as was promised.'

There were numerous beggars, too, at the Palazzo Simonetta two miles outside Milan, for no Tourist would leave the town without going there to hear the famous echo. 'It is at a palace which was not finished on account of the dampness of the soil,' Boswell noted in his journal in January 1765. 'It has three tiers of pillars in front and would have made a noble thing.' Following Addison's example, Boswell discharged his pistol into the air, and 'the sound was repeated fifty-eight times'.

On leaving Milan, Boswell made for Piacenza where he found 'one fine street, a new elegant church by Vignola, and the Cathedral [with] many good pictures'. From Piacenza, he set out for Parma at three o'clock in the morning, having obtained permission from the commander of the garrison, an Irishman who had been in the Spanish service, for the gates to be specially opened for him.

At the time of the carnival the Tourist left Milan direct for Venice, passing through Verona, which Mrs Piozzi thought was the gayest town she had ever lived in, and staying at Vicenza, where many of the finest buildings were the work of the town's illustrious son, Andrea Palladio, whose graceful designs were so deeply and widely admired.

The last stage of the journey from Padua to Venice was usually made down the Brenta in a *burchio*, an elaborately fitted barge, horse-drawn up to the entrance to the lagoon and then towed by a *remulcio* to the custom-house. A gondolier in white trousers and waist-coat with gold rings in his ear and on his fingers, would then take the Tourist to his hotel; and the Tourist lounging on the black damask cushions, looking at the bridges and palaces gliding by, would feel the 'excitement of Venice already within him', sensing its spell, as Elizabeth Barrett Browning did, wrapping itself around him 'at first sight'.

The third city in Italy, although by the eighteenth century declining from its former greatness, Venice was crammed with thirty thousand visitors at the time of the carnival, and the streets were filled with masked ladies hobbling about on immensely tall pattens, 'half as high again as the rest of the world', and with 'such a multitude of Jews, Turks, and Christians; lawyers, knaves, and pickpockets; mountebanks, old women, and physicians; strumpets bare-faced; and, in short, such a jumble of senators, citizens, gondoleers, and people of every character and condition, that your ideas are broken, bruised, and dislocated in the crowd'.

The carnival at Venice began on Twelfth Night, and so long as it lasted a Tourist wearing a black or white mask was welcomed anywhere. In the daytime there were numerous spectacles to watch, acrobatic displays, bullfights, boxing and wrestling tournaments, wild beast shows, and the ceremonial processions to which the Venetians, and, indeed, all Italians, were so devoted. In the evenings there were dances, gambling parties, fireworks and exhibitions in the courtesans' houses.

John Evelyn was in Venice in 1645 and the carnival he described had altered little a hundred years later:

'At Shrovetide all the world repair to Venice, to see the folly and madness of the Carnival; the women, men, and persons of all

Philipp, Baron von Stosch, caricatured here by Pier Leone Ghezzi receiving various collectors and dealers, spent about eleven years in Rome at the beginning of the eighteenth century. An insatiable collector and expert connoisseur, he was at the same time secretly employed by the British Government to keep watch on English Tourists in Italy who might be using the Grand Tour as a cover for intrigue with Jacobites living in exile there.

Venice

The carnival at Venice, depicted here by Giovanni Domenico Tiepolo, began on Twelfth Night and was a time of 'great frivolity and irregularity . . . the crowd of masqueraders is often so great there is no passing in the piazza . . . Tumblers and mountebanks are constantly to be enjoyed.'

conditions disguising themselves in antique dresses, with extravagant music and a thousand gambols, traversing the streets from house to house, all places being then accessible and free to enter. Abroad, they fling eggs filled with sweet water, but sometimes not over-sweet. They also have a barbarous custom of hunting bulls about the streets and piazzas, which is very dangerous, the passages being generally narrow. The youth ... contend in other masteries and pastimes, so that it is impossible to recount the universal madness of this place during this time of license. The great banks are set up for those who will play at basset; the comedians have liberty, and the operas are open; witty pasquils [lampoons] are thrown about, and the mountebanks have their stages at every corner ...

[Late one night], conveying a gentlewoman who had supped with us to her gondola at the usual place of landing, we were shot at by two carbines from another gondola, in which were a noble Venetian and his courtezan unwilling to be disturbed, which made us run in and fetch other weapons, not knowing what the matter

was, till we were informed of the danger we might incur by pursuing it further.'

If the Tourist arrived at Venice early in the morning he would find the canals covered with rafts and barges filled with fruit and vegetables. In the Grand Canal William Beckford could

'scarcely distinguish a wave. Loads of grapes, peaches and melons arrived, and disappeared in an instant, for every vessel was in motion; and the crowds of purchasers hurrying from boat to boat, formed one of the liveliest pictures imaginable. Amongst the multitudes I remarked a good many whose dress and carriage announced something above the common rank; and upon enquiry I found they were noble Venetians, just come from their casinos, and met to refresh themselves with fruit before they retired to sleep for the day.'

These nobles – in 1714 there were 1,731 of them who were entitled to take part in the Grand Council – aroused the curiosity of every visitor to Venice, though they would have little to do with strangers.

'The great diversion of Venice during the carnival is masquerading. Then they forget all marks of distinction, care and business, and resign themselves up to joy and liberty, frequently attended with folly and great disorder.' Painting by Giovanni Battista Tiepolo.

'They do not know what it means to offer a meal,' Charles de Brosses complained. 'I have sometimes been at a *conversazione* at the Procuratress Foscarini's, a house of enormous wealth, and she is an extremely charming lady; as the only titbit, at 3 p.m. i.e., about eleven o'clock at night in France, twenty valets bring in, on an immense silver platter, a large sliced pumpkin known as *anfouri* or water-melon, a detestable dish if ever there was one. A pile of silver plates accompanies it; everyone grabs at a slice, washes it down with a small cup of coffee and leaves at midnight with empty head and belly to sup in his own home.'

William Beckford did not think that this lack of hospitality in Venice was any great loss, since most noblemen 'unstrung by disease and the consequence of early debaucheries' were listless and dull. They passed their lives 'in a perpetual daze'. They seemed to spend most of the day in bed or half asleep in a gondola. The nights were passed either in gambling or in the pursuit of some intrigue, while their wives, like most Italian ladies, remained at home once the carnival was over.

'Their gaming-houses are called *Ridotti*,' Nugent warned, 'apartments in noblemen's houses, where none but noblemen keep the bank, and fools lose their money. They dismiss the gamesters when they please, and always come off winners. There are usually ten or twelve chambers on a floor with gaming-tables in them, and vast crowds of people; a profound silence is observed, and none are admitted without masks. Here you meet ladies of pleasure, and married women who under the protection of a mask enjoy all the diversions of the carnival, but are usually attended by the husband or his spies. Besides these gaming-rooms, there are others for conversation, where wine, lemonade, and sweetmeats are sold. Here the gentlemen are at liberty to rally and address the ladies, but must take care to keep within the bounds of decency, lest they meet with bravoes or assassins.'

When a nobleman wanted to make love to one of these ladies of pleasure or the masked wife of one of his acquaintances he would steal away with her, so Beckford said, to 'a little suite of apartments in some out-of-the-way corner' of which his family were 'totally ignorant' and of which even the gondoliers, 'though the prime managers of intrigue' were 'scarce ever acquainted'.

Those who could not afford to keep a mistress for their own 'particular use', Nugent continued, 'join with two or three friends and have one in common amongst them. When the nobility have done with their concubines, they become courtesans. Of these there are streets full, who receive all comers; and as the habits of other people are black and dismal, these dress in the gayest colours with their breasts open, and their faces bedaubed with paint, standing by dozens at the doors and windows to invite their customers.' In the early seventeenth century there were as many as twenty thousand courtesans

A Venetian ridotto, a set of rooms in a nobleman's palace used for gambling and for assignations. Courtesans and married women in masks were met here and then taken off to 'a little suite of apartments in some out-of-the-way corner'.

in Venice, Coryat estimated, 'whereof many are esteemed so loose,' he confided to his readers, 'that they are said to open their quivers to every arrow.' There was a foundling hospital especially devoted to the care of any babies they were unfortunate enough to bear; but it was rarely full, for 'according to the old proverb the best carpenters make the fewest chips'.

To save their sons from 'contracting distempers with common harlots', a rich mother would make a bargain with one of her poor neighbours for a daughter of the house to become his bedfellow for a sum which depended upon the attractions of the girl. This girl would ultimately join the ranks of the courtesans, and so add one more justification for Venice's reputation as 'the brothel of Europe', the place where you had to beware of the 'Four Ps' – the *pietra bianca* (the slippery white stone of the steps up to the 450 bridges), the *prete*, the *pantaleone*, and, above all, the *putana* (the whore). There was a time at the beginning of the eighteenth century when the courtesans in Venice were members of a rich and respected profession, when the Prince of Denmark was entertained by them at a far more magnificent banquet than he had enjoyed elsewhere; but those days had soon passed, and by the third decade of the century the courtesan had lost

The church of S. Marco, 'an almost square structure built after the *Greek* fashion,' was not widely admired by English Tourists. The horses of brass gilt over the main gate, however, were universally esteemed for their 'incomparable workmanship'.

most of the prestige she had enjoyed in former times.

As well as being considered 'the brothel of Europe', Venice also had the reputation of being one of the dirtiest and smelliest cities.

John Howard, the prison reformer, with thoughts of gaol fever in mind, advised a young Tourist who was staying in the same house as himself not to remain in Venice longer than four days; and a later arrival there described the city as 'a stinkpot'. Goethe said that flat-bottomed boats, manned by country people from the neighbouring islands, occasionally came into the canals and took away the filth which was heaped up in corners by the bridges to use it on their land as manure. 'But there is no regularity or strictness about these arrange-ments,' he added, 'and the filthy state of the town is all the more unpardonable because it is as well situated for cleanliness as any town in Holland.'

Nor were the stenches and filth limited to the canals and streets. Even the Doge's palace, as Baron von Archenholz was not the only visitor to observe, was noisomely fetid: 'The very stairs are like a sink. Go where you will, you will find whole rills of stinking water, and smell its noxious exhalations. The nobles, who honestly contribute their share, never regard these nuisances, and paddle through them with uplifted gowns.' In James Smith's opinion St Mark's Church was quite as filthy as the Doge's palace, 'perhaps the most dirty place of public worship in Europe, except the Jews' synagogue at Rome'.

Few Tourists spoke well of St Mark's even when they did not complain of the filth inside it. The arrangement of the buildings around the square was fine enough. The Doge's residence and the tall columns at the entrance, together with the arcades of the public library, the 'lofty Campanile and the cupolas of the ducal church', formed, as Beckford expressed it, 'one of the most striking groups of buildings that art can boast of'. But Anne Miller, who was in Venice in the early 1770s, expressed a common enough opinion when she

complained of the 'absurd old Gothic style' of St Mark's. James Smith condemned its 'barbarous, inelegant style'; Eustace wrote of its 'gloomy, barbaric magnificence'. James Boswell, after a visit to it in July 1765, made this laconic entry in his diary: 'To St Mark's church. Old mosaic. Luckily, a solemn service.'

The Doge's palace, although it contained what were admitted to be 'some good pictures' – the genius of Veronese, Titian and Tintoretto being less subject to the vagaries of taste than many other artists – was not as a building much commended, either, except by those few Tourists who were beginning to appreciate the spirit of the Gothic style.

It was the graceful buildings along the Grand Canal, the Ponte di Rialto, the church of Santa Maria della Salute, Palladio's new fronts to the churches of San Francesco della Vigna, Santa Lucia and San Giorgio Maggiore, and such new buildings as Giorgio Massari's palaces, which had combined to alter the appearance of eighteenth-century Venice far more than that of any other Italian town – it was these examples of Venetian taste that aroused wider admiration than the grandeur of St Mark's. While it was the Arsenal, 'the greatest and most beautiful in Europe', which aroused in many Tourists the more real interest. The guides who showed them round told them that it contained 2,500 cannon, enough arms and equipment for 100,000 infantry soldiers and 25,000 cavalry, and – to show how efficient was its foundry – they pointed out a cannon which had been entirely made while the Doge was having his dinner.

Even so, there was nothing in Venice as intriguing as its people – the Doge himself clothed in purple silk trimmed with ermine, a cloak of cloth of gold, a tall horn-shaped cap, a jewelled belt, and painted sandals; the noblemen in their silk- and fur-lined ankle-length togas coloured black, red, cream or violet according to their rank; the graceful ladies of the court with their painted faces almost hidden

The Ponte Rialto, the white marble bridge spanning the Grand Canal. It was built by Contino, nicknamed da Ponte, the architect of the Bridge of Sighs, in 1588–91. In the middle of the eighteenth century it was the only Venetian bridge to be railed.

behind their veils and their scented hair covered by pale blonde wigs; the itinerant minstrels in the streets; the oriental rope-dancers, jugglers, fortune-tellers and magicians in St Mark's; the exotic, cheering, extraordinarily discordant crowds at the bull-baitings, the goose-catchings, the gondola races and the prize-fights.

On leaving Venice for the south, the Tourist would first visit Padua. In Fynes Moryson's time there were always numerous Englishmen at Padua, for here, it was considered, the best Italian was spoken. 'English swarme here,' a diplomat reported in 1614. Moryson, himself, attended the university where, in his own words, 'Gentlemen of all nations come ... some comming to study the civill Law, others the Mathematickes and Musick, others to ride, to practise the Art of Fencing, and the exercises of dancing and activity, under most skilful professors of those Arts'. It was a happy place to be in, Moryson thought, and the people were kind and honest: 'The Hostesse dresseth your meat in the bargaine for your chamber, and findes you napkins, tableclothes, sheetes and towels; and either in your chest or her owne, will lay up the meat and the very bread you leave ... and little boyes attend in the market places with baskets, who for a soll will carry home the meat you buy, and dare not deceive you though you goe not with them.' Others, though, found Padua less pleasing. William Lithgow, who sailed for the Continent in 1608, thought it the 'most melancholy City of Europe'. The students at the university were notorious for their violence, and as for 'beastly Sodomy' it was as 'rife here as in Rome, Naples, Florence, Bologna, Venice, Ferrara, Genoa, Parma not being excepted, nor yet the smallest village of Italy: A monstrous filthiness, and yet to them a pleasant pastime, making songs, and singing sonnets of the beauty and pleasure of their Bardassi, or buggered boys'.

Both the town and university were still flourishing when John Evelyn visited Padua in 1645. But a hundred years later the university had lost its reputation. Tourists noticed with stern disapproval the grass growing in the streets and the comte de Caylus wrote of its 'very poverty-stricken appearance'. 'It is badly built,' the comte added, 'its houses lack any trace of beauty and it is extraordinarily badly paved.'

Since medieval art meant little to all but a few of them, scarcely any Tourists bothered even to look at Giotto's frescoes; and only Palladio's church of St Justina, 'one of the finest pieces of architecture in Italy', still received the kind of praise which Evelyn had bestowed upon it.

Ferrara received even stronger condemnation than Padua. Many of its canals were abandoned, and mosquitoes buzzed drearily above their stagnant water; while its streets were so poor and desolate that Misson thought it could not be viewed without compassion. Baron von Archenholz thought that the authorities ought to put a notice on the gates: 'This Town is To Be Let'; and Mrs Piozzi was on the point of praising it for its cleanliness until she reflected that there was

Padua

Baldassare Longhena's Church of Santa Maria della Salute in Venice was built in 1623 to commemorate the end of the plague in 1630. This painting of it is by Michele Marieschi, probably one of Canaletto's pupils, whose work was a formative influence on that of Francesco Guardi.

nobody to dirty it. She looked around for half an hour and did not encounter a single beggar – 'a bad account of poor Ferrara'.

Bologna Bologna, on the contrary, presented a very different picture. Nugent considered it 'one of the handsomest cities in Italy' and those who followed him there agreed with him. There was an excellent university, celebrated for its schools of law; there were as many beautiful palaces as churches – the staircase in the Aldrovandi Palace was superb – and in the church of Corpus Domini those with a taste for such things – and few Tourists did not share the taste – could inspect the embalmed body of a nun, St Katerina di Vigri who had died in 1469. Apart from St Katerina, the main things which the Tourist remembered about Bologna were the ice in the boiled wine, the sausages, the machines on the hotel tables for driving away the flies, the men carrying fans in the streets, and, of course, the pictures. The most admired of these pictures, which were scattered about in the numerous churches and monasteries of the town, were by Guido Reni, Guercino and the Caraccis. Although not so highly esteemed to-day, they were considered then to be as fine as any works to be found in Italy. Mariana Starke, for instance, thought that one of Annibale Caracci's pictures could 'vie with the finest productions of Raffaele, while it [surpassed] them all in beauty of colouring'.

Many Tourists who passed through Bologna in the 1780s had the pleasure of being entertained by Marquis Albergati who owned a beautiful villa just outside the town. The marquis's male guests were roused at nine o'clock by a bell which was gently tolled to inform them that two servants were ready to shave them and dress their hair. Their toilet complete, they went downstairs to have a drink in a room which was kept constantly open for this purpose. At ten o'clock they had a cup of chocolate while enjoying a conversation with their host; and at eleven they went with him to Mass in his private chapel. After Mass they played cards, or billiards, walked in the garden or read in the library. Soon after two o'clock they sat down to luncheon, an exquisite meal whose excellence was fully enjoyed, since during the eating of it their host sensibly forbade all serious talk.

After lunch everyone retired for a siesta; and then either on horseback, in a sedan chair or a barouche – whichever was preferred – they all went out for a drive, meeting at an agreed spot where servants had prepared an *al fresco* meal.

From Bologna the Tourist would drive to Rome either through Florence, Siena and Viterbo, or Rimini, Pesaro, Ancona, Loreto, Macerata and Terni. The second route allowed a visit to the chapel of Our Lady of Loreto, the house at Nazareth in which Mary had been born and which, after it had been converted into a church by the apostles, was carried across the sea to Italy by a flight of angels. Half a million pilgrims came to Loreto every year; but since the innkeepers, as Dr Moore put it, did not 'disturb their devotion by the luxuries of either bed or board', it was not a popular place with Protestants. Most of these were likely already to have been shown

The last stage of the journey from Padua to Venice was usually made down the Brenta in a *burchio*, an elaborately fitted barge, horse-drawn up to the entrance to the lagoon and then towed by a *remulcio* to the custom-house. The river journey provided opportunities to see the famous villas that lined the Brenta's banks.

during their Tour so many other Marian relics – as well as chairs on which her son had sat, nails from His cross, strands of St Peter's beard, the rock struck by Moses, pictures painted by St Luke, marble spotted with the blood of St John the Baptist, and arrows that had pierced the flesh of St Sebastian – that they preferred to take the road which took them through Siena, a 'most sweet City', as Fynes Moryson called it.

Although Gibbon found the 'women were so ugly and the men so ignorant' that he had no desire to stay in Siena, most visitors were so taken with it that even the cathedral's Gothic style, often condemned as barbaric in the Doge's palace at Venice and elsewhere, was usually found not only acceptable but pleasing. 'The most remarkable thing we met with at Siena,' wrote Breval, 'is the Dome; of a Gothic style indeed, but very beautiful in its kind, and would be still more so in my Opinion, were the Marble all of one Colour.'

Whichever route he took to Rome from Bologna, the Tourist had to cross the Apennines, an experience which nearly all of them found almost as great an ordeal as crossing the Alps.

William Beckford, toiling over the foothills, found 'nothing but dreary hillocks and intervening wastes ... parched fern and grasses ... desolate fields; and now and then a goggle-eyed pilgrim trudging along, and staring about ... During three or four hours that we continued ascending, the scene increased in sterility and desolation ...'

'A chill wind blew from the highest peak of the Apennines, inspiring evil, and made a dismal rustle amongst the woods of chestnut that hung on the mountain's side, through which we were forced to pass. I never heard such fatal murmurs, nor felt myself so gloomily disposed ... How long I continued in this strange temper I cannot pretend to say, but believe it was midnight before we emerged from the oracular forest, and saw faintly before us the huts of Lognone, where we were to sleep. This blessed hamlet is suspended on the brow of a bleak mountain, and every gust that stirs, shakes the whole village to its foundations. At our approach two hags stalked forth with lanterns and invited us with a grin, which I shall always remember, to a dish of mustard and crows' gizzards, a dish I was more than half afraid of tasting, lest it should change me to some bird of darkness, condemned to mope eternally on the black rafters of the cottage.'

Dr Burney, making his way through the Ligurian Apennines on mule-back, was buffeted in the face by the boughs of trees and kicked by the vicious mule's hind legs:

'Such bridges! Such rivers! Such rocks! ... Two days and two nights we were clambering up and sliding or tumbling down these horrid mountains ... the road always on the very ridge of the mountain and the sea always roaring beneath, with a strong loud wind, which I often thought would have carried me, mule and all, into it ... However, at length, about eleven at night, we arrived at a wretched inn or pigsty, half stable and half cowhouse, with a fire but no chimney, surrounded by boors and muleteers, all in appearance cut-throat personages, with no kind of refreshment but cold veal and stinking eggs.'

But at last the weary traveller from the north came down from Viterbo towards the Lago di Bracciano, and there, within easy reach of Rome, all the discomforts of his journey seemed worthwhile.

Rome

To some travellers, though, their first sight of Rome was something of an anti-climax. From a distance, Charles Dickens thought, 'it looked – I am half afraid to write the word – like LONDON!!! There it lay, under a thick cloud, with innumerable towers and steeples and roofs of houses, rising up into the sky, and high above them all, one Dome.'

Nor when he drove down the Via Flaminia through the Porto del Popolo was the Tourist likely to be fired with his first impressions of Rome at close quarters. The Piazza del Popolo, and the three long streets that fanned out, and still fan out, from it to the south – the Via del Corso, the Via Ripetta, and the Via Babuino – were fine enough,

'Races on the Tiber', by Vernet. To the sound of music from the bank young men endeavour to knock each other into the Tiber in a contest as old as history. The bridge is the Ponte S. Angelo, formerly the Pons Aelius. Vernet, who entered the studio of the marine painter Bernardino Fergioni as a young man, lived in Rome for twenty years until 1753.

despite the goats wandering in the Piazza, the one-storey hovels of washerwomen on its circumference, and the seedy houses of prostitutes in the side alleys beyond. But, as Father Labat observed in 1715, 'they were badly paved and extremely dirty', while the handsome houses were interspersed with others which were ugly, low and jerry-built. The air was thick with dust, and although in the evening a few carts trundled about followed by a man who swung from side to side a leather tube attached to a water barrel, the Romans did not really 'know what sweeping means, they leave it to Providence. Heavy rain showers act as brushes in Rome'.

When he reached the custom-house, made out of the hall of Antonius Pius, the Tourist had his things tumbled about on the floor by meddlesome officials pretending to search for contraband goods, yet in reality waiting for the customary bribe, as anywhere else in Italy.

'The narrowness of the streets, the thinness of the inhabitants, the prodigious quantity of monks, and beggars,' all gave, Dr Sharp suggested, 'a gloomy aspect to this renowned city.' All the shops seemed empty, 'and the shopkeepers poor'.

De Brosses's first impressions were also far from favourable. 'The Government is the worst possible. Of the population a quarter are priests, a quarter are statues, a quarter are people who do nothing.'

William Hazlitt was even more condemnatory:

S. Maria Maggiore, the largest of the eighty churches in Rome dedicated to the Virgin. The façade was built by Fuga in 1741–3. Gian Paolo Pannini produced numerous topographical views of the city and architectural studies which found their way into English collections.

'It is not the contrast of pigstyes and palaces that I complain of, the distinction between the old and new; what I object to is the want of any such striking contrast, but an almost uninterrupted succession of narrow, vulgar-looking streets, where the smell of garlick prevails over the odour of antiquity, with the dingy, melancholy flat fronts of modern-built houses, that seem in search of an owner. A dunghill, an outhouse, the weeds growing under an imperial arch offended me not; but what has a greengrocer's stall, a stupid English china warehouse, a putrid trattoria, a barber's sign, and old clothes or old picture shops or a Gothic palace, with two or three lacqueys in modern liveries lounging at the gate, to do with ancient Rome?'

Other Tourists complained not of the two or three lacqueys lounging about outside the Gothic palaces, but the multitudes of them, as in Paris, crowding round offering their services. They are 'sad fellows', Nugent warned, and would be sure to lead you to a bad inn for the sake of their commission, or give information against you to the Inquisition.

Fear of the Inquisition in Rome was, however, unreasonable. In the sixteenth and early seventeenth centuries, some English Protestants certainly came to Rome in disguise, and following Fynes Moryson's example, left before Easter to avoid the house-to-house search for non-communicants. Sir Henry Wotton, who began his travels in 1587, came disguised as a German Catholic, wearing a 'mighty blue feather' in his black hat, explaining the reasons for the feather as follows: 'First, I was by it taken for no English. Secondly, I was reputed as light in my mind as in my apparel (they are not dangerous men that are so). And thirdly, no man could think that I desired to be unknown, who, by wearing of that feather, took a course to make myself famous through Rome in few days.'

But Montaigne was allowed through the customs with material that would have warranted a charge of heresy; and later travellers, even when detected in their heretical beliefs, had little to fear from the authorities provided they kept their views to themselves. In Lent it was easy enough to obtain a licence to eat meat; and there were in any case plenty of taverns and butchers' shops prepared to sell or serve meat without bothering about the licence.

Few of the shops in Rome had windows and scarcely any of them bore the name of their proprietor, who advertised his trade by a symbol – a cardinal's red hat for a tailor, a man (usually a Turk) smoking a pipe for a tobacconist, a bleeding arm or foot for a surgeon, a Swiss in the uniform of the papal guard for a lace merchant, and a shaving plate (together, on one shop front, with the bald announcement 'Here we castrate the singers in the papal chapels') for a barber.

The shops and stalls of a particular trade were all grouped together in the same area. The cabinet-makers, for example, could all be found between Via Arenula and Piazza Campitelli, the watchmakers in Piazza Capranica, and the booksellers around the Chiesa Nuova. Some trades were all crowded together in the same street; as the names of Roman streets still testify. Via dei Coronari, between Piazza Navona and Via Curato, was where the rosary makers worked, and in the Via dei Capellari, between the Campo dei Fiori and Via Pellegrino, the hatters could be found. On Wednesdays in the market in Piazza Navona the Jews came out to set up stalls for the sale of secondhand clothes.

The Roman Jews were treated far more harshly than anywhere else in Italy. Locked up every night in their ghetto, obliged to hear a Christian sermon every afternoon – which, however, they attended to, said Evelyn, with 'so much malice in their countenances, spitting, humming, coughing, and motion that it is almost impossible they should hear a word from the preacher' – and forced to wear a distinguishing yellow hat, the Jews of Rome were 'a pack of poor wretches, permitted to deal only in old goods and cast off cloathes'.

More likely to enlist the sympathy of the average Tourist were the young girls who took the veil in the convent of St Ursula. Dr Burney watched one girl being offered here in what he called a 'human sacrifice'. She had beautiful light brown hair and was wearing an expensive dress and diamonds, all of which were cut off her. At the altar she changed colour several times, and seemed to pant and to be in danger of bursting into tears or fainting. But at the convent door 'she appeared to give up the world very heroically'.

Catharine Wilmot watched a similar ceremony and reported that 'not only the women, but many of the young Englishmen were in indignant tears.'

'One just by me,' Miss Wilmot went on, 'instinctively layed his hand upon his sword, swearing that such heartrending superstitious cruelties ought to be extirpated from off the face of the earth. All was in a moment silent as death, and everyone was obliged to see, and everyone obliged to hear, the snapping of the scissors, which separated a hundred glossy braids and curls from her head, which fell amongst her bands of Roses at the feet of the Abbess, who continued with unrelenting piety to strip her of every ornament, and then bound her temples with sack-cloth and threw over her the black austerities of her holy order, placing a crown of thorns upon her head, a branch of white lilies in her hand, a large crucifix by her side, and all the insignia of a heavenly office. She then

A young English Tourist and his suite arrive in Rome during the carnival. The Piazza di Spagna was a well known gathering place for the English. It contained several English inns and cafés, and was always haunted by numerous *cognoscenti* offering for sale the dubious 'masterpieces' here shown under examination on the left.

disappeared amongst a black procession of deep veiled Nuns, each with lighted torches in their hands, preceded by the Elevation of the Host. This that takes up two minutes to relate, took four hours to witness.'

Fortunately Rome provided less heartrending spectacles. The carnival which began eleven days before Ash Wednesday was as exciting as that held in Venice. Men and women wearing fantastic disguises paraded up and down the decorated streets, particularly in the Corso where flowers, ribbons, foliage and garlands hung down from the buildings over the rows of chairs and daïses. Every kind of costume could be seen – sailors', soldiers', pierrots', pirates', Turks', punchinellos', hangmen's, even cardinals' although these were forbidden – handsome women dressed as guardsmen and young men as nuns. Some revellers walked on stilts, others rode on their servants' shoulders, or on the running boards of carriages; but all threw confetti, streamers, handfuls of flour, rice, or sweets at each other, shouting and laughing beneath the lanterns and the illuminated churches.

The Piazza del Popolo, inside the gate that carried the road from the north through the wall of Rome. It was the first sight which many Tourists had of the beauty of Rome, a 'so much vaunted bonbonnière', as Stendhal called it. The obelisk was was brought to Rome by Augustus from Heliopolis; to the left are the steps leading up to the Pincio Gardens.

The leading families of Rome decorated floats and their younger members appeared on them as Chinamen, or janissaries, medieval knights or Grecian nymphs, drawn by horses in harnesses of gaily coloured leather covered with silver bells.

Every afternoon Barbary horses, tightly swaddled in white cloth and with painful nail-encrusted saddles to make them run 'like mad creatures', were taken to the obelisk in Piazza del Popolo and from there raced down the Corso; and every evening the crowds came out once again into the streets carrying candle ends, peering into masked faces in the passing crowd, shouting out insults and invitations, making assignations, dancing until dawn.

At less exciting seasons of the year, there were the Roman theatres to be enjoyed – though these were sometimes disappointing as the female parts had to be played by eunuchs as women were not allowed on stage. There were also the processions of blood-spattered flagellants who carried on their conversations with the most intriguing unconcern as they whipped themselves through the streets.

One of the most frequently attended spectacles was the representation of the washing of the Apostles' feet by Christ. The parts of the Apostles were taken by twelve old pilgrims, 'caught on purpose for the occasion, and ranged upon a long Form, their heads bare and long grey reverential beards'. Christ was represented by the Pope, 'barefoot, holding in both his hands a basin of water with napkins on his arms and a white apron tied about his waist'.

After the ceremony of washing, the Pope took the Apostles in to dinner and, still barefoot, carved their meat, offered them wine on salvers, took away their plates, 'in short performed the office of a servant excessively well'.

For many Tourists the highlight of their visit to Rome was their

138

Johann Joachim Winckelmann, the German archaeologist who was murdered at Trieste in 1768, was superintendent of antiquities in Rome and librarian to Cardinal Albani. He acted as guide to various distinguished Tourists.

presentation to the Pope. In the days of Pius VII they would be received by him in the Vatican gardens, finding him dressed in 'a scarlet large flowing mantle trimmed with gold, scarlet shoes with gold crosses embroidered on each, and a Friar's Dress underneath his mantle'. He was pleasantly unaffected and entertaining, yet made it seem entirely proper that visitors should prostrate themselves on their knees to kiss his toe, and that servants and gardeners should fall on their knees, as soon as he came into view in any part of the grounds, and remain kneeling until he had disappeared from sight.

Permission was frequently sought for a tour of the convent of the Capuchins where visitors were shown a cross made by the devil, a painting by St Luke, and the subterranean cemetery whose galleries were filled with skeletons. In these catacombs, there were grottos made entirely of knuckles, knee caps, ribs, grinning skulls and cross-bones. In each compartment, standing erect against the wall, were six skeletons in Capuchins' habits, with the skin dried tight upon the bones, long beards hanging to the girdles, rosaries clutched in spindly fingers. The live monks who conducted visitors through these grue-some caverns cheerfully pointed out the skeletons of former friends and the vacant niches where their own bones would soon be displayed.

For conducting him round the better-known sights of Rome, the Tourist was advised to employ a skilful antiquarian whose knowledge and honesty were unquestionable.

While staying in Rome with his beautiful mistress, Gertrude Corradini, John Wilkes was fortunate enough to have for his guide Johann Joachim Winckelmann who was appointed superintendent of Roman antiquities in 1763. Winckelmann's enthusiasm was infectious,

139

A painting by David Allan showing country people enjoying themselves in the Piazza in front of the Theatre of Marcellus. The theatre was begun by Julius Caesar and completed in 13 BC by Augustus. It accommodated between 13,000 and 14,000 spectators.

and Wilkes decided that he was 'a gentleman of exquisite taste and sound learning'. He endeared himself all the more to Wilkes for when the two lovers – to both of whom Nature had given the 'noble passion of lust' – disappeared for a few minutes, Winckelmann affected not to notice their temporary absence. 'This was the more obliging,' Wilkes commented, 'because he must necessarily pass such an interval with the mother of Corradini who had as little conversation as beauty.'

Winckelmann had not got on so well with a less interested Tourist, Frederick Calvert, sixth Lord Baltimore, whom he had conducted round the antiquities a few years earlier.

'My Lord is an original and deserves to be written up,' Winckelmann reported to friends. 'He thinks he has too much brain and that it would have been better if God had substituted brawn for a third part of it. He has wearied of everything in the world; we went through the Villa Borghese in ten minutes ... Nothing pleased him but St Peter's and the Apollo Belvedere ... He finally got so unbearable that I told him what I thought of him and shall have no more to do with him. He has £30,000 sterling of annual rent [as proprietor of the Colony of Maryland] which he does not know how to enjoy ... His retinue consists of a young and pretty English girl but he is looking for a male travelling companion; he will have difficulty in finding one.'

It was rare to find a guide as knowledgeable as Winckelmann. Rome was full of men who called themselves antiquarians, Northall warned in his *Travels through Italy*, 'who offer themselves to strangers of quality, to serve them as guides in surveying the curiosities of the place. Too many of our young English noblemen have been deceived and imposed upon by these persons ... These Antiquarians will make such novices believe a copy to be an original of Raphael, Angelo, Titian, or some other great master, which they purchase at an extravagant price.'

But honest and knowledgeable guides were to be found; and when one was employed the Tourist and his tutor were ready to set out, equipped with maps, magnifying glasses, a mariner's compass and quadrant, and all things needful to measure the dimensions of the antiquities they would be shown.

These antiquities were less obvious than they are today, for in the eighteenth century Imperial Rome was almost lost beneath crumbling medieval walls, the array of sixteenth-century buildings erected during Paul v's and Urban viii's pontificates, and the rubble and rubbish of hundreds of years. The arches of the theatre of Marcellus were filled in and inhabited by numerous poor families; the Palatine Hill was overrun with gardens and weeds; twice a week there was a market in the Forum; the Arch of Severus was half buried; and the Coliseum was let out to citizens who kept sheds for their animals there.

'A hermit has a little apartment inside [the Coliseum]', Boswell noted in his journal. 'We passed through his hermitage to climb to where the seats and corridors of the theatre once were ... It was shocking to discover several portions of this theatre full of dung.'

There was still much to see and admire all the same, and, as Nugent wrote in his guide – before prosaically listing the columns, arches, obelisks, churches, palaces, squares, bridges, fountains, villas, baths and temples of the Eternal City – 'no place in the universe affords so agreeable a variety of ancient and modern curiosities ... In fact one cannot walk fifty paces without observing some remains of its ancient grandeur.'

It was here in 1764 amongst these ruins, that Edward Gibbon felt inspired to write his great work.

'After a sleepless night, I trod, with a lofty step, the ruins of the Forum; each memorable spot where Romulus stood, or Tully spoke, or Caesar fell, was at once present to my eye; and several days of intoxication were lost or enjoyed before I could descend to a cool and minute investigation ...

It was on the fifteenth of October in the gloom of the evening, as I sat musing on the Capitol, while the barefoot fryars were chanting their litanies in the temple of Jupiter, that I conceived the first thought of my history. My original plan was confined to the decay of the City; my reading and reflection pointed to that

The Triumphal Arch of Titus, a single arch of Pentelic marble, was erected to commemorate the defeat of the Jews in 70 AD. It was the kind of monument of which the Tourist was expected to make notes and sketches.

aim; but several years elapsed, and several avocations intervened, before I grappled with the decline and fall of the Roman Empire.'

The less impressionable Tourist soon grew weary of going to see the antiquities, measuring them, drawing them, making notes about them, and ticking them off in his guide-book. He began to feel like Walpole who confessed:

> 'When I first came abroad everything struck me, and I wrote its history; but now I am grown so used to be surprised that I don't perceive any flutter in myself when I meet with any novelties; curiosity and astonishment wear off, and the next thing is, to fancy that other people know as much of places as one's self; or, at least, one does not remember that they do not ... I see several things that

The Grand Tour was not often undertaken by a man with a family, but such visitors were not, of course, uncommon in Rome. Here, in a sketch by Archibald Skirving, a tourist is seen giving information from his guide-book in 1792 to his wife and young son.

please me calmly, but *à force d'en avoir vu*, I have left off screaming Lord! this and Lord! that.'

Dr John Moore knew one English gentleman who did not much care for sightseeing or art and thought that two or three hours a day was too much time to spend 'on a pursuit in which he felt no pleasure, and saw very little utility'. On the other hand he did not want to leave Rome after six weeks unable to claim that he had not seen all that his fellow Tourists had seen. So

'he ordered a post-chaise and four horses to be ready early in the morning, and driving through churches, palaces, villas, and ruins, with all possible expedition, he fairly saw, in two days, all that we had beheld during our crawling course of six weeks. I found afterwards, by the list he kept of what he had done, that we had not the advantage of him in a single picture, or the most mutilated remnant of a statue.'

As many such a Tourist found there were many enjoyable ways of spending a day in Rome without benefit of antiquary, note-book and ruler. It was as easy to find a pretty, complaisant girl here as it had been in Paris and Milan.

'I sallied forth of an evening like an imperious lion,' Boswell told Rousseau. 'I remembered the rakish behaviour of Horace and other amorous Roman poets, and I thought that one might well allow one's self a little indulgence in a city where there were prostitutes licensed by the cardinal-vicar.'

On the morning of Ash Wednesday 1765 Boswell decided to have a girl every day; and for the next few days his notes about his outlays on 'girls' – always in the plural – show that he fulfilled his resolve.

A '*fille charmante*' cost fourteen paoli (7s) on 19 February; 'des filles' cost a sequin (10s) on 20 February; and on the 21st and 22nd he recorded expenditure of three and four paoli. Later he became a satisfied customer of a small brothel run by three sisters named Cazenove. He had first been taken to their house by a young student at the French Academy in Rome who had previously found him a 'charming girl', the sister of a nun, near Cardinal Colonna's palazzo.

Although few Tourists recorded their sexual adventures with Boswell's detailed frankness, there can be no doubt that his experiences were far from exceptional.

Rome had other advantages, too. The people were very friendly and life was cheap. A handsome furnished house cost no more than six guineas a month; and Robert Adam enjoyed a pleasant apartment and the services of a cook, valet, coachman and footman for only twelve shillings a day. A poorer Scottish architect, Robert Mylne, managed to provide both for himself and his brother with no more than £30 a year. There was plenty of good food in the markets – excellent kid and pork, the best veal in Europe, tender poultry and game, fresh good bread and fruit, a greater variety of wines than

The Pantheon, here depicted by Pannini, was rebuilt by Hadrian *c.* 115–125 AD after the original structure had been struck by lightning in 110 AD. Since 609, it has been the Christian Church of S. Maria-Rotonda. The dome was the first of such a size to be erected.

other towns in Italy. And after a good meal a delightful few hours could always be spent in the Piazza Navona, dozing by the fountains, idly inspecting the medals, pictures and curiosities on sale in the market, listening to the prattle of the mountebanks as they offered for sale their dubious charms and prophylactics.

For the more adventurous there was the excitement of a visit to the catacombs, as described by Evelyn:

'We therefore now took coach a little out of town, to visit the famous Roman Sotteranea ... Here, in a cornfield, guided by two torches, we crept on our bellies into a little hole, about twenty paces, which delivered us into a large entry that led us into several streets, or alleys, a good depth in the bowels of the earth ... We ever and anon came into pretty square rooms, that seemed to be chapels with altars, and some adorned with very ordinary ancient painting. Many skeletons and bodies are placed on the sides ... Here in all likelihood, were the meetings of the Primitive Christians during the persecutions, as Pliny the younger describes them. As I was prying about, I found a glass phial, filled (as was conjectured) with dried blood and two lachrymatories. Many of the bodies, or rather bones (for there appeared nothing else) lay so entire, as if placed by the art of the chirurgeon, but being only touched fell all to dust. Thus, after wandering two or three miles in this subterranean meander, we returned almost blind when we came into the daylight, and even choked by the smoke of the torches. It is said that a French bishop and his retinue adventuring too far in these dens, their lights going out, were never heard of more.'

Englishmen were always welcome in the palaces of the nobility and the cardinals. They were frequently entertained both at Cardinal Alessandro Albani's splendid villa (now known as Villa Torlonia) built for him just outside Porta Pia by Carlo Marchionni between 1746 and 1758, and at Princess Colonna's; while the Princess Borghese's palace, a French writer observed, was their recognised meeting-place. They were always 'in great numbers there, most of them very rich'.

The Borghese palace, though like so many huge Italian palaces, was more like an art gallery than a home.

'All these great compartments which are so vast and so superb,' complained Charles de Brosses, 'are only there for foreigners: The masters of the house cannot live in them, since they contain neither lavatories, comfort nor adequate furniture; and there is hardly any of the latter even in the upper storey apartments which are inhabited ... The sole decoration in the rooms consists of pictures with which the four walls are covered from top to bottom in such profusion and with so little space between them that to tell the truth they are often more tiring than attractive to the eye. On top of this they spend hardly anything on frames, the majority of them being old, black

The Tourist was expected to bring home from Rome a portrait of himself painted against the background of one or other of the city's notable antiquities, preferably by Pompeo Batoni. Conversation pieces, such as this one of a group of aristocratic 'English Cognoscenti' in Rome in about 1750, were more unusual.

The beauty of Naples was caught for many Tourists by the Dutch artist Gaspar van Wittel, known as Vanvitelli, who spent several years working here before his death in Rome in 1736.

and shabby, and, for all the tremendous number they crowd in, they have to mix a fair quantity of mediocre works with the beautiful ones.'

But for all these forbidding surroundings, foreigners – and in particular, English Tourists – were always made to feel welcome at the Borghese palace as elsewhere in Rome. Rome, indeed, seemed in large part designed to make the English feel at home. There were English coffee-houses where English journals could be read, English inns where English cooking could be enjoyed, taverns run by Englishmen where English students met. The expensive Albergo Londra was always full of English guests; while the elegant apartments at Casa Guarneri, near the Spanish steps, were occupied by a succession of English Tourists. Also, there were numerous English people who had made their homes in Rome. The dukes of Dorset kept a villa there and this, like Princess Borghese's, was filled most evenings with English people; as was the English College with English Roman Catholics.

The most distinguished exile of all was the Cardinal Duke of York, brother to the Pretender who was born in Rome and became bishop of Frascati in 1761. He held court there in a truly regal style, insisting that everyone should address him as Your Royal Highness, as, of course, all Jacobite exiles did.

As well as driving out to Frascati to pay court to the Duke of York, the industrious Tourist would pay a visit to Albano, Palestrina, the Pope's palace at Castel Gandolfo, and the Este palace and gardens at Tivoli which, like Palladio's palaces in the north, had a profound influence on the rich young man contemplating the building of a country house of his own in England. To such a young man, however, there were even more powerful influences yet to come.

Naples

When the wind was fair the quickest way to reach Naples was by sea; but there were disadvantages. As in sailing from Marseilles to Genoa, there was the danger of being attacked by corsairs; and there was the danger, too, that a sudden change of wind would drive the felucca

149

into some squalid port where neither bed nor food could be found. Also, a sea journey meant that the Tourist would miss seeing the palace at Caserta, the vast structure of 1,200 rooms which Luigi Vanvitelli had designed for the king of Naples as a rival to Versailles. Work had begun on it in the 1750s and was still continuing in the early nineteenth century. Its splendid staircase has been described as the most magnificent in all Italy, and the gardens and cascades behind it were enchanting. Mrs Piozzi was enthralled and described Vanvitelli's aqueduct as 'prodigiously beautiful . . . magnificent . . . superb'.

Nugent recommended the Tourist to make the journey to Naples by land, and suggested that the traveller with a limited amount of time at his disposal could not do better than to book for one of the fifteen-day trips organised by *vetturini* who, for fifteen crowns, undertook to provide eight meals on the journey south and eight meals on the way back, the ferry charges at all river crossings, a day's outing to Vesuvius, another day at Pozzuoli, and five days at Naples.

But it was generally felt that five days in Naples were not nearly enough. As soon as they caught sight of it they wanted to stay much longer. The biggest town in Italy, the third biggest in Europe, it was almost universally agreed to be captivating. Nugent himself was categorical:

> ''Tis generally allowed that Naples is the pleasantest place in Europe. The air is pure, serene, and healthful; it is scarce ever cold in winter, and in summer they have refreshing breezes both from the mountains and the sea, which is not subject to storms. The neighbouring country is the richest soil in Europe, abounding with corn, wine, and oil, which are excellent. Their wines particularly are the best in Italy, among which their Lachryma Christi is reckoned the most delicious ... In fine, there cannot in all respects be a more agreeable place to live in.'

It was an opinion shared by many. Keysler thought it much more beautiful than Paris or London; the streets of Rome and Florence were 'mean and contemptible' compared with Neapolitan streets. The Toledo, in Stendhal's opinion, 'the most populous and gayest street in the world', excelled 'most in Europe for its length and breadth'. And Lord Macaulay, who had been so critical elsewhere, formed 'very favourable' impressions of Naples. 'It is the only place in Italy that has seemed to me to have the same sort of vitality which you find in all the great English ports and cities. Rome and Pisa are dead and gone; Florence is not dead, but sleepeth; while Naples overflows with life.'

Goethe, too, was immediately conscious of the beguiling charm of the city although it slightly alarmed him. 'Naples is a paradise,' he wrote in his *Italianische Reise*; 'in it everyone lives in a sort of intoxicated self-forgetfulness. It is just like this with me. I scarcely recognise myself. I feel like a different man. Yesterday I said to myself "Either

you have always been mad, or you are mad now." Were I not im-
pelled by the German spirit and desire to learn and to do rather than
to admire, I would stay on a little longer in this school of light-hearted
and happy life, and try to profit from it still more.'

To some visitors, indeed, Naples seemed altogether too much overflowing with life, too full of 'little brown children jumping about
stark naked, the bigger ones dancing with castanets'. The population
of three hundred thousand included – as well as ten thousand prostitutes – forty thousand half-naked *lazzaroni* who noisily made their way
about the town amidst the hawkers, waiters, fishermen, musicians,
soldiers, priests, carriages and porters, and once a day they would go
down to the sea to take off what few clothes they wore and 'bathe
themselves without the smallest ceremony'. Afterwards, they could
be seen 'walking and sporting on the shore perfectly naked'. The
authorities were quite happy to tolerate this; but when in 1776 the

Goethe, depicted here in
the Italian countryside, set
out on his journey to Italy
in 1786, and arrived in
Naples in the Spring of the
following year. Naples he
thought a paradise, in
which everyone lived 'in a
sort of intoxicated self-
forgetfulness'.

Prince of San Lorenzo took to sitting naked in the Toledo, this was considered rather too extravagant behaviour even for Naples.

Partially clothed once more the *lazzaroni* swarmed about the taverns and inns in the evening, and it was impossible to walk along a street without seeing one of them being thrown out of a doorway by a waiter. They were expert pick-pockets, too, and the Tourist was advised to keep his handkerchief in his hat, his watch well secured by a strong guard, and his hand on his purse.

Of course, Naples was as dirty as any other Italian town. The porticoes and colonnades, as elsewhere, seemed 'made for people to relieve themselves whenever they [felt] the urge'. Grosley noticed that 'the courtyards of palaces and hotels, the porches of private houses, the staircases and their landings served alike as receptacles for the needs of passers-by, even people in carriages often got out to mix with the pedestrians for the same purpose, each citizen taking the same liberty in other peoples' houses as he would have done in his own.'

But the marvellous gaiety and exuberance of the Neapolitans, their captivating *simpatia*, were infectious. Even the rather staid Mariana Starke denied the truth of the Italian proverb, that Naples was a paradise inhabited by devils. 'The common people are good-humoured, open-hearted, and though passionate, so fond of drollery,' she thought, 'that a man in the greatest rage will suffer himself to be calmed by a joke.' They were naturally ignorant and superstitious – only one in fifty of them could read – and some of their customs seemed curiously primitive. The ceremonies and celebrations connected with the liquefaction of the blood of San Gennaro on the first Sunday in May and on 19 September seemed to English Tourists particularly strange and savage.

When John Wilkes witnessed the ceremony in 1765 the miracle

The Castel del'Ovo over-looking the Bay of Naples was built in the twelfth century, but having been destroyed by Ferdinand II was restored in the sixteenth.

James Gillray had a profound contempt for self-professed connoisseurs, men like William Baillie, a well-known copyist of old master drawings in private collections and an eager judge of the works brought back by Tourists from the Continent. Many of their works were fakes. The patrons of the sculptor Joseph Nollekens, so said one of his former pupils, 'being characters professing taste and possessing wealth, employed him as a very shrewd collector of antique fragments; some of which he bought on his own account; and, after he had dexterously restored them with heads and limbs, he stained them with tobacco water, and sold them, sometimes by way of favour, for enormous sums.'

A COGNOCENTI contemplating ye Beauties of ye Antique.

'Ballo di Napoli', an etching by Paolo Fabris of a young Italian couple dancing the Tarantella to a tambourine.

was somewhat delayed and as the cardinal agitated the 'phial the people grew quite outrageous. The women shriek'd hideously, beat their breasts and tore their hair. The men seemed equally frantic. They began the most frightful yelling, and several were cutting themselves with knives.'

Wilkes does not say what they were yelling; but according to Mathilde Sarao they commonly shouted abuse at the saint for not performing the miracle, and thus laying them open to fearful disasters, disease, impotence, even death. '*Faccia verde!*' they would scream, '*Faccia gialluta! Santo malamente!* Green Face! Yellow Face! Cursed saint! Do your miracle! Do it now, now, now!'

Really, Wilkes decided, the Neapolitans were scarcely human.

'They do not even dance to music,' Henry Swinburne observed, 'but perform the Tarantella to the beating of a kind of tambourine, which was in use among their ancestors, as appears by the pictures of Herculaneum. The Tarantella is a low dance, consisting of turns on the heel, much footing and snapping of the fingers. It seems the delight of their soul, and a constant holiday diversion of the young

Marco Ricci's impression
of an Italian male singer
in the role of a general.

women, who are, in general, far from handsome, although they have fine eyes and striking features.'

The restlessness and gaiety overflowed into the theatre. The audiences in Naples were noisy even by the standards of Italy, where to make themselves heard above the shouting, laughter and conversation, the actors, as Dr Burney put it, 'seem in a perpetual brawl. Each sentence pronounced is more like the harangue of a general at the head of an army of one hundred thousand men, than the speech of a hero or heroine in conversation'. At the performance of an opera, and at a time when Italy was setting standards for European music as Germany was to do in the next century, the audiences talked the whole time, shouting across the auditorium to friends in the opposite boxes, spitting orange peel onto the heads of the people beneath, listening only to their favourite arias, loudly booing an inexpert performance or the new work of any composer which displeased them, or going down to one of the gambling rooms with which most Italian theatres were equipped.

At the San Carlo in Naples, which was opened in November 1737, it was the custom to walk about the house first to one box, then to another, upstairs and downstairs, then back to the box you had first occupied which was now full of a quite different assortment of people. All the while there would be the sound of kissing, for the Neapolitans never shook hands, looking upon it as 'the most hoity toity impudent custom in the world', and kissed each other, men and women, with a smack which resounded about the room.

'Every lady's box is the scene of tea, cards, cavaliers, servants, lapdogs, abbés, scandal, and assignations,' Beckford affirmed, 'attention to the action of the piece, to the scenes, or even to the actors, male, or female, is but a secondary affair.' When the court was present 'a tolerable silence was maintained, but the moment his Majesty withdrew (which great event took place at the beginning of the second act) every tongue broke loose, and nothing but buzz and hubbub filled up the rest of the entertainment.'

The King of the Two Sicilies at this time was the Bourbon Ferdinand I, third son of Charles III of Spain. He reigned in Naples from 1759 until his death in 1825, and to one British Tourist, who saw him at a ball given by his prime minister, the English doctor's son, Sir John Acton, he looked like 'an overgrown ass', though 'exceedingly civil'. The Queen, the Austrian Maria Carolina, was 'a sturdy looking dame by no means elegant in her deportment, and trotted about in her black and blue robes, much more as if she were crying "tooky, tooky, tooky" after her Poultry, like a housewife, than a queen during the dignities of her drawing room'. The Prince danced with his Spanish wife like 'a cow cantering, kicking up his hoofs and making a sort of noise like the braying of an Ass'. Vulgar was 'no expression to apply to his appearance', for vulgarity became 'genteel within his presence'.

The court was clearly no place at which to spend a happy evening;

but on Sundays, Tuesdays and Thursdays from the end of June to 8 September, the Marina de Chiaia provided a pleasant alternative rendezvous. Here the most beautiful ladies in the town could be seen as they were driven up and down in their carriages; and sometimes they could be watched on the promenade of La Mergellina waiting for their admirers who came across the bay in decorated feluccas with musicians to serenade them.

Then there were – as well as the villas of such expatriates as Sir Francis Eyles whose home became known as the English coffee-house – many Neapolitan palaces of an astonishing grandeur whose doors were open to English visitors and where guests enjoyed themselves up till five o'clock in the morning while hordes of servants slept and snored on the marble tiles of the magnificent baroque halls until it was time to escort their masters home.

The Prince of Francavilla gave regular dinners for Tourists who were introduced to him by letters from mutual friends. Sharp reported one such 'splendid dinner which closed the carnival last week (perhaps more splendid than you see in London) provided for eighteen guests, ten of which were the English Gentlemen on their travels'. The Prince was immensely rich and extravagantly hospitable, taking his guests down to the casino after dinner, and then making his pages, 'all sweethearts of the Prince', dive into the sea and swim about in it. 'The Englishmen asked him if he would give us the same spectacle only substituting nymphs for his *amorini*,' a guest recorded after one such display, 'and he promised to do so the next day at his splendid house near Portici, where there was a marble basin in the midst of the garden … The next day he kept his promise, and we had the pleasure of seeing the marble basin filled with ten or twelve beautiful girls who swam about in the water.'

Another hospitable Neapolitan nobleman was the Duke of Monte Leone who, in Charles de Brosses's opinion, held 'the largest and most magnificent assembly in the town, which costs him, so they claim, more than fifty thousand francs in candles, ices and refreshments.' Yet even more hospitable was Gaetano Filangieri, author of *La Scienza della legislazione*, whose fascinating, wayward sister, the Principessa Ravaschieri di Satriano, delighted his many guests.

Quite as fascinating as the Principessa was the beautiful Irish-woman, Sara Goudar, who had started her career as a barmaid in London and in the 1770s lived in a villa at Posilipo with her French husband who made a very handsome living by running a casino which many English Tourists regularly frequented and by exploiting his wife's glorious sensuality. One evening Giovanni Jacopo Casanova, who had known her in her days as a barmaid, called at her villa and was 'stupefied; the metamorphosis was so great'.

'She was dressed with the utmost elegance,' Casanova continued, 'received company admirably, spoke Italian with perfect correctness, talked sensibly, and was exquisitely beautiful … In a quarter of an hour five or six ladies of the highest rank arrived, with ten or twelve

Caricature of a female singer by Ricci.

Lady H * * * * *
Attitudes

dukes, princes and marquises, to say nothing of a host of distinguished strangers. The table was laid for thirty, but before dinner Madame Goudar seated herself at the piano, and sang a few airs with the voice of a syren ... her singing was really admirable.' Goudar had worked this miracle. He had been educating and training her for six or seven years.

Another girl of lowly birth who became one of the leading figures in Neapolitan society was Emma Hart, a Cheshire blacksmith's daughter, who, after having been Charles Greville's mistress for several years, married Greville's uncle, Sir William Hamilton, British envoy in Naples between 1764 and 1800.

Almost every evening when they were not engaged elsewhere, it was the custom for English Tourists to meet at the Hamiltons' apartment in the Palazzo Sessa, overlooking the bay, to play cards or billiards, to talk or listen to a 'little concert'.

In April 1786, Emma Hamilton wrote to her former lover, Greville, of her life in Naples. 'We have company almost every day since I came – some of Sir William's friends. They are all very much pleased with me, and poor Sir William is never so happy as when he is pointing out my beauty to them. He thinks I am grown much more ansome than I was. He does nothing all day but look at me and sigh.'

Sir William, as well as being a diplomat, was an antiquary, and he took great interest in the excavations at Herculaneum and Pompeii. These excavations were of fairly recent date. When John Evelyn visited Naples in 1645, though a passionately thorough sightseer, he had no reason to visit either place. In 1775, when Robert Adam was there, the digging at Herculaneum had only recently begun and the site seemed to Adam 'like a coal-mine worked by galley slaves'.

It was Ferdinand I's mother, Maria Amelia, daughter of Frederick Augustus II, Elector of Saxony, who had aroused interest in the buried remains. On moving to Naples after her marriage to Charles III in 1738 she was intrigued by the amount of classical statuary which was lying about in the palace gardens, and suggested to her husband that they should dig for more.

A previous excavator, General d'Elboeuf, had discovered several interesting pieces buried under the lava deposit on one side of Vesuvius, so it was here that diggers were set to work. Before the end of that year, 1738, various fragments of bronze statues, marble busts, and painted columns were found; and soon an inscription reading THEATRUM HERCULANENSE indicated that a buried city was being revealed.

Ten years later excavations began at Pompeii. From then on Tourists flocked to see the new discoveries both in the rooms on the digging sites where they were repaired and in the various collections in Naples. Indeed, as Sacheverell Sitwell has suggested, the uncovering of Pompeii and Herculaneum might be accounted the second wave of the Renaissance so profound were its effects upon taste. Coming so soon after Palladio's works had made their deep impression on him,

Rowlandson's impression of Lady Hamilton adopting one of her 'attitudes', a series of *poses plastiques* representing classical figures, for the benefit of a young Tourist with artistic inclinations.

Sir William Hamilton, depicted here in a portrait by David Allan, was British Envoy to Naples between 1764 and 1800, and took Emma Hart, born Amy Lyon, the daughter of a Cheshire blacksmith, from his nephew Charles Greville as part of the arrangement for the settlement of his debts.

it destroyed any leanings the English aristocrat might have had towards rococo, and was responsible for that taste in interior decoration associated with the brothers Adam. It was also largely responsible for late eighteenth-century taste in both furniture and decorative pottery. The 'Etruscan' pottery made famous by Josiah Wedgwood and the style of certain pieces of furniture associated with the names of Sheraton and Hepplewhite are directly derived from these discoveries at Herculaneum and Pompeii. One of Sheraton's chair designs which reproduced various classical *motifs* recovered from the excavations was actually called 'The Herculanium'.

Every Tourist took it as a matter of honour after visiting the excavations, to make the ascent of Vesuvius, difficult and sometimes dangerous as it was.

John Wilkes, then living with Gertrude Corradini in Villa Pietracatella, a 'crazy old castle' at Vomero near Naples, made the climb with Boswell in March 1765.

'I had five men to get me up,' Wilkes told his daughter Polly, 'two before, whose girdles I laid hold of; and three behind who pushed me by the back. I approached quite to the opening from whence issues the sulphureous smoke ... I lay on my belly against the side on the edge and looked down, but could see very little; only now and then when the wind blew the smoke much on one side, I could see several ragged mountains of yellow (sulphur, I suppose). I endeavoured to go quite round but was almost suffocated by the smoke, and obliged hastily to retire. You descend with great difficulty, sometimes almost up to the knees in ashes ... The *lava* is not beautiful; yet, if you choose it I will send you some.'

Eighty years later Charles Dickens climbed Vesuvius with his wife and sister-in-law, Georgina Hogarth. The age of the Grand Tour was over; but the ascent was just as so many Tourists described it. It was made in winter when the sides of the mountain were covered in snow 'glazed with one smooth sheet of ice from the top of the cone to the bottom'. The tourists – six of them, accompanied by twenty-two guides – rode on saddle horses until the slope became too slippery and steep when the women were put into sedan chairs and the men provided with sharp-pointed sticks.

'By prodigious exertions,' Dickens told his friend Thomas Mitton, 'we passed the region of snow and came into that of fire – desolate and awful you may well suppose. It was like working one's way through a dry waterfall, with every mass of stone burnt and charred into enormous cinders, and smoke and sulphur bursting out of every chink and crevice, so that it was difficult to breathe ... the fire was pouring out, reddening the night with flames, blackening it with smoke, and spotting it with red-hot stones and cinders that fell down again in showers. At every step everybody fell, now into a bed of ashes, now over a mass of cindered iron.'

Dickens and two companions decided to go right to the top of the crater, despite the alarming roaring and the feeling 'at every step as if the crust of ground between one's feet and the gulf of fire would crumble in and swallow one up (*which is the real danger*)'. When they came back to the rest of the party, having looked into the flaming bowels of the mountain, they were 'alight in half a dozen places, and burnt from head to foot'. Dickens had never seen 'anything so awful and terrible'. His clothes were 'burnt to pieces'.

On the way down it was impossible to keep balance on the ice, and three of the party slipped and fell over the edge. One of them had still not been found at midnight.

As well as climbing Vesuvius, and visiting Pompeii and Herculaneum, the enterprising and dutiful Tourist made an expedition to Mergellina to see where Virgil had been buried on the small country estate, bequeathed to him by Siron, his teacher of philosophy.

On his return the Tourist might visit Lago d'Agnano and test the lethal properties of the Grotto del Cane in a way of which a modern traveller, more sensitive to the sufferings of animals, could scarcely be expected to emulate.

'We now came to a lake of about two miles in circumference, environed with hills,' John Evelyn wrote, describing this experiment; 'the water of it is fresh and sweet at the surface, but salt at bottom. The people call it Lago d'Agnano, from the multitude of serpents which, involved together about the spring, fall down from the cliffy hills into it. It has no fish, nor will any live in it. We tried the old experiment on a dog in the Grotto del Cane, or Charon's Cave; it is not above three or four paces deep, and about the height of a man, nor very broad. Whatever having life enters it, presently expires. Of this we made trial with two dogs, one of which we bound to a short pole to guide him the more directly into the further part of the den, where he was no sooner entered, but – without the least noise, or so much as a struggle, except that he panted for breath,

The site of Pompeii, having been lost for centuries, was discovered beneath the vineyards and mulberry fields at the foot of Vesuvius in 1748. In 1763 systematic excavations began on the orders of the King of the Two Sicilies and continued throughout the remaining period of the Grand Tour.

lolling out his tongue, his eyes being fixed – we drew him out dead to all appearance; but immediately plunging him into the adjoining lake, within less than half an hour he recovered, and swimming to shore, ran away from us. We tried the same on another dog, without the application of the water, and left him quite dead.'

Pompeii was as far south as most Tourists ventured. A few went on to Sorrento or sailed across the Bay to Capri; but the Gulf of Salerno, Basilicata, Calabria and Sicily were largely disregarded. When in 1828, Crawford Tait Ramage, tutor to the sons of the British consul in Naples, set off for the south 'in search of its ancient remains and modern superstitions', he was undertaking a dangerous adventure which all but the most intrepid Tourist refused to contemplate.

And so the road north began at Naples. Returning by a route which

A view of Vesuvius, seen smoking across the Bay from a house near the Castel Nuovo, the great fortress built by Charles I of Anjou in 1283.

top One of Sir William Hamilton's many interests was the study of earthquakes and volcanoes, and he employed artists to make such records as this one of Vesuvius erupting.
bottom The excavations at Pompeii continued throughout Sir William's time in Naples and with his help many Tourists acquired their memorials and antiquities.

would take him past towns he had not seen on his way down, the Tourist made his way back towards the Alps collecting on his way those mementoes of his journey which every tour of Italy was expected to provide – books of prints, medals, maps, paintings and copies of paintings at Rome, as well as scent, pomatums, bergamot, imperial oil, and *acqua di millefiori;* snuff-boxes and silk from Venice; glasses from Murano; swords, canes, soap and rock-crystal from Milan; mosaics of dendrite, and amber, musk and myrrh from Florence; point lace, sweet-meats and velvet from Genoa; snuff and sausages from Bologna; fire-arms from Brescia; milled gloves from Turin; masks from Modena; spurs and toys from Reggio nell'Emilia.

In the midst of his shopping, his sight-seeing, his long jolting journeys, his strange meals, his arguments with his tutor, his brief love affairs and lengthy *conversazioni*, he found time perhaps to write some such dutiful and grateful letter to his parents as this one which Gibbon wrote from Florence on 20 June 1764:

'… Every step I take in Italy, I am more and more sensible of the obligation I have to my father in allowing me to undertake the Tour. Indeed, Dear Madam, this Tour is one of the very few things that exceed the most sanguine and flattering hopes. I do not pretend to say that there are no disagreeable things in it; bad roads, and indifferent inns, taking very often a good deal of trouble to see things which do not deserve it, and especially the continual converse one is obliged to have with the vilest part of mankind – innkeepers, post-masters, and custom house officers, who impose upon you without any possibility of preventing it – all these are far from being pleasing. But how amply is a traveller repaid for those little mortifications by the pleasure and knowledge he finds in almost every place.'

Sir William Hamilton was a distinguished archaeologist and collector as well as a diplomat. It was partly due to the published illustrations of his collection of Roman, Greek and Etruscan antiquities that the treasures discovered in the excavations around Naples became generally known throughout Europe.

Leopoldstadt, the main
suburb of Vienna, 'divided
from the town by a little
plain and the river Danube.
It is ornamented with the
houses of the principal
people of quality.'

GERMANY
AND AUSTRIA

Insolence of German postilions – discomfort of country inns and luxuriousness of town ones – difficulties encountered with diversity of dialects and currencies – extreme hospitality of German families – the university towns, Göttingen, Leipzig and Jena – spas as an essential feature of the Tour – popularity of Munich – Vienna – Berlin and the visit to Potsdam – the Gothic Cathedral at Strasbourg – Frankfurt, Wiesbaden and Cologne.

Disagreeable as Gibbon and his fellow Tourists found travelling in Italy, they discovered that in Germany it was even more of an ordeal.

'To travel with a *Vetturino*, a *Procaccia*, or a *Corriere*, through the worst Italian roads,' Dr Burney thought, 'is ease and luxury compared with what is suffered in Germany.'

The roads in most parts of the empire were appalling; and to travel in bad weather, as *The Traveller's Guide to Germany* warned, was 'a perfect misery'. It was sometimes impossible to cover more than eighteen miles a day. Even on the main roads leading to such towns as Berlin and Hanover the wheels of the carriages would sink up to the axle in mud and wet sand.

'Before nine o'clock, it rained violently,' Dr Burney wrote of his journey to Berlin, 'and it became so dark, that the postilion lost his way, and descended from his place, in the front of the wagon, in order to feel for it, with his hands; but being unable to distinguish any track, he mounted again, and, in driving on, at a venture, got into a bog, on a bleak and barren heath, where we were stuck fast, and obliged to remain from eleven o'clock at night, till near six the next morning.'

Catharine Wilmot's experiences were even worse:

'In the midst of jolts, dust, and weakness from fatigue, the springs of my carriage broke, and threw me into the Ditch. After a considerable delay, we drove on again over such roads or rather rocks, that I felt as if my existence was to snap at every step, and before we could arrive at the next town, the wheel flew off, and again

flung me into the middle of the road. We then waited a couple of hours for reparations and so set off again, hoping all my misfortunes had ceased. But in the middle of the night the Pole snapped, and I was obliged to be drawn on for some miles, by ropes, men, and oxen, till at length we got into a Village. I literally was more dead than alive, and had not strength to take off my clothes.'

The carriages were as uncomfortable as the roads were bad. For those who did not have a chaise of their own, there was generally the severely limited choice – until diligences came into general use in the nineteenth century – between riding a post-horse or of travelling in a post-wagon, which was little better than a cart with rough seats for six or eight passengers. Post-wagons rarely had any covering and, pulled by four tawdry beasts, went 'but a slow pace, not much above three miles an hour, and what is still more inconvenient to passengers, they jog on day and night, winter and summer, rain or snow, till they arrive at the place appointed. In winter when the cold is very severe, the postilion stops pretty often, when he can get to a public house, where it is customary for passengers to alight and warm themselves on the stove, and call for a glass of brandy, for there is seldom anything else, in a great many parts, to be had for love or money.'

In these carts most Tourists found the company far from agreeable. 'My company,' complained one of them, 'consisted of a swine of an Oldenburgh dealer in horses, a clodpole Bremen broker, and a pretty female piece of flesh, mere dead flesh lying before me in the straw. There was not a word spoke all the way from Gottingen here [Cassel],

Of all the pleasures of their travels many Tourists enjoyed most of all their river journey down the Rhine, eating salmon, drinking hock and looking at small riverside towns and the crumbling castles on the hills above them. This is Bacharach, a few miles west of Mainz.

169

so that if the *dulcis et alta quies* had not been now and then interrupted by coughing, sneezing, belching, and the like, I should not have known that I had company with me.'

Other travellers had no doubt about the company, since the carts, so they said, were overcast by a haze of smoke or, as in Fyne Moryson's case, full of women alternately arguing, quarrelling, 'now brawling together, now mutually with tears bewailing their hard fortune'.

If the companions of the journey were annoying, the postilions were insupportable. Nor was it only the British Tourists who thought so. 'Travellers always speak with great indignation about the rudeness of the Prussian postilions,' the Russian Karamzin reported. 'The present King [Frederick William II] issued an order which obliges all postmasters to treat travellers with more respect and not keep anyone more than an hour at each station. It also forbids postilions to stop at will on the road. Nevertheless, the impertinence of the postilions was insufferable. They stopped at every tavern for beer, and the

unfortunate travellers had either to put up with this or bribe them to go on.'

German postilions, Catharine Wilmot agreed, were 'insolent beyond measure and dreadful cheats'. Dr Burney could not find words sufficiently strong with which to condemn their 'villainous and rascally behaviour'. Forced into paying for more horses than were necessary – as so many other travellers were, including William Wordsworth – he never forgot their 'heinous impositions'.

They also made a habit of taking their passengers to the worst possible inns where they could expect free food and drink as commission from the landlord. Many of these inns were, indeed, atrocious.

'When your carriage stops at the inn,' Ann Radcliffe said, voicing a familiar complaint, 'you will perhaps perceive instead of the alacrity of an English waiter, or the civility of an English landlord, a huge figure wrapt in a great coat, with a red worsted cap on his

In the eighteenth century bandits seem to have been less of a hazard in Germany than in France or Italy, but in the seventeenth century country roads in Germany were extremely dangerous. Throughout the Thirty Years War, and for several years after it ended in 1648, travellers were very likely to be attacked like this.

German inns were notoriously uncomfortable, and the Tourist was sometimes obliged to sleep in a barn or stable.

head and a pipe in his mouth, stalking before the door. This is the landlord. He makes no alteration in his pace on perceiving you, or, if he stops, it is to eye you with curiosity; he seldom speaks, never bows, or assists you to alight; and perhaps stands surrounded by a troop of slovenly girls, his daughters, whom the sound of wheels has brought to the door, and who, as they lean indolently against it, gaze at you with curiosity and surprise.'

Once inside the inn all the travellers' worst fears were confirmed. In Westphalia few inns had chimneys, the smoke being left to find its best way out through the broken windows; even fewer provided their guests with separate bedrooms, men and women being huddled together into a room which might well already contain a cow or some other animal that would wake him up in the middle of the night by trying to eat his pillow.

The food provided in German inns was frequently atrocious, comprising in some of them nothing but gingerbread with *Branntwein* or greasy black sausage with *Sauerkraut*. The wine, as this guest appears to have discovered, was often sickening.

The traveller in Germany, according to Nugent, had often to 'tumble pell-mell into a large kind of barn, where the landlord and landlady, men and maidservants, and passengers of both sexes, cows, sheep and horses pig all together on the ground.'

This was certainly Boswell's lot. After being 'laid upon a table covered with straw', at an inn in Vellinghausen, he was shown the floor to lie on at an even more squalid inn near Mameln in Hanover. 'On one side of me,' he noted in his journal, 'were eight or ten horses; on the other, four or five cows. A little way from me sat on high a cock and many hens; and before I went to sleep the cock made my ears ring with his shrill voice, so that I admired the wisdom of the Sybarites, who slew all those noisy birds. What frightened me not a little was an immense mastiff chained pretty near the head of my bed. He growled most horribly, and rattled his chain.'

In such inns straw took the place of beds; and when beds were provided these were often damp and verminous. One guide-book, *An Essay to Direct and Extend the Enquiries of Patriotic Travellers*, advised its readers to take to Germany with them two pairs of sheets, a silk coverlet, and two dressed hart's skins so as to avoid catching 'the itch, venereal or any other disease' which would result from direct contact with the bedclothes of previous lodgers.

The type of bed commonly found was no more to the Tourist's taste than the high beds to be found in France. A true German bedstead was 'a sort of wooden box or trough', equipped with a huge and heavy 'squab or cushion covered with a gay patterned chintz, and ornamented at each corner with a fine tassel – looking equally handsome, glossy, cold, and uncomfortable'.

As well as being uncomfortable, inns in the remote German countryside were also places where 'safety ought always to be suspected'. Tourists were recommended to have their servants sleep in the same room, to have a wax-candle burning there all night, to fix a pocket door-bolt to the door, or, if they did not carry a pocket door-bolt with them, to push the furniture in the room against the door to prevent attack by 'needy assassins'. Further, 'it will not be amiss in such lonesome places, to show his fire-arms to the landlord in a familiar discourse, without acquainting him of his well-grounded suspicion of insecurity; and to tell him, with a courageous look, that you are not afraid of a far superior number of enemies'.

In some villages there were no inns at all, and the unfortunate Tourist obliged to spend the night in an isolated place would have to seek shelter in a private house whose poor owners might have little to offer him but potatoes, salted bacon, brown bread made of bran, and beer which to an English palate tasted 'vile'.

However vile it seemed, though, the Germans themselves drank gallon upon gallon of it; and, unlike the Italians, were as often to be found incapably drunk as the English. Beside the common dining-table of many inns was still to be found the leather-covered sofa which the seventeenth-century inn nearly always provided for the guest too drunk to sit up.

Whether or not they liked the beer provided for them in private houses, most Tourists agreed that the food they ate there, scanty as it often was, was much better than that served in the average inn, at some of the worst of which the guests could get nothing to eat and drink but coarse *Branntwein* and gingerbread or greasy black sausage with *Sauerkraut*. The beef, mutton, fowls, lampreys, snails, and dried fish and venison offered in the better private houses were all considered excellent, while the *Zuckerwerk*, the *Pflaumenmus*, and the many fruit dishes were as original as they were appetising. Apples and apricots were halved, dried in the oven, and then served with butter and cinnamon. Black cherries were cut up with pears and boiled, then the juice was pressed through the holes of a pot and left to cool and jelly; reheated, it made a delicious sauce.

Drawings like this one by Daniel Chodowiecki, the German artist of Polish descent who has been termed the German Hogarth, reminded the Tourist of such happy days as that William Beckford spent with a peasant family in Bavaria.

William Beckford described the cheerful, simple hospitality of a country family in Bavaria:

'After a few hours' journey through the wilderness, we began to discover a wreath of smoke; and presently the cottage from whence it arose, composed of planks, and reared on the very brink of a precipice. Piles of cloven spruce-fir were dispersed before the entrance, on a little spot of verdure browsed by goats; near them sat an aged man with hoary whiskers, his white locks tucked under a fur cap. Two or three beautiful children with hair neatly braided, played around him; and a young woman dressed in a short robe and Polish-looking bonnet peeped out of a wicket-window. I was so much struck with the exotic appearance of this sequestered family, that, crossing a rivulet, I clambered up to their cottage and begged some refreshment. Immediately there was a contention amongst the children, who should be the first to oblige me. A little black-eyed girl succeeded, and brought me an earthen jug full of milk, with crumbled bread, and a platter of strawberries fresh picked from the bank. I reclined in the midst of my smiling hosts, and spread my repast on the turf: never could I be waited upon with more hospitable grace.'

This was in 1780, when the ravages of the Seven Years War were at last being made good in Germany. But even while the effects of that war could everywhere be seen, while large tracts of desolated country were inhabited by half-starving people just recovering from malignant fevers, it was still possible to enjoy the generous hospitality for which the Germans were famous.

Nor were all country inns in Germany as bad as some Tourists implied. Charles Burney complained of the three or four shillings he paid for 'a pigeon and half a pint of miserable sour wine', of the outrageous price charged for milk. Others wrote of the 'miserable pompernickel', the 'half-raw bacon', the 'wretched beer'. But it was nevertheless possible to buy a good meal for ten pence, if one knew where to go.

In the larger towns of the empire there were inns that could be compared with the best in Europe. The Emperor and The Red House at Frankfurt, The Hotel de Pologne at Dresden, The Stockholm at Cassel, the Darmstadter Hof at Karlsruhe were all excellent; the Three Kings at Augsburg was internationally famous, and so, in their heyday, were Wolf's and The White Bull at Vienna. There were three fine inns at Nuremberg and at least two at Munich. The Hotel Zum Rheinischen Hof at Mainz; and the Hotel de Bellevue at Coblenz both received high praise from more than one critical Tourist.

So comfortable were some of the hotels in the larger towns, indeed, that the prospect of moving out and continuing the Tour was made all the more uninviting. It was not just the bad roads, rattling wagons, bullying postilions and unpredictable inns that made the Tourist apprehensive, but the fear that his route would take him 'through forests without roads, extended plains, and wilds, without the trace of a wheel on the turf'. It was not just that he was afraid that he would pass nothing – as one traveller said he did on the way to Bonn – but 'beggarly children, high convent walls, scarecrow crucifixes, lubberly monks, dejected peasants, and all the delights of Catholicism', but that he would be robbed and murdered.

Setting out for Emms, William Beckford was given this warning by a woeful native:

'Sir, said he, your route is to be sure very perilous: on the left you have a chasm, down which, should your horses take the smallest alarm, you are infallibly precipitated; to the right hangs an impervious wood, and there, sir, I can assure you, are wolves enough to devour a regiment; a little further on, you cross a desolate tract of forestland, the roads so deep and broken, that if you go ten paces in as many minutes you may think yourself fortunate. There lurk the most savage banditti in Europe, lately irritated by the Prince of Orange's proscription; and so desperate, that if they make an attack, you can expect no mercy. Should you venture through this hazardous district to-morrow, you will, in all probability, meet a company of people who have just left the town to search for the mangled bodies of their relations.'

In fact, robberies and murders on the road seem to have been far less common in Germany than in Italy. Catharine Wilmot wrote of her 'great surprise' that when travelling all night through Saxony she met no robbers, although the road was in such densely wooded country that the carriage brushed the trees as it rattled along. But if not stopped by highwaymen, the carriage was constantly stopped by custom officials at the boundaries of the small states into which Germany, like Italy, was then divided.

Then, to add to the Tourist's disinclination to resume his journey, there were the language difficulties, the problems with money, the likelihood of being arrested at night in a strange town for the breach of some local law – such as being in the streets at ten o'clock without a lantern – not to mention the disproportionate expense.

For, as well as being far more uncomfortable than it was in France and Italy, German travel was also far more expensive. *Postgeld* (horse-hire) and *Wagengeld* were but two of the charges necessarily incurred. There was *Schossegeld* to pay at the turnpikes, *Schwagergeld*

Several shops in Nuremberg sold this unusual type of weights which many Tourists brought back as presents for their families.

to pay the postilion, *Schmiergeld* to pay for the greasing of the wheels, *Barriergeld* to pay for the tollgates, *Trinkgeld* to pay for drinks for the ostler.

These formidable obligations had to be met in a muddling variety of specie. Frankfurt, for example, being almost in the middle of Germany and surrounded by numerous petty states, was pestered with gulden, creitzers, batzes, groschen, reichstaler, pfennings, stivers, deniers, German gold ducats and Spanish philips. Germany as a whole was also pestered with so many disparate dialects that people from one province found it scarcely possible to understand those from another; while the Tourist, of course, could not understand any of them at all. Fortunately most Germans who had been reasonably well educated spoke French and a little Latin as well as their own mother-tongue and in Saxony English was widely understood as well.

But this did not lessen the irritation experienced each time a Tourist came to a frontier town where baggage was searched with a thoroughness and a slowness which Mariana Starke thought would be impossible to conceive by anyone who had not been through the ordeal. 'They seize gold and silver lace, snuff and tobacco,' she wrote after crossing the frontier into Carinthia where her baggage was opened in the street, 'and for unmade silks, gauzes, etc., they oblige you to deposit double the worth.'

The examination at Berlin, Charles Burney discovered, was even more rigorous:

'When I arrived at the gates of this city … I had hopes that I should be suffered to pass peaceably to an inn, having received a passport at Ireuenbrietzen, the first Prussian town I entered on the Saxony side, when I had submitted to a thorough rummage of my baggage, at the persuasion of the custom-house officers, who had assured me it would prevent all future trouble on entering Berlin. But this was merely to levy fees upon me, for, notwithstanding my passport, I was stopped three quarters of an hour at the barrier, before I was taken into the custody of the sentinel; who mounting my post-wagon, with his musket on his shoulder, and bayonet fixed, conducted me, like a prisoner, through the principal streets of the city, to the custom-house. Here I was detained in the yard more than two hours, shivering with cold, in all my wet garments, while everything was taken out of my trunk and writing box, and examined as curiously as if I had just arrived at Dover, from the capital of France.'

At Potsdam there were further questions and even longer delays. 'The examination here,' Burney went on, 'could not be more vigorous at the postern of a town besieged. Name, character, whence, where, when, to whom recommended, business, stay, and several other particulars were demanded to which answers were all written down.'

These irritating examinations and inspections could not be avoided if the Tourist travelled by boat; but in most other respects river travel

Charles Burney travelled widely on the Continent in the early 1770s in search of material for his *History of Music*. His *Present State of Music in France and Italy* was published in 1771 and *The Present State of Music in Germany, the Netherlands and United Provinces* in 1773.

was much to be preferred in Germany to journeys by road. Boats equipped with bunks and galleys transported passengers all over Germany, and principally along the Rhine, the Weser, the Danube, the Isar and the Elbe.

Lady Mary Wortley Montagu, going up the Danube from Regensburg to Vienna in 1716, travelled 'in one of those little vessels, that they very properly call wooden houses, having in them all the conveniences of a palace, stoves in the chambers, kitchens, etc. They are rowed by twelve men each, and move with such incredible swiftness that in the same day you have the pleasure of a vast variety of prospects.'

Charles Burney, going to Vienna from Munich down the Isar and the Danube in 1772, found river travel less pleasurable. His boat was a flat-bottomed raft of fir logs on which a booth was built as shelter for the passengers. Those who paid an additional four florins, as he did, could have a private cabin built; but this cabin was hot and stuffy and was 'constructed of green boards, which exuded as much turpentine as would have vanquished all the aromatics of Arabia'. There were two square holes for windows through which the rain poured so violently on occasions that there were three or four feet of water on the floor; and Burney longed for one of the hammock beds favoured by Benjamin Franklin so that he could lie, suspended by silk cords, above the lapping ripples.

Λ sudden thunderstorm reminded Burney that the year before thirteen churches had been struck by lightning in the electorate of Bavaria alone, and he got as far away as he could from his sword and pistols and anything else that might have served as a conductor. When the raft was moored for the night his servant went to the nearest village to buy food, but on his return he was rarely able to dish up anything more appetising than bread and beer, boiled up with two or three eggs, accompanied by 'black, sour pumpernickel', 'vile' cheese and 'bad' apples. When the raft was in the shallow Isar,

Much of the Tour in Germany was done by the boats, equipped with bunks and galleys, that transported passengers down the rivers. The Rhine, rolling along mirror-smooth through the heart of Europe, was considered 'the beautifullest river in the earth'.

Huge rafts like floating islands transported passengers down the Isar and Danube. Charles Burney's journey from Vienna to Munich on one of these rafts was the most disagreeable and alarming experience of his entire Tour.

Burney was in perpetual fear that it would get stuck fast on the bottom; and when it swirled out into the Danube, he was even more alarmed by the roaring noise the waters made as they rushed past the projecting rocks.

Nor did the landscape compensate for the alarm and discomfort. North of Munich the countryside beyond the Isar's banks provided a wretched view of willows, sand, sedge and gravel; at Passau, after the raft had moved into the Danube, the outlook was more attractive, but once Linz was passed the river became so wide that he could scarcely see the banks which soon disappeared from view altogether in a thick fog. The craft encountered on the way were gloomy-looking floats laden with damp timber and hogsheads, or barges full of salt being dragged up river from Salzburg by teams of forty plodding horses. Encouraged at long last by the sight of Vienna, Burney's spirits were immediately dashed again by the custom officers who confiscated his books.

Poor Burney's experiences were exceptional. Generally Tourists enjoyed their river travel, particularly on the Rhine, 'the beautifullest river in the Earth' which rolled along 'mirror-smooth (except that, in looking close, you will find ten thousand little eddies in it), voiceless, swift, with trim banks, through the heart of Europe,

181

and of the Middle Ages wedded to the Present Age'.

The author of *A Journey through Flanders to Switzerland* sailing down it in mid-winter in the 1790s, despite the sleet and snow and the 'few chips smouldering in a little smoàking stove', found the river and the ruined castles that towered above the well cared-for farms and vine-yards 'nor otherwise than supremely interesting, instructive and gay'. In the summer it was delightful; and the memories of his passage down the Rhine, of meals of trout and salmon, asparagus and strawberries, of delicious Rhenish hocks, of his visits to crumbling Gothic castles, of the 'honest, kindly' people he met in the riverside towns, were amongst the most pleasant and vivid recollections which the more romantic Tourist took home with him.

Nor was it only along the Rhine that the Tourist found the people friendly and generous. Although Dr Burney thought that Germans tended to avoid strangers in the way that the English did, nearly all other visitors emphasised their hospitality. 'A single letter of recommendation,' Nugent said, 'is sufficient to procure a person an agreeable reception among the Germans, which can hardly be said of the inhabitants of any other country. Their civility extends so far as to introduce a stranger directly into their societies or assemblies.'

Indeed, they were sometimes considered far too hospitable, insisting that their guests should eat far more than they wanted to and should not stop drinking from the moment of arrival in the house. It was customary in many towns to take a visitor away on first acquaintance to a wine-cellar, where strangers were warned to be upon their guard, 'for the Germans think they have never performed the duties of hospitality, till they have overpowered their guests with liquor'.

At Christmas time their hospitality was particularly marked; and many English Tourists were invited to spend Christmas with German families where they encountered customs which, familiar as they have since become in England, then seemed strange to them. Samuel Taylor Coleridge, writing at the end of the eighteenth century, said that 'the children make little presents to their parents, and to each other; and the parents to the children'.

'For three or four months before Christmas the girls are all busy, and the boys save up their pocket-money, to make or purchase these presents. What the present is to be is cautiously kept secret ... Then on the evening before Christmas-day, one of the parlours is lighted up by the children, into which the parents must not go. A great yew bough is fastened on the table at a little distance from the wall, a multitude of little tapers are fastened in the bough, but so as not to catch it till they are nearly burnt out, and coloured paper hangs and flutters from the twigs. Under this bough the children lay out in great order the presents they mean for their parents, still concealing in their pockets what they intend for each other. Then the parents are introduced, and each presents his little gift, and then

Tourists were often invited to spend Christmas with German families, whose customs seemed very strange to them. Samuel Taylor Coleridge was surprised to find trees bedecked with candles brought indoors, a custom that Prince Albert was later to popularise in England.

bring out the rest one by one from their pockets, and present them with kisses and embraces.'

It was all very engaging and *gemütlich*, and it confirmed the Tourist in his belief that the Germans were far from being as savage and unfeeling as so many elegant Frenchmen said they were. There were, all the same, customs and habits in Germany which the Englishman found it difficult to write about without distaste. Fox-hunting was all very well, but to surround a wild-boar or deer and then set upon the creature with guns, lances and spears, without giving it a chance to escape was 'rather medieval'. Floggings in the British Army were common enough; but in the Prussian Army soldiers were beaten like dogs on the parade-ground without trial and for the slightest offence. Nor was the sight of a soldier being made to run the gauntlet – and being savagely cut in the process – at all unusual; and although bear-baiting was still practised in England, the Tourist of 1772 was a little shocked to read with what gusto similar, and even more savage, exhibitions were advertised in the handbills which could be picked up in the streets of a Sunday night.

'This day, by imperial licence, in the great amphitheatre, at five o'clock will begin the following diversion.

1st.   A wild Hungarian ox, in full fire (that is, with fire under his tail, and crackers fastened to his ears and nose, and to other parts of his body) will be set upon by dogs.

2nd. A wild boar will in the same manner be baited by dogs.

3rd. A great bear will immediately after be torn by dogs.

4th. A wolf will be hunted by dogs of the fleetest kind.

5th. A very furious and enraged wild bull from Hungary will be attacked by fierce and hungry dogs.

6th. A fresh bear will be attacked by hounds.

7th. Will appear a fierce wild boar, just caught, which will now be baited for the first time by dogs defended with iron armour ...

11th. And lastly, a furious and hungry bear, which has had no food for eight days, will attack a young wild bull, and eat him alive upon the spot; and if he is unable to complete the business, a wolf will be ready to help him.'

Women took their knitting with them to these exhibitions, as they did to the theatre; and looking at them, complacently clacking away with their needles, 'well-complexioned, of a sober behaviour, faithful to their husbands, and good housewives', many a Tourist regretted the painted voluptuaries he had left behind in Venice. German women in the towns were 'reckoned very handsome, and to excel those of several other parts in Europe, inasmuch as they use neither paint, nor foreign ornaments to embellish their persons', but they were also reckoned very virtuous; and there was little hope for a lusty young Englishman who wanted to pursue the kind of intrigues he had enjoyed in France and in Italy.

In the larger towns, prostitutes and *Bordells* were easily found; but these were often undesirable even to Boswell's less than fastidious taste. In Berlin he declined the services of a 'Black Girl' whose *gesunde Beschaffenheit* he was not prepared to take on trust; and the bawdy house he was taken to by some German friends was 'a poor little house' with 'an old bawd, and one whore'. So when a clean-looking woman came into the bedroom of his inn to sell him some chocolate, he was delighted. He 'toyed with her and found she was with child: Oho! a safe piece. Into my closet. "Habs er ein Man?" "Ja, in den Gards bei Potsdam". To bed directly. In a minute – over. I rose cool and astonished.' In Dresden he found no chocolate sellers, and the two 'easy street girls' he did find both picked his pocket.

Those young Englishmen not prepared to run Boswell's risks, yet regretting the sensual pleasures of France and Italy, could not but admire the example set by Lord Baltimore, the vastly rich young rake who had so irritated Winckelmann in Rome. Baltimore, so it was rumoured, arrived in Vienna with a doctor, two Negro eunuchs and eight women. When asked by the chief of police to point out which was his wife, Baltimore replied that he was an Englishman, and it was not his practice to discuss his sexual arrangements. If he could not settle the matter with his fists he would set out instantly on his travels again.

In the country, the Tourist was not tempted by the women who

were, for the most part, dismissed as 'miserably ugly'. In many provinces they hid their hair inside tawdry cotton skull caps, wore neither shoes nor stockings, and worked in the fields, so Clara Crowninshield noted on a journey from Heidelberg to Schwetzingen, 'with apparently only one garment on their backs. Their bending posture, which exposed the nudity of their lower extremities, and the vehemence with which they wielded their instruments of agriculture gave them the look of wild creatures.'

The Tourist encountered a very different Germany, of course, in the university towns such as Göttingen, Leipzig and Jena, at the fashionable spas, and at the various courts which were scattered all over Germany from Weimar to Gotha and Schwetzingen, from Anspach to Darmstadt and Meiningen.

Indeed, the Tourist's route was largely governed by the waters he wanted to taste, the baths he wished to take and the princelings to whom he wished to present letters of introduction.

In Montaigne's day, Baden was already famous for its baths. The inn there had 177 beds, and provided meals for three hundred guests a day. People came from all over Europe to seek cures for all manner of diseases, and thousands came 'with no disease but that of love: and many times [found] remedy.'

'Weomen come hither as richly attired as if they come to a marriage,' Fynes Moryson wrote: 'for Men, Weomen, Monkes, and Nunnes, sit all together in the same water, parted with boords, but so as they may mutually speak and touch, and it is a rule here to shun all sadness, neither is any jealousie admitted for a naked touch. The water is so cleere as a penny may be seene in the bottome, and because melancholy must be avoided, they recreate

185

themselves with many sports, while they sit in the water; namely at cards, and with casting up and catching little stones, to which purpose they have a little table swimming upon the water, upon which sometimes they doe likewise eat. These Bathes are very good for Weomen that are barren.'

At Carlsbad, too, the waters were said to be good for barrenness. Containing 'a composition of chalk, red bolus or mountain earth, nitre, allum, vitrol, iron and a volatile spirit of sulphur', they were also good 'for all obstructions, particularly for the gravel'.

As at Baden, at Langenschwalbach, and at Wiesbaden (where the waters were like 'hot Epsom salts') the jaded Tourist could overcome the effects of his self-indulgence under the Italian sun, and, once rejuvenated, he could proceed upon his round of the German courts. In the eighteenth century there were no less than sixty of these.

James Boswell – who loved ceremonial and dressing up, who welcomed the opportunity to style himself Baron and to have the common people bowing to his state coach as it passed – went from Brunswick to Potsdam, and then on to Dessau, Dresden, Gotha, Mannheim and Karlsruhe, on his Tour in 1764, revelling in the 'shows and gaiety and ribbons and stars', and even finding satisfaction

Wiesbaden, near Mainz in Hesse-Nassau, was one of those German watering-places whose hot springs and mild climate attracted many Tourists anxious to spend a few weeks recuperating from the exertions of travelling and the debilitating life of the German courts.

Karl Wilhelm Ferdinand, Duke of Brunswick and Lüneburg, depicted here in a painting by Battoni, was host to many Tourists and a most generous patron of the arts. Boswell was presented to him in 1764 and enjoyed much hospitality at his court. The Duke was a worthy man, Boswell was informed, 'but passionate, and sometimes gives way to terrible rages'.

for his *nostalgie de la boue* in the hardships and squalor of travel. 'I am really campaigning in Germany,' he wrote after having spent ten days without undressing. 'I like it much.'

At Brunswick he was seated at dinner next to Prince Ferdinand, the Duke's brother, and was 'absolutely electrified'. 'I live with princes, and a court is my home,' he later recorded in his journal after being honoured with a 'pretty long conversation' with the Duke. 'They asked me to return to Brunswick in August, when I should see the Fair. I said I probably should have that pleasure. I went home in vast spirits. I could scarcely speak.'

At Potsdam he saw King Frederick the Great, 'a glorious sight. He was dressed in a suit of plain blue, with a star and a plain hat with a white feather. He had in his hand a cane. The sun shone bright. He stood before his palace, with an air of iron confidence that could not be opposed. I was in noble spirits, and had a full relish of this grand scene which I shall never forget. I felt a crowd of ideas. I beheld the king who has astonished Europe by his warlike deeds.'

At Dessau he hunted and dined and danced with the *noblesse* of the Prince's court; at Dresden he went to the court of Saxony dressed in the uniform of an English officer – 'great palace ... sweet prince'; at the court of Saxe-Gotha he wore 'a suit of flowered velvet of five colours' and was delighted when the Princess asked him to come up to the table where she was playing cards and said to him, 'Mr Boswell! Why, how fine you are!' At Karlsruhe he was presented to the Margrave of Baden-Durlach. 'A grave, a knowing, and a worthy prince,' he wrote of him. 'He has seen my merit.' Only at Mannheim was Boswell disappointed. Here the Elector Palatine was 'very high and mighty' when 'Baron Boswell' was presented to him, while the Electress, who 'was much painted', was also 'exceedingly lofty'. Boswell decided that although the entertainments at Mannheim – the operas, French comedies and concerts – were admittedly 'really magnificent', a court which invited strangers to dine so seldom must be reckoned 'very bad'.

'I have not been asked once,' he grumbled to his friend John Johnston. 'What an inhospitable dog! I have been obliged to dine at an ordinary, amongst fellows of all sorts and sizes. It was one of the best tables in town, but the company disgusted me sadly. O British, take warning from me and shun the dominions of the Elector Palatine.'

Boswell's condemnation now seems unreasonable; but the Tourist had come to expect that a rich German prince who spent great sums of money on his court and palace, his soldiers, his band, and his hunt, should keep open table for foreign visitors who were presented to him. Most princes did so; and as Crabb Robinson observed, 'Everywhere in Germany English travellers are treated as if they were noble, even at the small courts where there is no ambassador. No inquiry is made about birth, title, or place.'

The Tourist had, accordingly, come to organise his route so that he visited as many of these hospitable courts as possible. If he left Italy from Venice his first stop would usually be at Augsburg in Bavaria to which a coach ran, past the Dolomites and through the Tirol, every week. He would probably stay at the Three Moors whose visitors' book was later to contain the names of Napoleon, Josephine, Marie Louise, Talleyrand and Wellington. Augsburg had once been, after Nuremberg, the centre of the trade between Italy and northern Europe, and the finest city in the empire. But it was now in decline. Tourists found it dull, and after visiting the fine Renaissance townhall and the miniature town (the 'Fuggerei', built by the Fugger brothers in 1519), after noting that 'the colossal paintings on the walls of almost every considerable building gave it a strange air', and that the Roman Catholic inhabitants walked about the streets carrying a rosary, 'as an ornament as much as an instrument of devotion', the Tourist was glad to move on either north to Nuremberg, or east to Munich and Vienna.

Dresden as it appeared before Prussian guns laid much of it in ruins during the siege of 1760. The artist is Bernardo Bellotto, Canaletto's nephew, who was court painter to the Elector of Saxony at Dresden from 1747 to 1756.

There was no place in the world where people lived more luxuriously than at Vienna, according to Nugent. The poultry market, held in the Neuer Markt, was always crowded.

Nuremberg – although now admired as a fine example of a late sixteenth-century fortified town, although *The Travellers' Guide Through Germany* dutifully extolled the fairness of its streets, the uniformity of its buildings, and the industry of its sixty thousand inhabitants – was no more admired by most Tourists than Augsburg. Crabb Robinson thought it 'very unpleasant', its theatre 'wretchedly supplied with actors', and its women 'notoriously and universally ugly'. The vast houses were 'without beauty and almost all painted on the outside', while the 'frightful horn', which was sounded every evening from each gate of the city in turn to give notice of its closing, was as irritating as it was discordant.

Munich

Munich was very much more to the Tourist's taste. 'The splendour and beauty of its buildings, both public and private, surpassed anything in Germany'; the Elector's palace was magnificent. In Nugent's opinion the palace furniture was 'rich beyond imagination'; and Beckford thought that its chapel was 'richer than anything Croesus ever possessed, let them say what they will. Not a corner but shines with gold, diamonds, and scraps of martyrdom studded with jewels. I had the delight of treading amethysts and the richest gems under foot.'

Beckford was delighted, also, by the animation of the people of Munich.

'Immediately after supper,' he wrote, 'we drove to a garden and tea-room, where all degrees and ages dance jovially together till morning. Whilst one party wheel briskly away in the valz, another amuse themselves in a corner with cold meat and rhenish. That despatched, out they whisk amongst the dancers, with an impetuosity and liveliness I little expected to have found in Bavaria. After turning round and round, with a rapidity that is quite astounding to an English dancer, the music changes to a slower movement, and then follows a succession of zig-zag minuets, performed by old and young, straight and crooked, noble and plebeian, all at once, from one end of the room to the other. Tallow candles snuffing and stinking, dishes changing, heads scratching, and all sorts of performances going forward at the same moment; the flutes, oboes, and bassoons, snorting and grunting with peculiar emphasis; now fast, now slow, just as Variety commands.'

Vienna   Vienna, too, was a gay city, and a very luxurious one. 'I have seen more splendid equipages and horses here,' wrote Baron Riesbeck, 'than there are in all Paris.'

'Especially on court days,' Nugent agreed, 'one sees the greatest profusion and extravagance in this kind of pageantry, the servants being ready to sink under the weight of their liveries, bedawbed all over with gold and silver.

'There is no place in the world where people live more luxuriously than at Vienna. Their chief diversion is feasting and carousing, on which occasions they are extremely well served with wine and eatables. People of fortune will have eighteen or twenty different sorts of wine at their tables, and a note is laid on every plate mentioning every sort of wine that may be called for. In the winter when the several branches of the Danube are frozen over, and the ground covered with snow, the ladies take their recreation in sledges of different shapes, such as, griffins, tygers, swans, scollop shells, etc. Here the ladies sit dressed in velvet lined with rich furs, and adorned with laces and jewels, with a velvet cap on their heads. The sledge is drawn by a single horse, set off with plumes of feathers, ribbons and bells, and as the diversion is taken chiefly in the night time, footmen ride before the sledge with torches, and a gentleman sitting on the sledge behind, has the direction of the horse.'

In contrast with this excitement and splendour, the town itself, in Charles Burney's opinion, seemed 'dark, dirty and narrow'. Of the streets only the Prat – 'frequented by people of quality, as the Mall is at London' – was kept clean; while in Baron Riesbeck's judgment there were 'scarce eight buildings in the whole town' which could be 'called beautiful or magnificent ... The emperor's palace is an old black building, that has neither beauty nor stateliness ... There are hardly three squares or places which make any figure at all.'

There were, though, many fine palaces on the outskirts of the town of which the two splendid baroque Belvedere palaces were the most admired. The Lower Belvedere, completed in 1716, and the more grandiose Upper Belvedere, built between 1719 and 1724, were

Operas were as well produced and sung at Vienna as anywhere else in Europe. The first performance of Mozart's *Così fan Tutte* was produced at the old Burgtheater on 26 January 1790.

both designed by Johann Lucas von Hildebrandt for Prince Eugen of Savoy, part of whose immense collection of works of art they housed. In the beautifully laid out gardens of the Belvedere, visitors could see rare plants and trees which had come from all over the world; and in the menagerie they could inspect as wide a variety of strange beasts as could be found in any zoo in Europe.

Vienna was considered an excellent place for the English Tourist to settle for a time. There were splendid theatres and libraries, first class riding and fencing schools. It was, in Martin Sherlock's view, 'perhaps the best city in Europe to teach the young traveller the manners of the great world'. An Englishman was sure to be introduced 'into all the best houses' and to meet with 'the most flattering reception'. Dr Moore agreed with him: 'I imagine there is no city in Europe where a young gentleman, after his university education is finished, can pass a year with so great advantage.'

Prague

North from Vienna, the Tourist usually made for Dresden by way of Prague. An extremely beautiful city, though much damaged in the Seven Years War, Prague seems to have delighted nearly every Tourist who visited it. Its white stone houses, the fruitful countryside around it, its copper-roofed churches glittering in the sun, 'the fine Italian-like buildings, the Gothic Cathedral, the Regal residence, the people so handsome, the shops so good, and everything looking so happy and delightful', induced one appreciative Tourist to describe

Prague as the 'handsomest city in Europe'.

Dresden, although devastated, like Prague, during the Seven Years War, also was much admired.

Boswell, staying at the Hotel de Pologne in 1764, decided it was a 'beautiful city'. He admired the Elector's library, and the new Catholic church, and the noble bridge over the Elbe; he cut a fine figure at the court; enjoyed meals with the British envoy in Dresden, Philip Stanhope, Lord Chesterfield's natural son to whom the earlier of the famous letters were addressed. He was 'luxuriously entertained' at the picture gallery, the best in Europe outside Italy, though he thought that strangers paid monstrously dear to see all the treasures – this was 'shameful' since they were the property of a prince – and he found the street-girls exceptionally inviting.

At Leipzig, a common place of call between Dresden and Berlin, street-girls were far less numerous than they were in the surrounding countryside. For 'in most of the inns in the neighbouring villages about the town good agreeable wenches are provided for the conveniency of the students [many of them English students attending the university] whose flames, 'tis thought, would be more pernicious in town, were they not quenched in this manner.' The town itself – one of the most populous and handsomest cities of the empire – was gay enough, all the same. The rich merchants of the town gave frequent balls and dinner-parties, and, in general, Nugent wrote, 'live in a

Many a Tourist spent his mornings in Vienna looking at the passing scene from the lemonade stall on the Graben.

opposite top Dresden on the Elbe was on most Tourists' itineraries since it was the usual residence of the Elector of Saxony. It was 'surrounded by hills, beautifully filled with vineyards.'

bottom The Michaelerplatz in Vienna. The building in the centre is the Burgtheater founded by Josef II.

splendid manner. The women dress vastly gay, and are very sumptuous in respect to gold and silver lace, with which they adorn their
caps and gowns.'

Berlin was considered not so gay as Leipzig, but quite as beautiful
as Dresden. Indeed, Boswell thought it the 'finest city' he had ever
seen. It was situated on a 'beautiful plain', its streets were 'spacious',
and its houses 'well-built'. Karamzin, visiting Berlin twenty years
later, agreed with him, despite the fact that he had to hold his nose
because of the fearful smell arising from the canals which were 'filled
with all sorts of filth'. Even the charming Unter den Linden, which
ran parallel to a canal, was spoilt because of this. But the Tiergarten
was wholly delightful. Here there was a kind of little Vauxhall where
a Berliner who called himself Corsica served supper 'with great
neatness of table-furnishing and china'. 'All the people of superior
ranks go and the rich burghers as well,' Count Lehndorff wrote in
his diary. 'This garden with its more than fifty small tables, all laid,
where everyone sups with company to his liking, makes a very pleasant
impression on a visitor. The foreign diplomatic corps goes there
frequently.' As popular a meeting-place in the mornings was the
military parade where, Nugent said, 'the Tactic art appears to its full
perfection.' This daily 'exercising of the soldiers [provided] one of the
pleasantest sights at Berlin.'

No one left Berlin without paying a visit to Potsdam, the 'German

Leipzig was one of the most populous cities of Germany but 'of so small a circumference that one may easily walk round it in the compass of an hour. To remedy this inconvenience, they build their houses very lofty six or seven stories high', as here in the Markt Platz.

Versailles', where Frederick the Great had laid out the park of Sans Souci and had built at vast expense his New Palace. The town had been enlarged by his father, King Frederick William I, and it bore the stamp of his military tastes in the exact and formal regularity of its streets, and in the impressive façades of its brick and stucco houses, so much more imposing than the rooms that lay behind them.

Visitors were conducted around the palace, taken into the concert-room, and shown, through a glass door, Frederick the Great's bed-room and library. Most of them were more interested in catching a glimpse of the great man himself – one man had travelled all the way from England for no other reason and returned home satisfied after his ambition had been achieved – but Frederick, who felt that he had been forsaken by England when he had most needed her friendship, did not particularly care for Englishmen; and few English Tourists were able actually to meet him.

After his visit to Berlin and Potsdam, there was little more on the Tourist's normal route other than the towns along the Rhine, from Strasbourg in Alsace to Düsseldorff in Westphalia. A few went up to Bremen and Hamburg, in Wordsworth's opinion 'a *sad* place' (whose inhabitants Fynes Moryson had found so 'unmeasurably ill affected to the English' that it was unsafe to walk about after noon when the common people were 'warmed with drinke'); a few more went on to Copenhagen; but most turned inland again and – after visits to the

Boswell, who was there in 1764, was 'struck with the beauty of Berlin. The houses are handsome and the streets wide, long and straight. The palaces of some of the royal family are very genteel'. The Royal Mint was a fine example of Berlin neo-Classicism.

wilderness and unending fields – came to the Rhine.

At Strasbourg the fine Gothic cathedral was one of 'the wonders of Germany'. Its tower, 489ft. 8in. high, was believed to be the highest in the world. At Heidelberg the castle fascinated both Longfellow and Dorothy Wordsworth who wrote in admiration of its 'noble round tower', its ivy-clad walls adorned with the figures of saints and warriors. The grounds were the most delightful Miss Wordsworth had ever seen. The German students at Heidelberg were fascinating, too. With their passion for beer and duelling, their long blonde hair and strange clothes they seemed the very spirit of rebellious youth.

A few miles from Heidelberg was Mannheim, 'one of the most handsome little towns of Europe', neat, regular, orderly, cheerful, with a large and splendid theatre. 'Numbers of well-dressed people were amusing themselves with music and fireworks in the squares and open spaces', when William Beckford was there. 'Other groups appeared conversing in circles before their doors, and enjoying the serenity of the evening. Almost every window bloomed with carnations; and we could hardly cross a street without hearing a German flute. A scene of such happiness …'

Frankfurt, further downstream, also struck the Tourist as a rich and cheerful town, surrounded by fruitful vineyards and pretty villages. Unlike so many other German towns, Frankfurt contained no beggars, although, as Nugent remarked, it was full of poor Jews confined to a ghetto and reduced to selling goods to foreigners in the taverns and during the two annual fairs. 'The Christians have a great contempt for these wretches, putting them to the vilest drudgeries,

Tourists were recommended to take a carriage four miles out of Berlin to the delightful palace of Charlottenburg. The Kaffeegarten Muskau was a well known rendezvous in the district.

top Frankfurt on the Main, one of the free cities of Germany, in whose great red sandstone church of Saint Bartholomew the Emperors were crowned. *bottom* The Castle at Heidelberg stands over 300 feet above the Neckar on the Jettenbühl. Begun in the thirteenth century and ruined in the eighteenth, it was on every Tourist's itinerary between Mannheim and Karlsruhe.

198

The Castle of
Heidelberg was much
damaged during Louis
XIV's invasion of the
Palatinate and then struck
by lightning in 1794.
Dorothy Wordsworth was
fascinated by its crumbling
tower, its ivy-clad walls
decorated with the figures
of saints and warriors.

Sachsenhausen · FRANCFORT

Cologne

and particularly employing them in extinguishing fires.'

Leaving Frankfurt by way of Wiesbaden, Coblenz and Bonn, the Tourist made for Cologne. And here, also, he found the Jews badly treated. In fact, in Cologne the pleasures of Germany were over. Baron Riesbeck castigated it as the ugliest town in Germany, full of disgusting filth and noisome stenches.

'A great part of the inhabitants are privileged beggars, who form a regular corporation ... They roam through the city and besiege the travellers with an insolence and rudeness not to be conceived. Upon the whole, Cologne is at least a century behind the rest of Germany. Bigotry, ill manners, clownishness, slothfulness are visible everywhere; and the speech, dress, furniture of the houses, every-thing, in short, is so different from what is seen in the rest of Germany, that you conceive yourself in the middle of a colony of strangers.'

There were weeds growing everywhere, William Beckford noticed, while the houses were gloomy and ill-contrived, and the shops dirty. Not even the exquisite workmanship of the unfinished medieval cathedral, nor the church of St Ursula whose walls were lined with the bones of the eleven thousand virgins, could overcome the Tourist's universal distaste for Cologne. 'The town is beastly,' W. M. Thackeray concluded in a final condemnation which an earlier generation would have wholeheartedly endorsed, 'the cathedral unfinished, the weather was hot beyond all bearing – I was consequently in my own room a great part of the day employing myself between sleeping, smoking, reading, eating raw herring and onions.'

Düsseldorff

Twenty miles further north, Düsseldorff was scarcely better. 'Nothing but the famous gallery of paintings could invite strangers to stay a moment within its walls', William Beckford decided. 'More crooked streets, more indifferent houses, one seldom meets with; except soldiers, not a living creature moving about them; and at night a complete regiment of bugs "marked me for their own".'

There was a good art gallery at Düsseldorff containing 'several valuable productions of the Italian school'; but this was not to Beckford's taste either. And the pictures on display in the Rubens room there he found less imposing than absurd:

'three enormous representations of the last day, where an in-numerable host of sinners are exhibited as striving in vain to avoid the tangles of the devil's tail. The woes of several fat luxurious souls are rendered in the highest gusto. Satan's dispute with some brawny concubines, whom he is lugging off in spite of all their resistance, cannot be too much admired by those who approve this class of subjects.'

Those who did approve this class of subjects soon had many more examples to admire in the Netherlands.

The best times to visit Frankfurt were at Easter or in September when the famous fairs were held. The book-sellers' displays seemed to Thomas Coryat, who visited the autumn fair at the beginning of the seventeenth century, 'a very epitome of all the principal libraries of Europe'. The Roman Emperor at Frankfurt enjoyed the reputation of being one of the best inns in the world.

'The streets, even, straight, and well paved, the houses so uniform and planted with lime trees as nothing can be more beautiful.' John Evelyn's delight in Dutch towns and particularly in Amsterdam was shared by thousands of later Tourists.

THE LOW COUNTRIES

Improved roads and carriages – Dutch inns amongst the best in Europe – beauty of the scenery – Amsterdam – the famous universities – Rotterdam, birthplace of Erasmus – 'neither dirt nor beggary to be seen' – the Austrian Netherlands – buying trophies from the battlefield of Waterloo – recuperating from the Tour at Spa and Aix.

Once he had crossed over the empire's frontiers into the United Provinces, the Tourist's worst ordeals were at an end. The roads in Flanders and Holland were in general much better than those in Germany. The Antwerp-Brussels road, for instance, was 'paved in the middle as well as the best streets in London, and kept in better repair'; while the road from Brussels to Ghent was 'all a fine causeway thirty miles long, broader than any street, and well paved'.

The carriages, too, were better than the German ones. The diligences in Flanders, in fact, were agreed to be 'much more convenient than those used in England, and heavier hung'. They had eight chairs, each one separated from the next and all of them facing the front. Every chair had its own sash window which the passenger could open or shut as he chose, and through which he could enjoy a view of the pleasing countryside.

And this view, Lady Mary Wortley Montagu thought, was a delight. Nothing could be more agreeable than travelling in the Low Countries, she wrote. 'The whole country appears a large garden; the roads are well paved, shaded on each side with rows of trees and bordered with large canals, full of boats, passing and repassing. Every twenty paces gives you the prospect of some villa, and every four hours that of a large town, so surprisingly neat, I am sure you would be charmed with them.'

Even William Beckford – although he was not in the best of tempers since he complained that his carriage travelled at such a slow pace over the sandy heath that a tortoise might have kept up with it without once being out of breath – could not but admire the 'glory of

canals, trackschuyts [*trek-schuits* – draw-boats], and windmills'.

'The minute neatness of the villages,' Beckford continued, 'their red roofs, and the lively green of the willows which shade them, corresponded with the ideas I had formed of Chinese prospects; a resemblance which was not diminished upon viewing on every side the level scenery of enamelled meadows, with stripes of clear water across them, and innumerable barges gliding busily along. Nothing could be finer than the weather; it improved each moment, as if propitious to my exotic fancies; and, at sun-set, not one single cloud obscured the horizon. Several storks were parading by the water-side, amongst stags and osiers; and, as far as the eye could reach, large herds of beautifully spotted cattle were enjoying the plenty of their pastures.'

Travelling by water was no less enjoyable than travelling by land. The pace was slow – about four miles an hour compared with the hundred miles a day a diligence could cover on a good clear road, even allowing for the change of horses every twelve miles – but the comfort was remarkable. The *trek-schuits* were horse-drawn and carried about twenty-five passengers who could sit on deck in summer and in a large, clean saloon in winter. The one that plied between Ghent and Bruges was esteemed 'the most remarkable boat of the kind in all Europe'. 'It is a perfect tavern, divided into several compartments', the *Travellers' Guide Through the Low Countries* reported, 'with a very good ordinary dinner of six or seven dishes, and all sorts of wines at moderate prices. In winter they have fires in their

No country in Europe was neater or cleaner than the Netherlands. The well-swept streets of the villages, the trim, gabled houses with their polished windows made one Tourist think that 'a giant must have been along with a scrubbing-brush'.

Chimneys, and the motion of the vessel is so small, that a person is all the way as if he were in a house.'

The cost was about a penny a mile, and a meal – which might well include soup and pickled herrings, duck and salmon, as well as veal, mutton, beef, vegetables, fruit, nuts, crumpets and cheese – rarely cost more than 1s 6d; and the beer, like the bread, was free.

For those who preferred to eat a quick meal ashore, the boat stopped at certain villages for half-an-hour or so. And the passenger just had time to have his snack before the bell rang to warn him that he must get back on board again.

Dutch inns were amongst the best in Europe. At some of them there were disadvantages – a common complaint was that they had few separate bedrooms, guests being obliged to sleep in communal rooms and in cabins set into the wall, and placed so high that 'a man may break his neck, if he happens to fall out of them'. Then, there was the smell of tobacco everywhere – for the Dutch, 'even Dutch gentlemen', were constantly smoking – and on all the tables were laid unsavoury spitting-pots. But the rooms were invariably clean, the floors sanded and scoured, the linen fresh, the beds soft, and the food as plentiful as it was excellent – although to some guests the habit of

The Tourist felt gratified that most Dutch inns were so much better than those in Germany for he was rarely invited to any form of entertainment in a private house. Establishments such as this, however, provided an amusing evening.

serving fish with their heads on and mouths stretched open, and of presenting birds with their heads tucked behind their wings as though they were asleep, was a little disconcerting.

Thomas Nugent gave a word of warning, against the Dutch innkeeper who was not a man to have a dispute with, either about the amount of the bill or any other particular.

'If you find fault with his bill,' said Nugent, who clearly had made a complaint himself on more than one occasion, '(tho' properly speaking they make no bills, but bring in the sum the reckoning amounts to by word of mouth) he will immediately raise it, and procure a magistrate to levy his demands by force, if they are not readily paid. For this reason I should generally prefer to be accommodated in an English house when travelling through Holland, because I have not only found it, by experience, to be every bit as cheap, if not cheaper; but moreover, you have the pleasure of having victuals dressed after the English way; as also of laying out your money with your own countrymen, and of having to do with reasonable people.'

There were English inns in nearly all the larger towns in Holland, the most famous being the Golden Ball at Leyden, the Queen of Hungary at the Hague, the King's Head at Middleburg, Mrs Cator's in Wine Street, Rotterdam, and the English Bible and the Queen's Head in Warmoes Street, Amsterdam. In all of these a traveller could live very comfortably on five or six shillings a day in the middle of the eighteenth century, a third or less of what it would cost him to live at the King's Arms in Pall Mall or at Pontac's in the City of London.

Even those Tourists who had preferred the company of the native population in France and Italy and Germany, resorted to these English inns in Holland, for they found it difficult to enjoy much contact with the Dutch.

'The gentility and nobility are not numerous,' Nugent said, 'many of these families having been extinguished in the Wars with Spain.' Those that remained were 'remarkable for their frugality and order in their expences', so that the Tourist could not expect much hospitality. In any event, or so he was led to suppose, he would not find the company of the Dutch nobility much to his taste. They tried to imitate the French but did so very awkwardly, for the 'passions of both sexes run lower and cooler here than in any other country: Their tempers being not airy enough for joy, or any unusual strains of pleasant humour; nor warm enough for love'. They drank and ate too much; they allowed their women to wear the breeches; they wore the plainest clothes with neither 'shape nor plaits; and their long pockets [were] set as high as their ribs'. Moreover, like all their countrymen, they affected 'to be neat in their houses and furniture to a degree of excess'.

As in France, so here, the guide-books painted a portrait which most Tourists who took the trouble to get to know Dutch people failed to recognise. There were some Tourists who dismissed the Dutch as 'uncouth bipeds', who, detecting in their features 'a certain oysterishness of eye and flabbiness of complexion', affected to believe that there might have been 'a period when Holland was all water, and the ancestors of the present inhabitants fish'. There were others who professed themselves irritated by the Dutch people's obsessive passion for cleanliness and neatness, their continual washing and scrubbing of floors and benches, their horror of seeing even so much as a piece of orange-peel in the streets, their habit of taking their shoes off before going upstairs, of offering visitors mats to wipe their boots on and straw slippers to wear before stepping on the spotless floor of the hall, their excessive fastidiousness in tying up the tails of their cows to the barn roof.

William Beckford, though he came in the end to admire their uncompromising neatness, could not at first disguise the exasperation occasioned by the complacent regularity of the houses and gardens of the opulent citizens of Amsterdam which, with carefully arranged flower-beds and immaculately clipped hedges, stretched mile after mile along the road to Utrecht – 'endless avenues and stiff parterres scrawled and flourished in patterns like the embroidery of an old maid's work-bag'.

Yet, despite these rather intimidating indications of an aseptic conformity, the Dutchman turned out to be a far more engaging and lively person than his reputation allowed. Hardworking and conscientious he certainly was; a trifle too preoccupied with becoming rich he may have been; but the Dutchman – as the Tourist soon recognised after his arrival in Amsterdam or The Hague – certainly did not allow his industry to dull his sense of pleasure. Amsterdam, for all the doll's-house regularity of its streets and canals, its neat little trees all trimmed to exactly the same size, was as teeming with life as its harbour was teeming with ships. 'The streets are filled with the common people,' Clara Crowninshield wrote of this 'most singular-looking town', the greatest port in the world. 'At the corners of the bridges are stalls where fruit is sold. I saw a woman making pies and frying pancakes in one of these places.'

At another corner a money-changer would be rattling his great black bags of coins; coachmen would be drinking tea, sailors drinking gin; elsewhere the huge lighted windows of the packed shops threw square beams of light onto the cobbles, over which scores of sledge-carriages were dragged with a fearful screeching sound, and young girls ran laughing into the noisy *speelhuizen* to dance and drink and find boys.

When the Tourist went out in the morning to see the sights, he would find women in wooden shoes with pointed toes washing the stones in the streets, and rope-dancers, musicians and puppeteers entertaining the passers-by. These buskers were reputed to give a third of all that they received to the poor; for the people of Amsterdam

'Tis generally thought,' wrote Nugent, 'that next to London and Paris, Amsterdam is the biggest city in Christendom. It is certainly the greatest port in the known world for trade, and inferior to none in Europe for wealth and riches.'

were famous for their charity. Many playhouses gave a half of their profits to the needy; and outside most private houses there was a poor-box into which the inhabitants put money whenever they had cause to feel particularly conscious of their own good fortune. These boxes were unlocked and emptied each month by the official overseer.

Less well organised was the Spin-House, where 'incorrigible and lewd women' were locked up and made to spin for the benefit of the poor. For here the custodians, although they looked like 'grave and sober matrons', permitted the Tourist for a trifle of money to have access to their charges, 'on which occasions it is customary for these lewd women to entertain their visitors with such abominable discourses and indecent actions as are shocking to men of any sense or morality.'

The more respectable Tourist quickly passed by the Spin-House on his way to less reprehensible sights, to the English Presbyterian Church (one of many in Holland), to the Old Church (built about 1300) and the New Church (built between 1408 and 1470), or to the Synagogue, the celebrated Bank (believed to contain more treasure

than any other in the world), the Guildhall (supported, as all the big buildings in Amsterdam were, on countless hundreds of wooden piers driven deep into the marshy earth), the Rasp-house where 'lusty knaves' were compelled to work, the Dool-house, 'for madmen and fools', or to the hospital, 'for lame and decrepit soldiers and seamen'.

Then, stocked with the goods for which Amsterdam was renowned – tiles, maps, optical glasses, precious stones, tulip bulbs, turtle doves and finely printed English books – the Tourist moved on.

He would usually move south. A few Tourists visited Zutphen, 'a large, handsome, well-built town'. A few went north to Edam, to see where those 'excellent cheeses that have a red crust' are made and to learn about the mermaid that was caught here in 1450 and was taught to spin and dress like a woman but never learned to speak. Others, if they had not already been there on their way from Germany, went to Arnhem, whose wholesome air attracted 'a great many persons of distinction', to Utrecht, where there were several British students at the university (including in 1763-4, James Boswell), or to Nijmegen, 'just like Nottingham'. But most Tourists, after a glance at Haarlem – where they made particular note of its siege works and its famous organ – turned south-west for Leyden, The Hague, Delft, Rotterdam and Middleburg.

Leyden's university, where there were many British, particularly Scottish, students – since Scottish law relies much on Roman law, and the Dutch were the great masters of this subject – was a university with an international reputation and two thousand scholars. James Boswell's grandfather and father had both studied here, as did John Wilkes in the 1740s; and the presence, throughout the eighteenth century, of numerous talented and high-spirited young men made Leyden, like Utrecht, a gay as well as an intellectually stimulating centre.

Well worth a visit were the astonishing variety of plants in the Physic-Garden, adjoining the university, and the even more astonishing items to be found in the Garden's Galleries and the Anatomy School where you could inspect an assortment of oddities ranging from a cat with wings, a mermaid's hand, the dried skin of a Scotsman, the feather of a phoenix and the rib of a rhinoceros, to the skeletons of animals as big as whales and as small as ants, 'a vegetable Priapus which is a curious plant', and a 'monster issued out of a hen's egg'.

At The Hague, too, there was a remarkable collection of curiosities in the Prince of Orange's cabinets, including a 'grave hippopotamus', bottled snakes, pickled foetuses, and the representation in wax of a human head. The head, William Beckford commented, was 'most dexterously flayed indeed. Rapturous encomiums have been bestowed by amateurs on this performance. A German professor could hardly believe it artificial; and, prompted by the love of truth, set his teeth in this delicious morsel.'

Nearly every Tourist liked The Hague, its charming buildings and

From Haarlem to Leyden boats sailed down the canal every two hours or so from six in the morning until dusk, with a night boat at eleven. The distance was fifteen miles, but the villages, windmills, pleasant houses and gardens 'which one meets with all along the canal, make the way appear short and the passage agreeable'.

The Oude Rhyn canal at Leyden, the second largest town in Holland in the eighteenth century. The university at Leyden, renowned in particular for its law school, was amongst the best in Europe. James Boswell's father and grandfather were both sent here, though Boswell himself went to Utrecht which had a gayer social life.

well-paved streets, its squares and walks shaded by beautiful trees. The people were polite, Nugent advised his readers, 'the coaches numerous, the houses and walks exceedingly fine, and the air very good, which makes it a most agreeable place.'

Unlike the inhabitants of other towns in Holland, the people of The Hague were much taken up with fasion. One scornful visitor believed that they observed 'forms here more than they [did] at the Court of Great Britain. Were a person of quality to appear in the Mall at The Hague equipped like his footman, everybody [would have] believed him out of his senses'. But most Tourists preferred this emphasis on fashion to the lack of interest in it displayed in other Dutch towns; and at least, while gambling was as much an obsession with the rich at The Hague as it was in Paris and Venice, no one considered it unfashionable or ill-bred of the Englishman if he chose not to play.

Rotterdam, where the great Erasmus was born, was also much admired. A stranger on first entering it could not fail to be astonished by the 'beautiful confusion of chimnies intermixt with tops of trees with which the canals are planted, and streamers of vessels, insomuch that he can hardly tell whether it be a fleet, city, or forest'.

After arriving there with his pupils in 1783, Dr Roget wrote that he was 'much rejoiced' to see it. 'The city is very beautiful,' he thought; 'fine canals running through the streets filled with a variety of pretty sailing boats, added to rows of large trees which give an agreeable shade to the houses, with the remarkable cleanliness of the whole, make the scene both entertaining and extraordinary.'

Half a century before Lady Mary Wortley Montagu had also been struck by the remarkable cleanliness of Rotterdam and its inhabitants.

'My arrival at Rodderdam presented me a new scene of pleasure,' she wrote. 'All the streets are paved with broad stones, and before the meanest artificers' doors seats of various-coloured marbles, and so neatly kept, that, I will assure you, I walked almost all over the town yesterday, *incognita*, in my slippers, without receiving one spot of dirt; and you may see the Dutch maids washing the pavement of the street with more application than ours do our bed-chambers … Here is neither dirt nor beggary to be seen. One is not shocked with those loathsome cripples, so common in London, nor teazed with the importunities of idle fellows and wenches, that choose to be nasty and lazy. The common servants and little shop-women here are more nicely clean than most of our ladies; and the great variety of neat dresses (every woman dressing her head after her own fashion) is an additional pleasure in seeing the town.'

Leaving Rotterdam by way of Dordrecht (where fresh salmon was so plentiful that servants had once felt obliged to make a bargain with their masters not to be made to eat it more than twice a week), the Tourist crossed over the frontier into the Austrian Netherlands and came to Antwerp.

No Tourist could leave The Hague without a visit to the Hall of Knights. It was originally built in the twelfth century, though many additions have been made to it over the centuries.

The brass statue of Erasmus, who was born in this small house in Rotterdam in 1467, stood on the bridge crossing the canal that ran through the market place.

In the sixteenth century Antwerp had been considered one of the
most beautiful as well as one of the most prosperous and populous
towns in all Europe. In the seventeenth it was still considered beautiful. John Evelyn, who was there in 1641, thought that he had never
observed 'a more quiet, clean, elegantly built, and civil place, than
this magnificent and famous city of Antwerp'. But in the eighteenth
century, while it still retained much of its beauty and charm, while
its well-proportioned buildings, its broad and regular streets, and its
lovely walks on the outskirts commanding a delightful prospect of the
surrounding country, were all still so much admired that the city
was often compared to Florence, it had lost all its former liveliness
and bustle.

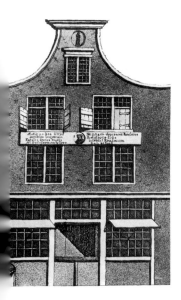

To James Edward Smith it seemed 'gloomy and lifeless'; to Dr
Roget 'thinly inhabited'; while William Beckford considered it the
quietest, dreariest place he had ever come across:

'Were any one to ask my advice upon the subject of retirement, I
should tell him: By all means repair to Antwerp. No village
amongst the Alps, or hermitage upon Mount Lebanon, is less
disturbed: you may pass your days in this great city without being

the least conscious of its sixty thousand inhabitants, unless you visit the churches. There, indeed, are to be heard a few devout whispers, and sometimes, to be sure, the bells make a little chiming; but, walk about, as I do, in the twilights of mid-summer, and be assured your ears will be free from all molestation.'

There were 212 streets in Antwerp, according to the guide-books, and twenty-two squares; and in most of them the grass grew in deep silence. Even the churches so much admired by previous generations did not appeal to Beckford who wondered what pleasure there could possibly be in wandering from 'one dull church to another'.

Only when there was a religious procession through the streets in honour of some saint did the citizens of Antwerp appear to enjoy themselves. Then the noise of 'riot and debauchery', bonfires, crackers and rockets filled the air till two o'clock in the morning. On other days no one was allowed out after half past ten at night without the written permission of the governor.

Outside Antwerp the people of the Austrian Netherlands seemed very much more cheerful. They were 'open and freehearted', friendly and hospitable; and in French Flanders, where the peasants sang cheerfully in the fields, their contentment appeared to be complete. Even the waspish Beckford was struck by the ease and good-humour of these happy Flemings: 'All is still and peaceful in these fertile lowlands: the eye meets nothing but round unmeaning faces at every door, and harmless stupidity smiling at every window. The beasts, as placid as their masters, graze on without any disturbances; and I don't recollect to have heard one grunting swine, or snarling mastiff, during my whole progress.'

But the towns of Flanders did not please him. In Ostend – 'so unclassic a place! Nothing but preposterous Flemish roofs [and] mongrel barbers' – he was 'smoked with tobacco and half poisoned with garlic'; and on entering a church in search of silence and solitude, here again he was 'disappointed: half-a-dozen squeeking fiddles fugued and flourished away in the galleries, as many paralytic monks gabbled away before the altars, whilst a whole posse of devotees, wrapped in long white hoods and flannels, were sweltering on either side'.

Ghent was even worse, in his opinion. Dorothy Wordsworth thought it picturesque; but to Beckford it was 'a large, ill-paved, dismal-looking city, with a decent proportion of convents and chapels, stuffed with monuments, brazen gates, and glittering marbles. In the great church were two or three pictures by Rubens, mechanically excellent.'

Brussels   Brussels, however, was much more attractive. Its people were affable and polite, its gardens and squares delightful, its fountains almost comparable with those of Rome, its inns and restaurants equal to any in France. Nugent, who thought the Market Place in Brussels 'one of the beautifullest squares' to be found anywhere, wrote with particular enthusiasm of the opera house:

'The markets of Holland,' according to the *Traveller's Guide Through the Netherlands*, 'are better supplied and better ordered than any in Europe... They are very fond of pickled herrings, Bologna sausages, and other savory dishes. Their butter and cheese is very good, and the common people seldom go upon a journey without a butter-box in their pockets.'

'The opera house is one of the noblest and largest in Europe. It was built by the duke of Bavaria in 1700, after the Italian manner, with rows of ledges or closets, most of them with chimneys, which the nobility hire by the winter for the conveniency of their families and friends, and keep the keys themselves. That of the prince de Ligne is wainscotted with a looking-glass, so that he can sit in a corner of his ledge or box, with half a dozen friends, and drink a bottle, or sup, which they often do by a warm fire, and see the whole representation in the looking-glass, without being seen by the actors or the company.'

In the years immediately following 1815, hundreds upon hundreds of English visitors came to Brussels each month to wander over the battlefield of Waterloo, searching like beachcombers for bullets and buttons, buying boots and badges and bits of uniform from the stall-holders at Hougoumont and La Belle Alliance, looking at the crumbling walls and scarred trees, and poking about, as George IV did on a visit with the Duke of Wellington, in the hope of coming across Lord Anglesey's leg. Byron, who had been 'damned sorry' when he heard of Napoleon's defeat, came here in 1816 and after riding over the battlefield, bought trophies to send back to England.

Before 1815 Waterloo was virtually unknown; for few Tourists bothered with the country south of Brussels. Having already done Antwerp, Ghent, Bruges to the north, having gone to Courtrai in the west (perhaps to buy some of the finest table linen in Europe) and to Tournai (where an inspection of Vauban's citadel, his masterpiece, was an essential requirement), they usually turned east for Louvain, Liège, Spa and Aix.

Louvain was famous for its university, which resembled an English one more than any other university abroad, and for its Hôtel de Ville, a marvellously rich and ornate example of fifteenth-century pointed Gothic. Liège, celebrated for its good inns, cheap food and fine wines, was recommended by Nugent as a place where a gentleman of small estate could live more comfortably than anywhere else in the world. But it was at Spa and Aix that a gentleman could best recuperate from the effects of his long Tour now almost completed.

Spa, perhaps, was a little too gay for a satisfactory cure; for the

More than one Tourist remarked on the air of timelessness that hung over many of the smaller villages in the Low Countries. A painting of a fair in a Dutch village.

benefits of the waters which were taken during the day were frequently offset by the dissipations of the night, though many Tourists seem to have led a healthy enough life here. In the summer of 1768 the Earl of Carlisle told George Selwyn that he had met many old friends at Spa, and added, 'I rise at six; am on horseback at breakfast; play at cricket till dinner; and dance in the evening till I can scarce crawl to bed at eleven. This is a life for you.'

At Aix the waters and the baths were taken more conscientiously; and the Tourists who underwent a serious course of them could expect to be cured of almost any disorder which their experiences might have occasioned. They were reputed to be beneficial, for both men and women, in

'all affections of the nerves, such as convulsions, palsies, numbness, tremblings, gouts, sciaticas, contractions, swellings, distempers of the bowels, stomach-aches, spleen, inveterate head-aches, vertigos, nephritical distempers, cold affections of the womb, stoppage or flux of the menses, barrenness, abortions, and scabs of all sorts. They are likewise said to cure stoppage of water and stranguries; as also the gout, scurvey, rheumatism, cholic, scrophulous distempers, imposthumes of the mesentery, etc. ... The time of drinking is from the first of May to the middle of June, and from the middle of August to the end of September; about the pumps where they drink the water, there are raffling shops, coffee-houses, and all other diversions, as at Bath and Tunbridge in England ... Intrigues are also carried on here with the ladies as at Bath.'

Refreshed by the waters, the Tourist left Aix for Ostend and from there sailed home to England.

Immense travelling chests such as this, while forming an essential part of a gentleman's luggage on the Grand Tour, necessarily slowed his progress.

Amongst the many
mementoes of his travels
which one Tourist brought
home with him was this
fan decorated with
pictures of some of the
places he had seen.

EPILOGUE
Popinjays and Patrons

As many an anxious parent asked himself when sending his son away on this last, expensive phase of his education, would it all be worth it? Would the boy return an affected, foppish, extravagant, drunken, lazy dilettante, full of foreign prejudices and pretensions and of pagan irreverence, believing that manners were more important than morals. Such fears had long been held. Lord Burghley had expressed them in the sixteenth century when he said that he feared his elder son, Thomas Cecil, would come back 'a spending sot, meet only to keep a tennis court', and in *The Merchant of Venice* Portia ridicules the young Englishman who 'bought his doublet in Italy, his round hose in France, his bonnet in Germany, and his behaviour everywhere'. In the seventeenth century Sir William Trumbull admitted that the Grand Tour had been of little profit to him: 'I went abroad and spent about two years in France and Italy where I learnt little besides the languages, partly from my youth and the warmth of my temper, partly from lazynesse and debauchery.'

Later, Lord Chesterfield, when bequeathing his property to his godson, Philip, insisted that 'by no means should he be allowed to go into Italy . . . the foul sink of illiberal manners and vices'. And Lord Cowper, on his deathbed, ordered that his son should never travel, for he had found that there was 'little to be hoped, and much to be feared' from it. Certainly, there could be no doubt that many Tourists did return so much the worse for their experiences.

Adam Smith, who resigned his professorship of Moral Philosophy at Glasgow to accompany the young Duke of Buccleugh on the Grand Tour, said that, although his own pupil had profited by it, most

Most eighteenth-century guide books gave lists of 'what it would be proper for the traveller to provide himself with' in the various Italian towns through which he passed. These three objects were all brought back from Italy, the bronze horse from Naples where its original was on display at the museum, the gloves from Turin, the chest from Florence.

Tourists returned home 'more conceited, more unprincipled, more dissipated, and more incapable of any serious application either to study or to business, than he could well have become in so short a time, had he lived at home'.

Oliver Goldsmith agreed with him. 'The greatest advantages which result to youth from travel', he thought, 'are an easy address, the shaking off of national prejudices, and the finding nothing ridiculous in national peculiarities. The time spent in these acquisitions could have been more usefully employed at home.'

Dr John Moore, who had been tutor to the Duke of Hamilton and Lord Lauderdale, went even further in insisting that no English gentleman who was to live in England ought to be educated outside it. 'It is thought that by an early foreign education all ridiculous English prejudices will be avoided. This may be true; – but other prejudices, perhaps as ridiculous, and much more detrimental will be formed.'

One of the principal objections to the Grand Tour was that it was undertaken at the wrong time in a man's life. The average age of the Tourist was about eighteen. Many left when they were only sixteen or even younger. Thomas Coke of Holkham Hall in Norfolk was fifteen when he began his Tour in the care of Dr Thomas Hobart, Fellow of Christ's College, Cambridge; the third Earl of Devonshire was fourteen when he began his; Robert Boyle, fourteenth child of the Earl of Cork, was only eleven when he set off after having spent three years at Eton. Few Tourists even in the later eighteenth century were over twenty-one. Yet although a boy was more likely to learn a foreign language well and acquire a good accent when he was much younger, he was more inclined to profit by his travels and not to resent the guidance of his tutor when he was much older. Dr Moore believed that no one should embark on the Tour before he was twenty. 'If it is a year or two later,' he added, 'there will be no harm.'

Adam Smith emphasised the point in *The Wealth of Nations*:

'By travelling so very young, by spending in the most frivolous dissipation the most precious years of his life, at a distance from the inspection and control of his parents and relations, every useful habit, which the earlier parts of his education might have had some tendency to form in him, instead of being rivetted and confirmed, is almost necessarily either weakened or effaced. Nothing but the discredit into which the universities are allowing themselves to fall, could ever have brought into repute so very absurd a practice as that of travelling at this early period of life.'

Dr Johnson supported this view. He felt convinced that for young men under twenty-four it was far more satisfactory to study at home than to travel abroad. Certainly the men he did meet who had travelled when they were young, profoundly irritated him by their inability to communicate anything of the excitement and wonder of the things they had been privileged to see. 'I never but once heard him

A richly ornamented piece of furniture, designed by Robert Adam in 1771 and made by Ince and Mayhew. The pieces of marble with which it is decorated were brought back by a Tourist from Florence for the Duchess of Manchester.

talk of what he had seen,' he once said of a much travelled lord, 'and that was of a large serpent in one of the Pyramids of Egypt.' 'Surely, the man who has seen Prague,' he complained on another occasion, 'might tell us something new and strange, and not sit silent for want of matter to put his lips in motion.'

'I never liked young travellers,' Gibbon concluded: 'they go too raw to make any great remarks, and they lose a time which is (in my opinion) the most precious part of a man's life.'

How much better, Lord Macaulay thought, to travel when the mind was mature and the brain stored with facts which would illuminate the foreign scene. He compared his own youthful reactions to travelling in France with those of a later time in his life:

'I had, indeed, seen what I was told were olive-trees, as I was whirled down the Rhone from Lyons to Avignon; but they might, for anything I saw, have been willows or ash-trees. Now they stood, covered with berries, along the road for miles. I looked at them with the same sort of feeling with which Washington Irving says that he heard the nightingale for the first time when he came to England, after having read descriptions of her in poets from his childhood. I thought of the Hebrews, and their numerous images drawn from the olive; of the veneration in which the tree was held by the Athenians; of Lysias's speech; of the fine ode in the Oedipus at Colonos; of Virgil and Lorenzo de Medici. Surely it is better to travel in mature years, with all these things in one's head, than to rush over the Continent while still a boy!'

And if he *were* a boy, the Tourist derived little benefit from his contacts with foreigners of intelligence and taste. Indeed, few young Tourists took the trouble even to make these contacts. Being awkward and not speaking the languages, Lord Chesterfield wrote, 'they go into no foreign company, at least none good; but dine and sup with one another only at the tavern.'

Scarcely one in a hundred of the youths who went abroad under tutors, in John Locke's estimation, ever even visited 'any person of quality, much less made an acquaintance with such from whose conversation he might learn what was good breeding in that country, and what was worth observation in it.' Those few who did were usually too young to appreciate the value of the lesson.

Callow, arrogant, rich, too excited to have escaped their parents' authority to accept that of a tutor whose narrowness of view was often a provocation to their own high-spirited instincts, the young Tourists were frequently seen as a tiresome blot on the face of Europe. Irritating foreigners by an ostentatious preference of all things English to anything not, they remained, so far as they could, in their own self-contained communities wherever they went.

Lady Mary Wortley Montagu wrote to Lady Pomfret from Venice to tell her of the inundations of English boys and governors who

John Moore, the father of the general, was a Scottish physician and writer who became a travelling tutor. He spent five years on the Grand Tour with the Duke of Hamilton and later accompanied the Earl of Lauderdale to France. His *View of Society and Manners in France, Switzerland and Germany* was published in 1779, and *A View of Society and Manners in Italy* in 1781.

'kept an inviolable fidelity to the language their nurses taught them. Their whole business abroad (as far as I can perceive),' she went on, 'being to buy new cloaths, in which they shine in some obscure coffee-house, where they are sure of meeting only one another; and after the important conquest of some waiting gentlewoman of an opera Queen, who perhaps they remember as long as they live, return to England excellent judges of men and manners . . . I look on them as the greatest blockheads in nature; and, to say truth, the compound of booby and petit-maitre makes up a very odd sort of animal.'

Smollett, too, thought that most of them were blockheads. He was forty-two when he and his wife left England, hoping to recover their health and spirits in France and Italy after the death of a dearly loved daughter, so he himself – like Laurence Sterne who was over fifty when he began the tour that was to provide material for *A Sentimental Journey* in which Smollett appears as the splenetic Smelfungus – could scarcely be considered a Grand Tourist in the usual sense of the term. 'I have seen in different parts of Italy,' he wrote, 'a number of raw boys whom Britain seemed to have poured forth on purpose to bring her national character into contempt.' They were ignorant, petulant, rash, and profligate. One of them would lose his money at gambling, another would be 'poxed and pillaged by an antiquated cantatrice', a third 'bubbled by a knavish antiquarian', and a fourth cheated by a picture-dealer.

Such criticisms were voiced by foreign observers also. 'In a hundred [English Tourists],' recorded a Frenchman in 1785, 'there are not two that seek to instruct themselves. To cover leagues on land or on water; to take punch and tea at the inns; to speak ill of all the other nations, and to boast without ceasing of their own; that is what the crowd of English call travelling.'

Much of the blame lay with the boys' tutors, many, if not most, of whom were considered to be quite incapable of controlling their charges. In the seventeenth century, Theophilus Gale, tutor to Lord Wharton's son, Thomas, and his younger brother, was honest enough to admit his incapacity in this respect in a letter to his employer:

'1st, my Lord, as to Conversation Mr Wharton judgeth himself fit and capable to choose his company and thinks it too hard an imposition to be tyed up to such as I shall judge meete; whereupon he has sometimes persons come to him whom I neither know nor can approve of. Also as to times for recreation he is unwilling to be tyed up to rules, but sometimes useth violent exercises as fencing etc. immediately after dinner and at other times most proper for study. Again, as to rising it is now usually well nigh 8 of the clock before he is ready, so that oft times we have not sufficient time for praying together, much lesse does he use private prayer. But my chiefest fears are to matters of Religion and a reverent observance of the duties thereof especially on the Lords Day. I find your sons encline to the French custome of giving themselves liberty (so far as they can get fit occasion) to recreate themselves on that day with musick etc., and I might mention also some neglect of your Lordship's instructions as to your son's diet, eating fleshe suppers, going to bed late.'

Admittedly there were many distinguished and capable men who became travelling tutors, besides Dr John Moore and Adam Smith.

Thomas Hobbes, the philosopher, was once the travelling tutor of both the second and third Earls of Devonshire; Robert Wood, author of *The Ruins of Palmyra*, accompanied the Duke of Bridgewater on his Tour; William Whitehead, the future Poet Laureate, went with Lords Villiers and Nuneham; John Horne Tooke, the politician and philologist, was engaged as a 'bear-leader' in France and Italy in 1764–5; Paul Henri Mallet, the Swiss historian, was appointed by the Earl of Bute to accompany his eldest son, Lord Mountstuart; Joseph Addison took charge of Edward Montagu, a young relative of the Earl of Sandwich, and George Dashwood, son of the Lord Mayor of London.

But the majority of travelling tutors were incompetent place-seekers who deserved the derision with which they were treated. 'There is an animal still more absurd' than an English boy on his travels, Walpole decided, 'and that is travelling governors, who are mischievous into the bargain, and whose pride is always hurt because they are sure of its never being indulged. They will not leave the world because they are sent to teach it, and as they come far the more ignorant of it than their pupils, take care to return with more prejudices, and as much care to instill all theirs into their pupils.'

The Tourist's English servant was often even worse. Ideally:

'a servant selected to accompany a gentleman on his travels should be conversant with the French language … write a legible and quick hand, in order to be able to copy whatever is laid before him: know a little of surgery, and to bleed well in case his master should meet with an accident where no chirurgical [aid] is to be expected. Gentlemen should endeavour to attach such useful servants to their persons, by showing the same care as a father has for a child, and promise him a settlement for life on their return.'

Occasionally such servants were to be found, since the opportunity of travelling and of learning foreign languages attracted bright young men who would not have been contented with a valet's life at home. But more often the Tourist had cause to complain as bitterly about his English servant as Byron complained about his:

'The perpetual lamentations after beef and beer, the stupid, bigoted contempt for everything foreign, an insurmountable incapacity for acquiring even a few words of any language, rendered him, like all other English servants, an incumbrance. I do assure you, the plague of speaking for him, the comforts he required (more than myself by far), the [dishes] which he could not eat, the wines which he could not drink, the beds where he could not sleep, and the long list of

A water flagon, such as this one made of Bristol glass, was a necessary part of the Tourist's equipment.

calamities, such as stumbling horses, want of *tea* ! ! ! &c., which assailed him, would have made a lasting source of laughter to a spectator, and inconvenience to a master.'

English periodicals of the time are full of satirical comments on this ridiculous trio – the fussy, lazy servant, the pompous, prejudiced tutor, and, most absurd of all, the spoilt young gentleman who showed how inferior he supposed Continentals to be while travelling on the Continent, yet affected French manners on returning home, and spoke broken Italian in place of the English he pretended to have forgotten.

It was proposed, for example, that parliament should pass a new 'Act against Rambling', which would make it an offence to debase the purity of the English language 'by a vile mixture of exotic words, idioms, and phrases', to make any unmeaning grimace, shrug or gesticulation, to use the word *canaille* more than three times in the same sentence, or wantonly to cast contempt on the roast beef of old England. Offenders against the Act were to be 'flogged like school-boys'.

In May 1753, the *World* contained an essay characteristic of many such contributions. It was in the form of a pretended letter from a country gentleman on educating his son abroad. The son had 'passed nine years at Westminster School, in learning the words of two languages, long since dead, and not yet above half revived'. So, on leaving school the father decided to send him directly abroad, having been at Oxford himself. His wife agreed, provided that she and her daughter could go too. The results, the father complained, were disastrous:

'I no longer understand, or am understood, in my family. I hear of nothing but *le bon ton*. A French valet de chambre, who, I am told, is an excellent servant and fit for anything is brought over to curl my wife's and my daughter's hair, to mount a dessert, as they call it, and occasionally to announce visits. A very slatternly, dirty, but at the same time, a very genteel French maid is appropriated to the use of my daughter. My meat, too, is as much disguised in the dressing by a French cook as my wife and daughter are by their pompoms, their scraps of dirty gauze, flimsy satens, and black callicoes; not to mention their affected broken English and mangled French, which, jumbled together, compose their present language.'

Another correspondent took up the complaint. Lamenting, so he said, his own lack of knowledge of the languages, manners, characters and constitutions of other countries, he entrusted his son to the care of a Swiss tutor and sent him off, at far greater expense than he could afford, upon the Grand Tour. It was a cruel disappointment.

In Paris the son took an Irish girl as mistress, never spoke to French people unless it was to swear at them in English, and got himself into several scrapes from which he was rescued only by the intervention of the English ambassador.

The tutor admitted his incapacity to control the boy in Paris and advised a move to Italy from where the son wrote to his father to tell him of his progress:

'Sir, – in the six weeks that I passed at Florence, and the week I spent at Genoa, I never had time to write to you, being wholly taken up with seeing things of which the most remarkable is the steeple of Pisa: it is the oddest thing I ever saw in my life; it stands all awry; I wonder it does not tumble down.

I met with a great many of my countrymen, and we live together very sociably. I have been here now a month, and will give you an account of my way of life.

Here are a great many agreeable English gentlemen; we are about nine or ten as smart bucks as any in England. We constantly breakfast together, and then either go and see sights, or drive about the outlets of Rome in Chaises; but the horses are very bad, and the chaises do not follow well. We meet before dinner at the English coffee-house; where there is a very good billiard-table and very good company. From thence we go and dine together by turns at each other's lodgings. Then after a cheerful glass of claret, for we have made a shift to get some here, we go to the coffee-house again; from thence to supper, and so to bed. I do not believe these Romans are a bit like the old Romans; they are a parcel of thin-gutted, snivelling, cringing dogs; and I verily believe that our set could thrash forty of them. We never go among them; it would not be worth while; beside we none of us speak Italian and none of those signors speak English which shows what sort of fellows they are.

We saw the Pope go by tother day in a procession, but we re-solved to assert the honor of Old England; so we neither bowed nor pulled off our hats to the old rogue. Provisions and liquor are but bad here; and, to say the truth, I have not had one thorough good meal's meat since I left England. No longer ago than last Sunday we wanted to have a good plum-pudding; but we found the materials difficult to procure, and were obliged to get an English footman to make it.

Pray, Sir, let me come home; for I cannot find that one is a jot better for seeing all these outlandish places and people. But if you will not let me come back, for God's sake, Sir, take away the impertinent mounseer you sent with me. He is a considerable expense to you, and of no manner of service to me. All the English here laugh at him, he is such a prig. He thinkes himself a fine gentleman, and is always plaguing me to go into foreign companies, to learn foreign languages, and to get foreign manners; as if I were not to live and die in Old England, and as if good English acquaint-ance would not be more useful to me than outlandish ones. Dear Sir, grant me this request, and you shall ever find me

Your most dutiful son,
G.D.'

The contents of this letter are not entirely fanciful. In his *Lettres sur L'Italie*, Charles de Brosses said that there were young Englishmen in Rome when he was there in 1739, who would leave it without having 'seen any but English people and without knowing where the Coliseum is'. They would leave Italy with no better understanding of the classical poets or of Dante than they had had when they were at school.

It is clear, in fact, that William Cowper's picture of the youthful Tourist in *The Progress of Error* is drawn from life:

> From school to Cam or Isis, and thence home;
> And thence with all convenient speed to Rome.
> With reverend tutor clad in habit lay,
> To tease for cash, and quarrel with all day;
> With memorandum book for every town,
> And every post, and where the chaise broke down;

His stock a few French phrases got by heart,
With much to learn but nothing to impart;
The youth, obedient to his sire's commands,
Sets off a wanderer into foreign lands,
Surprised at all they meet, the gosling pair,
With awkward gait, stretch'd neck and silly stare,
Discover huge cathedrals built in stone,
And steeples towering high much like our own;
But show peculiar light by many a grin
At popish practices observed within …
Returning he proclaims by many a grace,
By shrugs and strange contortions of his face,
How much a dunce, that has been sent to roam,
Excels a dunce, that has been kept at home.

No eighteenth-century painter was more to the taste of the Grand Tourist than Canaletto. Hundreds of Canalettos, and imitations of Canaletto by his pupil Giuseppe Moretti, his nephew Bernardo Bellotto and others, poured into the country houses of England, many of them through the hands of Joseph Smith, British Consul at Venice from 1740 until 1760, the 'Merchant of Venice' as Walpole unkindly called him.

So also drawn from life, we may be sure, is the Tourist depicted by Pope in *The Dunciad*:

> Led by my hand, he saunter'd Europe round,
> And gather'd ev'ry Vice on Christian ground;
> Saw ev'ry Court, heard ev'ry King declare
> His royal sense of Op'ras or the Fair;
> The Stews and Palace equally explor'd
> Intrigu'd with glory and with spirit whor'd;
> Try'd all hors d'oeuvres, all liqueurs defin'd,
> Judicious drank, and greatly daring din'd;
> Dropt the dull lumber of the Latin score,
> Spoil'd his own language and acquir'd no more;
> All Classic learning lost on Classic ground,
> And last turn'd Air, the Echo of a Sound!
> See now, half-cur'd and perfectly well-bred,
> With nothing but a Solo in his head.

And so, having profited nothing from their Tour, having spent their time drinking, whoring, playing cards, driving in their carriages, watching for the arrival of the diligence so as not to miss meeting their fellow countrymen, rushing over the sights and paying them not the least attention, damning the foreigner, his food, his inns, his manners and his pope, making wholesale judgments on the basis of a single experience, considering the completion of the Tour as evidence of good breeding rather than as a means of education, the Tourists returned – so we are led to suppose – as stupid as they were when they left home and far more affected, 'transformed', in Milton's phrase, into 'mimics, apes, and kickshows'.

'There is indeed a kind of animal, neither male nor female, a thing of the neuter gender, lately started up amongst us,' the *Oxford Magazine* reported in June 1770. 'It is called a Macaroni. It talks without meaning, it smiles without pleasantry, it rides without exercise, it wenches without passion.'

But was this, the modern observer feels constrained to ask, a fair picture of the Macaroni and of the effects which his Tour had had upon him? Was John Locke right in complaining that the advocates of the Grand Tour were not concerned with 'building up men', but merely with 'tricking out a fine set of *gentlemen*'?

Certainly there were Macaronis like the ones described in the *Oxford Magazine*, idle and effete young men with painfully tight suits and elaborately curled hair, who chose to keep two watches in the pockets of their exquisitely embroidered waistcoats – one to tell them what the time was, the other, as Walpole supposed, to tell them what the time was not – but not every Macaroni was a wastrel. Charles James Fox, who once had posted all the way from Paris to Lyons just to buy patterns for his waistcoat, who returned to London wearing red-heeled shoes and blue hair powder and who thereafter sported

top Berne, the home town of Boswell's Swiss servant Jacob Hänni. It was a pretty town, Boswell thought, the houses 'excellent, good stone without and wood within'. The great Münster towering above the River Aar was begun in 1421.
bottom The Lake of Thun in the Canton of Berne. This water colour, and the one above, are by the wealthy amateur, the Rev. Edward Thomas Daniell, who was taught by John Crome at the Grammar School at Norwich.

As eagerly acquired as Canalettos were the engravings of Giovanni Battista Piranesi, master, with Pannini and Vanvitelli, in the special field of topographical and imaginary vedute. Demand for his work was so great that all his children and several of his pupils had to be called into his studios to help meet it.

a big feather in his hat in the House of Commons, was a man not merely of remarkable accomplishments but of painstaking industry. Many of his contemporaries who had shared his experiences of a European Tour returned, whether as Macaronis or not, so much the richer in mind if not in pocket.

A fair proportion of them continued to meet in London when their Tours were over. They met at Almack's in Pall Mall, eventually forming a club of their own which became known as Brooks's; they joined the Dilettanti Society which was formed in 1732; later they joined the Travellers' Club founded after the Grand Tour had been disrupted by the Napoleonic Wars. They brought to English life and culture a cosmopolitan influence, an intellectual curiosity and refinement of manner, which – for all the absurdities of the more pretentious Macaronis – were of inestimable value and importance. There were Tourists, of course, who came back quite unimpressed and unchanged by their travels; there were others who came back either with all their prejudices against foreign life and art confirmed or with an undiscriminating preference for all things Continental to everything at home. But the taste of the discerning Tourist eventually caused a lasting transformation in English art and manners.

An understanding and appreciation of music acquired in Italy, of painting in the Louvre and the Uffizi, in Dresden and Düsseldorf, of architecture in Vicenza and Rome, of the art of cooking in Brussels, of dressing in Paris, and of the universality of beauty everywhere, slowly but unmistakably extended the range of the Englishman's – and, the American's – aesthetic vision and sources of pleasure.

There were other influences, too. Milton's tour of Italy in 1638 and 1639, during which he frequented the most distinguished literary societies and took part in their proceedings, was of incalculable value to the author of *Paradise Lost;* while the scientific societies to be found in so many Continental cities were a direct spur to the formation of the Royal Society in London, just as their art galleries were a spur to the formation of many fine art collections in Britain.

The reputation of many painters and sculptors so much admired in the eighteenth century has since fallen. Correggio, Guido Reni, Guercino, the Caraccis were all far more revered then than they are today; and although the reputation of such masters as Donatello and Benvenuto Cellini, Raphael and Rubens has remained fairly constant, the now undoubted genius of others – Carpaccio and Bernini among them – was then not fully recognised. Shelley even condemned Michelangelo: 'He has not only no temperance, no modesty, no feeling for the just boundaries of art ... but he has no sense of beauty, and to want this is to want the sense of the creative power of mind.' Nor was it until the Victorian Age had long since begun that Botticelli was rated highly; nor, until Ruskin so convincingly demonstrated his talents, that the full force of Tintoretto's power was understood.

Yet, despite these fluctuations in taste, despite the numbers of fake Caraccis and Guercinos which found their way into the country houses of England – and the inferior landscapes bought at an absurdly inflated price in Rome from the egregious art dealer, Thomas Jenkins – the enormous increase in the nation's artistic wealth as a direct result of the Grand Tour was undeniable. Few wholesale purchases, such as those made by Thomas Coke and George III's acquisition of the collections made by 'Consul' Smith in Venice and by Cardinal Albani in Rome, have been recorded; but scarcely a Tourist came home without at least one genuine work of art as a memento of his travels. Admittedly, the average Tourist did not much care for contemporary French art – Watteau and Fragonard were almost totally disregarded; certainly, what he usually wanted in Italy was some personal record of his visit, a portrait done in Rome – preferably by Pompeo Batoni with a ruin, the Colosseum perhaps, in the background – a landscape, a view of Venice or Florence, the kind of painting in which Italian artists had hitherto not troubled to excel. But the Englishman's demands – and his money – did result in hundreds of excellent paintings by such artists as Canaletto and

The romantic landscapes of Nicolas Poussin and his adopted son, Gaspar, were also avidly acquired by rich English Tourists, whose houses they decorated and the designs of whose gardens they strongly influenced.

Zuccarelli finding their way across the Channel. Moreover the romantic landscapes by Poussin, Claude and Salvator Rosa which the Tourist brought back with him to remind him of the beauties of the Continental scene had a positive influence upon the development of English landscape gardening.

It was in architecture, however, that the influence of the Grand Tour can be most clearly and definitely discerned. Sir Roger Pratt, one of the most successful architects of the seventeenth century, expressed the belief that foreign travel was as essential for those who hoped to live in a well-designed modern building as it was for those who intended to design one. He himself had travelled throughout Europe inspecting, measuring, drawing, comparing the finest buildings, noting the differences between various ornate French exteriors and the severer Italian style; and had returned home to design Kingston Lacy near Wimborne, Lord Allington's house at Horseheath, Clarendon House, Piccadilly – a model for several other London houses built during the Restoration – and Coleshill, Berkshire.

Inigo Jones, whose work Pratt much admired, had also travelled widely on the Continent. He had visited Venice and Florence while in his twenties when 'naturally inclined to study the Arts of Design'; in his thirties he returned to France; and in 1613–14 he was once more in Italy in the suite of the young Earl of Arundel, who was to become one of the greatest patrons and art collectors of his time.

Inigo Jones had made a reputation for himself in England with his designs for the scenes and costumes of court masques, some of them clearly based on ideas he had acquired at the Medici court in Florence where masques were regularly performed in the Palazzo Vecchio and the Palazzo Pitti; but it was to the design of buildings that he felt increasingly drawn.

In the England of his boyhood and youth buildings had been designed by builders or by surveyors who, in most cases, had come out of the building trade, and who had never been abroad. 'Architect' was an unusual and rather pretentious word. There were those, however, who were beginning to call for a new approach to architectural design. Henry Wotton, who may have discussed the subject with Inigo Jones in Venice – he was later to become ambassador there – published his *Elements of Architecture* in 1624. In this book Wotton called for a proper appreciation of Vitruvius, the great Roman architect whose treatise *De Architectura Libri Decem* was to have so profound an influence on the originators of the classic revival.

Inigo Jones had carefully studied Vitruvius; and in Italy he threw himself deeply into the theory and philosophy of the classical style. He read and re-read Andrea Palladio's great work *Quattro libri dell' architettura*, and visited the buildings illustrated in it; he also studied the works of Alberti, Serlio, Labacco and the French theorist Philibert de L'Orme; in Venice he met Scamozzi whose *Idea dell'architettura universale* was to influence him as much as Palladio's *Quattro libri*.

When he returned to England to become Surveyor of the King's Works and the country's leading architect, the effect of his studies was unmistakable. Those few examples of his genius which still survive – such as the Queen's House at Greenwich, the Banqueting House at Whitehall, and St Paul's, Covent Garden – all demonstrate the sources of his inspiration. They are stamped with the marks of his own individuality, with his own remarkable invention; but they each have their model. The Queen's House, as Sir John Summerson has put it, is a '*quattrocento* idea of a Roman patrician villa, brought to the Thames, subjected to the full rigour of Palladio and Scamozzi, and resolved into such a serene and simple statement that it might as easily belong to 1816 as 1616.' The Banqueting House contains strong echoes of the Palazzo Thiene in Vicenza; while the church and piazza at Leghorn, as John Evelyn noted, 'gave the first hint to the building both of the church and Piazza in Covent Garden'.

Once the idea of neo-Classicism had taken root it was to dominate English architecture for more than two centuries. Christopher Wren, although his foreign travels during his apprenticeship were limited to France, had a library full of the recognised Italian authorities; and

Robert Adam, whose genius transformed English architecture and furniture in the second half of the eighteenth century, spent three years studying in Rome in the 1750s and met there many of his future clients. His influential *Ruins of the Palace of Diocletian* was published in 1764.

many of his City churches are strongly influenced by the simple, robust Tuscan style. Vanbrugh's best known work, Blenheim Palace, bears an unmistakable resemblance to Palladio's designs for Villa Trissino in Meledo, while the great marble entrance hall at Castle Howard was almost certainly inspired by the hall by Louis Le Van at Vaux-le-Vicomte. The work of William Kent, both as architect and garden designer, shows unmistakably how influenced he was by his travels in Italy at the expense of his patrons between 1710 and 1719.

In America, too, neo-Classicism proliferated. The plantation owners of Virginia, some of whom had been on the Grand Tour themselves and seen examples of Andrea Palladio's manner, built themselves mansions in the Palladian style. Charles Bulfinch, who provided Boston with many of its most imposing buildings, received his architectural training and inspiration during a long European Tour undertaken after his graduation at Harvard in 1781. President Jefferson, who had travelled all over western Europe, had the University of Virginia designed on the lines of one of Palladio's villas and would like to have had the president's house in Washington built as a replica of another of them.

Several rich English Tourists did, in fact, succeed in this ambition of building a replica of one of the master's Vicenza villas. In 1716, Richard Boyle, 3rd Earl of Burlington, a passionate advocate of Palladio, had the front of Burlington House built more or less as a copy of the Palazzo Porto; and his country house at Chiswick is modelled on Villa Capra. The beauty of Palladio's most famous villa, the Rotonda, can be admired in Kent where Colen Campbell – the Scottish architect of Wanstead House, prototype of many neo-Palladian houses in England – built Mereworth Castle from the illustrations in the *Quattro libri dell'architettura*. The work of William Chambers also shows how deeply both he and his clients were influenced by their months in Italy.

The ornamental decorations of the Tourists' new houses as well as their external design were strongly affected by Continental originals and often transformed by Continental artists. The whole character of the interior of West Wycombe Park, for instance, was changed by Joseph Borgnis whom Sir Francis Dashwood had met on the Grand Tour in 1726 and persuaded to come to England during a second visit to Italy ten years later.

Pierre Lescot's figures in the Salle des Cariatides at the Louvre were constantly imitated in other country houses, as were fine pieces of French furniture and Italian statuary. Nicholas Stone, having exhausted his stock of ornamental motifs, sent his son to Italy to make a fresh collection of drawings and books. And much of Robert Adam's time during a long sojourn in Italy in the 1750s was spent gathering ideas for the decoration of houses as well as for their outward appearance.

By 1759, when Robert Adam returned from Italy, many Tourists were growing tired of the rather heavily pretentious forms into which neo-Palladianism had fallen since the death of William Kent, Lord Burlington and James Gibbs; and Adam and his successors were able to provide them with something more extravagant and ornate. For twenty years this new style – inspired by ancient temples, baths and triumphal arches, early Christian tombs and churches, as well as by Renaissance villas – dominated architectural taste. Then with George Dance, James Wyatt, John Soane and John Nash, all of them born between 1740 and 1755, there came a new wave of neo-Classicism, a wave which incorporated certain aspects of the picturesque which earlier generations of Tourists would not have appreciated.

For up till the last decades of the eighteenth century only a few Tourists – of whom Horace Walpole was a conspicuous example – responded favourably to any style of architecture developed earlier than the fifteenth century. Before that Ruskin's interest in Gothicism – and almost any ancient building not in the classical tradition was referred to as Gothic – would have been considered highly eccentric. James Adam, Robert's younger brother, who followed him on his *Giro d'Italia*, was interested in Gothic as well as classical architecture, and thought that he had never seen 'a more superb style of ornament' than Siena cathedral; but this was an interest which up till then few Tourists had shared.

Sir Roger Pratt had written of his contempt for Gothic arches, which, 'both for the natural imbecility of the sharpe Angle itself and likewise for their very uncomeliness ought to be exiled from judicious eyes and left to their first inventors, the Goths and Lombards, amongst other Reliques of the barbarous age.'

Other travellers echoed this opinion. John Evelyn thought St John Lateran much inferior to St Peter's, being 'of Gothic appearance'.

Several rich Tourists succeeded in their ambition of building a country house in England modelled upon one of Palladio's beautiful villas which they had seen on their way to Venice. Mereworth Castle in Kent was based by Colen Campbell on the Villa Rotonda, Vicenza.

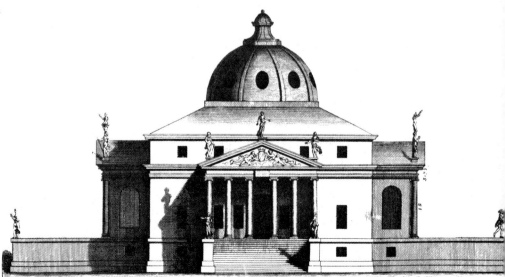

Robert Adam's brother, James, was also strongly influenced by his Continental Tour and on his return from Rome worked closely with his brother.

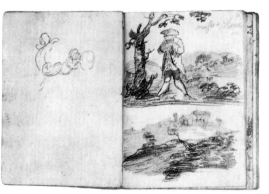

The Tourist himself, if he had any talent at all, was expected to make drawings of the places he visited and the buildings he saw; here one tries his hand at depicting the perspective of colonnades at Pompeii.

Joshua Reynolds left for Italy in 1749 and, after spending over two years in Rome, made a tour of the other important cities of Italy. Wherever he went he took his sketch book with him, and filled it with such drawings as these.

This painting of Vesuvius was commissioned by Sir William Hamilton for use in his studies of volcanic phenomena in South Italy and Sicily.

Wyndham complained that the cathedral at Monreale exhibited 'a very disagreeable specimen of the Gothic taste'; while Northall in 1752 compared the dim old churches of Florence built in the Gothic style with the 'more modern churches built in good taste', and wrote of the cathedral that 'there is nothing in this city so extraordinary as the cathedral ... though [it] can only be looked upon as one of the masterpieces of Gothic architecture'. Gothic remains and follies were all very well in gardens, but such edifices as Walpole's Strawberry Hill were but examples of perverse extravagance.

Towards the close of the century, James St John, in his *Letters from France*, expressed an opposing view. After visiting Chantilly he wrote enthusiastically:

'The Castle is a great pile of Gothic building, with huge round towers at the angles to serve as bastions. The venerable aspect of this groupe of Gothic castles, dark, and solemn, in the middle of a fine sheet of water, impresses the beholder with awe and admiration . . . It appears antique, solemn and romantic; and the noblest piece of Corinthian architecture does not appear so awful and majestic as the antique wall and ramparts of Chantilly.'

After a visit to Notre-Dame, St John wrote of its lofty majesty and beauty, adding 'I would rather spend my life even in an old Gothic castle in a romantic situation, with rocks and woods and cataracts round me than in all the formal grandeur and stupid regularity of Versailles.'

But these were sentiments quite out of tune with the spirit of the Grand Tour. They reflect the sentiments of a new age, an age in which men would prefer to follow in the wayward steps of Byron, rather than to trace the route so well worn for so long. By the time the nineteenth century had begun, the Revolutionary Wars had brought the Tour to a halt, except for a few adventurous spirits such as Henry Brougham; and when the wars were over it never again assumed its former peculiar significance. Less than twenty years after Waterloo, railway tracks were being laid all over Europe and new hotels were being built at every terminus; a generation after Napoleon's death, Thomas Cook, a former book salesman and lay preacher, was following up his successful hiring of a special train to carry the delegates to a temperance meeting from Leicester to Loughborough and back, by advertising 'A Great Circular Tour of the Continent'; by the 1860s, Rome could be reached from London in sixty hours, and a man could go all the way round the world in a shorter time than it had taken him to get to Naples and back in 1750. As an aristocratic institution the Grand Tour was already dying when the map of Europe was redrawn at Vienna in 1815; the steam engine and the railway hotel delivered the *coup de grâce*.

List of Sources

Ackerman, James, S. *Palladio* (1966)
Addison, Joseph *Remarks on Several Parts of Italy, 1701-1703* (1705)
Archenholz, Baron J. W. von *A Picture of Italy* (Trans. Joseph Trapp, 2 vols., 1791)

Babeau, Albert *Les Voyageurs en France, etc.* (1885)
Baretti, Giuseppe Marc' Antonio *An Account of the Manners and Customs of Italy*
    (2 vols., 1769)
    A Journey from London to Genoa, etc. (2 vols., 1770)
Barthelemy, M. L'Abbé *Travels in Italy* (1802)
Bates, E. S. *Touring in 1600* (1911)
Berchtold, Count Leopold *An Essay to Direct and Extend the Inquiries of Patriotic*
    Travellers (1787)
Birkbeck, Morris *Notes of a Journey through France, etc.* (1815)
Bisoni, Bernardo *Aventures d'un Grand Seigneur Italien à travers l'Europe* (1899)
Bonnaffé, Edmond *Voyages et Voyageurs de la Renaissance* (1895)
Bonnard, Georges A. (ed) *Edward Gibbon: Memoirs of My Life* (1966) *Gibbon's*
    Journey from Geneva to Rome: His Journal from 20 April to 2 October 1764 (1961)
Boorde, Andrew *Fyrst Boke of the Introduction of Knowledge* (? 1541)
Bourrit, Marc Théodore *A Relation of a Journey to the Glaciers in the Dutchy of Savoy*
    (1775)
Bray, William (Ed.) *The Diary of John Evelyn* (1818)
Breval, John Durant *Remarks on Several Parts of Europe, etc.* (2 vols., 1738)
Bromley, William *Several Years' Travels, etc.* (1702)
Brosses, Charles de *Lettres historiques et critiques sur l'Italie* (3 vols., 1799)

Carnarvon, Earl of (Ed.) *Lord Chesterfield's Letters to his Godson* (1890)
Carr, John *The Stranger in France, etc.* (1803)
Caylus, Comte de *Voyage d'Italie, 1714–1715* (1914)
Chapman, Guy (Ed.) *The Travel Diaries of William Beckford of Fonthill* (1928)
Clenche, John *A Tour in France and Italy, etc.* (1676)
Coe, Richard N. (Ed. and Trs.) *Rome, Naples and Florence by Stendhal* (1959)
Cogan, Thomas *The Rhine, etc.* (1793)
Coghlan, Francis *Hand-book for Italy* (1847)
Connell, Brian *Portrait of a Whig Peer* (1957)
Cork and Orrery, Earl of *Letters from Italy in 1754 and 1755* (1774)
Coryat's Crudities. Hastily gobled up in five Moneths travells in France, Savoy, Italie (2 vols.,
    1905)
 Coxe, William *Travels in Switzerland* (1789)

de Beer, G. R. (Ed.) *A Journey to Florence in 1817* (1951)
du Chesne, André *Les Antiquités et Recherches des villes, Chasteaux, et Places plus*
    Remarquables de toute la France (1647)
Duclos, Charles Pineau *Voyage en Italie* (1766)
Dupaty, L' Abbé *Travels through Italy in a series of Letters, 1785* (1789)

Ebel, Johann Gottfried *The Traveller's Guide through Switzerland* (1818)
Eliot-Drake, Lady (Ed.) *Lady Knight's Letters from France and Italy 1776–1795* (1905)
Essex, James *Journal of a Tour Through Parts of Flanders and France, etc. in 1773*
    (1888)
Este, Charles *A Journey in the Year 1793 through Flanders, Brabant and Germany to Switzer-*
    land (1795)
Eustace, Rev. J. C. *A Classical Tour through Italy, etc.* (1819)

Fleming, John 'Lord Brudenell and his Bear-Leader' in *English Miscellany*, 1958
    Robert Adam and His Circle in Edinburgh and Rome (1962)

Gentleman's Guide in His Tour through France, etc., The (1770)
Gentleman's Pocket Companion for Travelling into Foreign Parts, The (1722)
Glover, Cedric Howard *Dr Charles Burney's Continental Travels* (1927)

Goethe, Johann Wolfgang *Italian Journey 1786–1788* (Trans. W. H. Auden and Elizabeth Mayer, 1962)

Graf, Arturo *L' Anglomania e l'influsso inglese in Italia nel secolo XVIII* (1911)

Grosley, P.-J. *Observations on Italy and the Italians made in 1764* (1770)

Gunn, Peter *Naples: A Palimpsest* (1961)

Halsband, Robert (Ed.) *The Complete Letters of Lady Mary Wortley Montagu* (1965, etc.)

Hawkins, E. (Ed.) *Brereton's Travels in Holland, 1634–1635* (1844)

Hazlitt, William *Notes of a Journey through France and Italy* (collected works, vol. 9. 1904)

Heylyn, Peter *A full Relation of Two Journeys, etc.* (1656)

Hilen, Andrew (Ed.) *The Diary of Clara Crowninshield* (1956)

Holcroft, Thomas *Travels from Hamburg through Westphalia, Holland and the Netherlands* (1804)

Howard, Clare *English Travellers of the Renaissance* (1914)

Howell, James *Instructions for Forreine Travell* (1642, Ed. 1867)

Hunt, James Henry Leigh *Autobiography* (Ed. J. E. Morpurgo, 1949)

Hurd, Bishop Richard *Dialogue on the Uses of Foreign Travel* (1764)

Jesse, J. H. *George Selwyn and His Contemporaries* (1843)

Jones, Rev. William *Observations on a Journey to Paris, etc.* (1777)

Keysler, John George *Travels through Germany, etc.* (1760)

Knox, Vicesimus *Liberal Education, etc.* (1789)

Lalande, Jérôme Lefrançais de *Voyage d'un Francais en Italie fait dans les anneés 1765 et 1766* (1768)

Lambert, R. S. (Ed.) *The Grand Tour: A Journey in the Tracks of the Age of Aristocracy* (1935)

Lassells, Richard *The Voyage of Italy, etc.* (1670)

Lee, Vernon *Studies of the Eighteenth Century in Italy* (1880)

Lewis, W. S. (Ed.) *The Correspondence of Horace Walpole* (1937, etc.)

Lithgow, William *Travels and Voyages through Europe* (1771)

Locke, John *Some Thoughts Concerning Education* (1693)

Logan, Henry *Directions for such as shall Travel to Rome* (1654)

Low, D. M. *Edward Gibbon* (1937)

Mahon, Lord (Ed.) *Lord Chesterfield's Letters to His Son* (1845–1853)

Martyn, Thomas *Sketch of a Tour through Swisserland* (1787) *A Tour through Italy, etc.* (1791) *A Gentleman's Guide in his Tour through France* (1787)

Massingham, Hugh and Pauline *The Englishman Abroad* (1962)

Maugham, H. Neville *The Book of Italian Travel, 1580–1900* (1903)

Mead, William Edward *The Grand Tour in the Eighteenth Century* (1914)

Mikhailovich, Nikolai (Ed.) *Letters of a Russian Traveller* [N. M. Karamzin] (Trans. Florence Jonas, 1957)

Miller, Lady Anne *Letters from Italy* (1776)

Misson, François Maximilien *A New Voyage of Italy, with curious observations on Germany, Switzerland, Savoy, France, Flanders and Holland* (1724)

Montesquieu, Charles Louis de Secondat *Voyages* (1894–6)

Moore, John *A View of Society and Manners in Italy* (1792) *A View of Society and Manners in France, Switzerland and Germany* (1792)

Morris, James *Venice* (1960)

Moryson, Fynes *An Itinerary Containing His Ten Yeeres Travell, etc.* (1617, Reprinted 1907)

Northall, Captain John *Travels through Italy* (1766)

Nugent, Mr [Sir Thomas] *The Grand Tour containing an exact description of most of the Cities, Towns and Remarkable Places of Europe* (4 vols., 1749)

Ortolani, Giuseppe *Voci e visioni del settecento veneziano* (1926)

Parks, George Bruner *The English Travellers to Italy* (1954)

Piozzi, Mrs Hester Lynch *Observations and Reflections made in the Journey through France, Italy, and Germany* (1789)

Pottle, Frederick A. (Ed.) *Boswell on the Grand Tour: Germany and Switzerland, 1764* (1953)
(with Frank Brady) *Boswell on the Grand Tour: Italy, Corsica and France, 1765–1766* (1955) *James Boswell, The Earlier Years* (1966)

Pratt, Samuel Jackson *Gleanings through Holland and Westphalia* (1795)

Quennell, Peter *Byron in Italy* (1941)

Radcliffe, Ann *A Journey made in the summer of 1794 through Holland, etc.* (1796)
Ray, John *Travels through the Low Countries, etc.* (1738)
Raymond, John *An itinerary contayning a voyage made through Italy in the yeares 1646 and 1647* (1648)
Remarks on the Grand Tour lately performed by a Person of Quality (1692)
Richardson, Jonathan *An Account of The Statues, etc., in Italy, France, etc.* (1722)
Riesbeck, Baron [Johann Caspar Risbeck] *Voyages en Allemagne* (1792)
Rigby, Dr Edward *Letters from France, etc., in 1789* (1880)
Robinson, Henry Crabb *Diary, etc.* (1872)
Roget, S. R. (Ed.) *Travels in the Last Two Centuries of Three Generations* (1921)
Russell, John *A Tour in Germany, etc.* (1828)

Sadleir, Thomas *An Irish Peer on the Continent (1801–1803). As Related by Catherine Wilmot* (1924)
Sherlock, Martin *Letters from an English Traveller* (1780) *New Letters from an English Traveller* (1781)
Short Account of a Late Journey to Tuscany, Rome, etc. (1741)
Smith, James Edward *Sketch of a Tour on the Continent* (1807)
Smith, Logan Pearsall *Life and Letters of Sir Henry Wotton* (1907)
Smollett, Tobias *Travels through France and Italy* (1766)
Southey, Robert *Journal of a Tour in the Netherlands* (Ed. 1849)
Starke, Mariana *Letters from Italy, 1792–1798* (1800)
Stephen, Leslie *The Playground of Europe* (1871)
Sterne, Laurence *A Sentimental Journey through France and Italy* (1768)
St. John, James *Letters from France, etc., in 1787* (1788)
Stoye, John Walter *English Travellers Abroad 1604–1667* (1952)
Summerson, John *Inigo Jones* (1966)
Swinburne, Henry *Travels in the Two Sicilies, 1777–1780* (1790)

Taylor, Thomas *The Gentleman's Pocket Companion for Travelling into Foreign Parts* (1722)
Temple, R. C. (Ed.) *The Travels of Peter Mundy, etc., 1608–1667* (1907–1924)
Thicknesse, Philip *Observations on the Customs and Manners of the French Nation, etc.* (1766) *A Year's Journey through France* (1777) *Useful Hints to Those who Make the Tour of France* (1768)
Thierry, Luc Vincent *Almanach de Voyageur à Paris, etc.* (1785)
Tour through Germany, containing Full Directions, etc. (1793)
Tovey, D. C. *Gray and his Friends* (1890)
Travels of Edward Brown, Esq., formerly a Merchant of London, The (1753)
Trease, Geoffrey *The Grand Tour* (1967)
Trechmann, E. J. (Ed. and Trans.) *The Diary of Montaigne's Journey in 1580–1581* (1929)
Trevelyan, George Otto *The Life and Letters of Lord Macaulay* (1876)

Vaussard, Maurice *Daily Life in Eighteenth Century Italy* (Trans. Michael Heron, 1962)
View of Paris and Places Adjoining. Written by a Gentleman lately residing at the English Ambassador's (1701)

Warcup, Edmund *Italy in its Original Glory, Ruine and Revival* (1660)
[Windham, William] *A Letter from an English Gentleman giving an Account of . . . the Ice Alps in Savoy* (1744)
Wordsworth, William *Letters* (Ed. Ernest de Sélincourt, 1935, etc.)
Wraxall, Nathaniel *Tour through the Western, Southern, and Interior Provinces of France* (1777)

Young, Arthur *Travels in France in 1787–1789* (1889)

Photographic Acknowledgements

The author and publishers wish to thank all those listed below who have kindly supplied photographs from their collections, or who have allowed objects from their collections to be specially photographed for this book. The photographs were collected by Jacquemine Charrot-Lodwidge.

Anderson, 135; Ashmolean Museum, 59, 155; coll. Sir Edward Bacon, 215 *top*; Bibliothèque Nationale, 45; British Museum, 22, 26–7, 29, 33, 42, 46, 47, 49, 51, 54–5, 73 *top and bottom*, 76, 77, 78–9, 81, 84–5, 86, 87, 88, 89, 90, 91, 100, 111, 112, 126, 127, 132, 139 *top and bottom*, 145, 152, 158, 161, 162, 163 *top and bottom*, 169, 180, 181, 185, 204–5, 212 *top and bottom*, 214, 215 *bottom*, 243 *bottom*, 244 *bottom*, 245 *top and bottom*; coll. Major General Sir John Burns, 218; Ca' Rezzonico, Venice (photos.: André Held), 122, 124–5; Calcografica Nazionale, Rome, 237; Courtauld Institute, 187, 244 *top*; Deutsche Fotothek, Dresden, 195 *top*; Gabinetto Fotografico Nazionale, Rome, 143; Giraudon, Paris, 57 *bottom*, 67, 189; Graphische Sammlung Albertina, Vienna, 121, 195 *above*; Historisches Museum der Stadt Wien, 191, 193, 194; coll. the late Earl of Ilchester, 219; coll. Earl of Leicester, 23; Mansell Collection, 119, 239; coll. Mr and Mrs Paul Mellon, 147; Marzari, 97; Musée de Compiègne, 8–9, 36, 37, 63, 64, 65, 70–1, 75 *top*; Museo de Arte, Barcelona, 123; Museo Civico di Torino, 99; Museum Boymans-van Beuningen, Rotterdam, 94–5; National Gallery, London, 134, 232–3; National Galleries of Scotland, 83; National Portrait Gallery, 14, 21, 41, 105, 160, 179, 227, 241; Norwich Castle Museum, 43, 186, 235 *top and bottom* (R.J.Colman Collection); Duke of Northumberland (coll. Syon House), 17; Petworth House, 149, 170–1; coll. Lord Rosebery, 15; Royal Academy of Arts, 115 *top*; Scala, Milan, 129; coll. Lord Scarsdale, 11 *above*, 18; Sir John Soane Museum, 109; Staatliche Museen, Berlin, 173; Städeliches Kunstinstitut, Frankfurt, 151; Stourhead Castle (National Trust), 107, 142; Ullstein Bilderdienst, Berlin, 166–7, 172, 175, 183, 196, 197, 198, 200; Walter Steinkopf, 247; Windsor Castle (Royal Library), 72, 93, 116–17, 137, 140, 207, 208, 211, 217; Victoria and Albert Museum, 13, 75 *bottom*, 103, 115 *bottom*, 118, 156, 157, 199 *top and bottom*, 201 *top*, 202, 220–1, 223 *right*, 225.

Index